TIBET
UNCONQUERED

TIBET UNCONQUERED

AN EPIC STRUGGLE FOR FREEDOM

DIANE WOLFF

FOREWORD BY
ROBERT THURMAN

palgrave
macmillan

First published in 2010 by
PALGRAVE MACMILLAN®
in the United States—a division of St. Martin's Press LLC,
175 Fifth Avenue, New York, NY 10010.

Where this book is distributed in the UK, Europe and the rest of the
world, this is by Palgrave Macmillan, a division of Macmillan Publishers
Limited, registered in England, company number 785998, of Houndmills,
Basingstoke, Hampshire RG21 6XS.

Palgrave Macmillan is the global academic imprint of the above companies and
has companies and representatives throughout the world.

Palgrave® and Macmillan® are registered trademarks in the United States, the
United Kingdom, Europe and other countries.

ISBN: 978–0–230–62273–9

Library of Congress Cataloging-in-Publication Data

Wolff, Diane.
    Tibet unconquered : an epic struggle for freedom/ by Diane Wolff;
foreword by Robert A.F. Thurman.
        p. cm.
    Includes bibliographical references and index.
    ISBN 978–0–230–62273–9 (hbk.)
    1. China—Relations—China—Tibet. 2. Tibet (China)—Relations—
China. 3. Tibet (China)—History. 4. Tibet (China)—Politics and
government. 5. China—Politics and government. 6. Imperialism—History.
I. Title.

DS740.5.T5W65 2010
951'.505—dc22   2010013066

A catalogue record of the book is available from the British Library.

Design by Newgen Imaging Systems (P) Ltd., Chennai, India.

First edition: September 2010

10 9 8 7 6 5 4 3 2 1

Printed in the United States of America.

CONTENTS

China and Its Neighbors

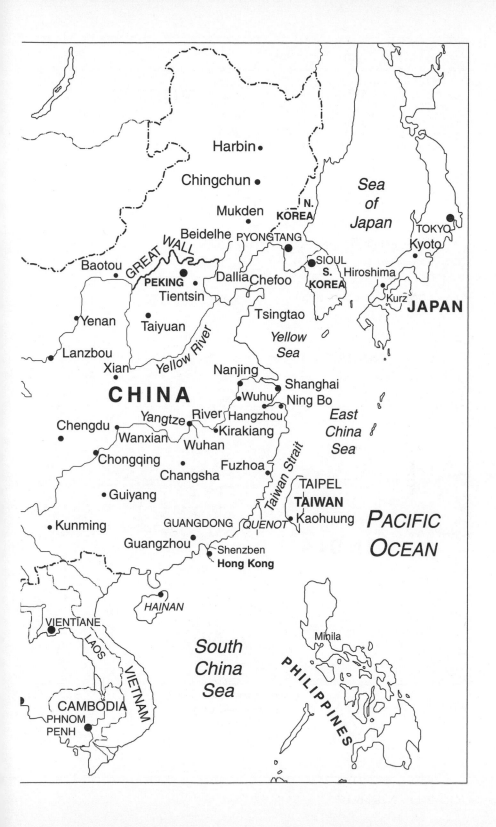

Ethnic Tibetan Areas of China

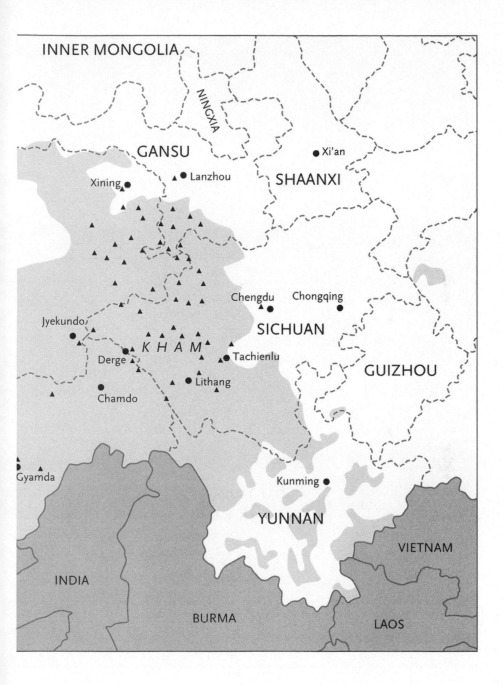

FOREWORD

I am pleased and honored to introduce Diane Wolff's brilliant work, as she gallops us across an 800-year swathe of history of China and Tibet. She carries us along in a knowledgeable and inspirational charge to share her vision of a win-win future awaiting the governments and peoples of the two nations, a solution for the current struggle between them based on the realities of history and the exigencies of the present. We begin by riding with Chinggis Khan across the steppes in his early period of the unification of the Mongolian nations, his conquest of north China, and his pragmatic engagement with Yeh-lu Chu-tsai in creating the "loose reins" pattern of workable empire. We end in a plausible future where the present People's Republic of China's government has discovered the ethical superiority and practical workability of a modern network version of the historical pattern of China-based empires of "loose-reins" management of the border states under its protection (rather than the unethical, increasingly impractical, realistically obsolete twentieth-century attempt by would-be superpower nation states to incorporate and assimilate neighboring nations).

After an exhilarating ride through history, when she comes down to the present, she makes many interesting points in her road map for a solution to China's Tibetan problem. She explains clearly how the thinking of the current Chinese leadership is still influenced by the Leninist approach to the ethnic question, and she strongly points out how the twentieth century proved that ethnicity is a more enduring human characteristic than class. Hard-line assimilation of ethnic groups has not worked anywhere on the planet and will not work in Tibet. Stubborn clinging in the twenty-first century of global media transparency to the effort of replicating the United

States' nineteenth-century genocidal policy regarding the Native American peoples (which still has not succeeded and remains one of the United States' greatest sources of shame and denial to this day) is particularly self-defeating.

Wolff's urging that economic development alone will not satisfy either China's own people or her "ethnic minority nationalities" without political reform and empowerment through replacing centralized command control with the modern network model of classical Chinese "loose-reins" control is realistic. Her ensuing vision, inspired by the suggestion of South Korea's political theorist Dr. Han, of using a truly autonomous, regionally empowered, satellite Tibet to create a "mountain coastal" region of interaction with the South Asian Association for Regional Cooperation (SAARC) is brilliant. China would be offering a true portal of economic interaction with the seven nations of SAARC which would create a natural prosperity in the region, and save China the continuing embarrassment of an oppressed and restive Tibetan people and the huge waste of the subsidies required in the futile effort to turn Tibet into a hermetically sealed-off colony of China, filled with altitude-challenged Han colonists suffering in the rarified air.

Wolff cogently argues that, left to their own devices with relaxed supervision, protection, and support from the Chinese federal center, the Tibetans themselves would restore their threatened environment that should nurture the headwaters of China's and all of Asia's major river systems, would re-create their inspiring, peaceful, and radiant Buddhist culture and educational systems, and would make Tibet a prosperous zone of sustainable economic development based on ecological, spiritual, and health tourism, while restoring Tibet's traditional role as a hub of trade in the Himalayan region. The mineral and resource exploitation that the PLA businesses are concerned about could still continue, though a modern "green" environmental policy monitored by Tibetan agencies would involve some additional investment to avoid pollution and damage to the ecosystem. This extra cost would be more than compensated for by the greater ease of partnerships with global mining concerns who would no longer be constrained by the ethical and public relations problems of working in an oppressive human rights atmosphere. Her main point is that "China's Tibet," thus released into a truly autonomous, regionally empowered satellite status, would be transformed from being an embarrassment for China into being a jewel in her crown, a regional leader of its neighboring Himalayan states and an efficient portal for China's trans-Himalayan trade with India and other SAARC members.

Wolff intriguingly perceives what few other observers have, that Tibetans, despite their Buddhistically restrained, basically nonviolent approach to resistance, have long been engaged in a unique kind of insurgency. Thus, the rule that the United States and others have been too slow to discover in Vietnam, Iraq, and Afghanistan, also applies to Tibet, that "You cannot kill your way out of an insurgency. You have to make friends. You have to develop economically and politically!" She is also well attuned to the extreme importance of the Tibetan plateau to the environmental health of China herself and the whole of Southeast and Southern Asia, since the headwaters of the Yellow, Yang-tze, Mekong, Salween, Iriwaddy, Brahmaputra, Ganges, Sutlej, and Indus River systems lie in Tibet. The frenzied pace of China's capitalist development and her intense hunger for basic resources of timber, meat, leather, and minerals has caused Chinese extractive industries to operate with no concern for the environment or sustainability. Fifty years of such policies have wreaked untold harm on the sensitive high-altitude ecosystems. Reform in these policies and systematic investment in repairing the damage would do wonders for China's own water crises, both floods and extreme shortages, and those of her southern neighbors and vastly improve China's international image.

On one of the main sticking points blocking the Chinese leadership's adopting a more pragmatic approach, that of their fragile pride in dealing with His Holiness the Dalai Lama, Wolff makes the following memorable statement, worth repeating in full: "For Tibetans, the Dalai Lama is the symbol of their culture. If he returns and accepts Chinese sovereignty, his return would guarantee peace in Tibet and bring the loyalty of the Tibetan masses—loyalty that the Chinese have sought since the time of Chairman Mao. The old lamaist system is gone. What would come is a new governmental form, one that could be tolerated as surely as the government of Hong Kong is tolerated within the Chinese system."

The great strength of Wolff's proposals is their way of being grounded in historical facts and in principles both of traditionally pragmatic Chinese statecraft and in pragmatic modifications of Marxist-Leninist theories. I am impressed with her argument that the PRC politburo's relaxing of central planning in Tibet and devolving of control to a regional model would parallel the successful creation of the Special Economic Zones on the Chinese coast. And she then makes this interesting statement, complete with an impressive acronym; "Tibet might be designated as a Special Ethnic, Trade, and Ecological Zone (SETEZ). This gradual approach to the emergence of a market economy would require loosening the reins of the command economy."

She crowns her argument with the following marvelous statement: "Tibet, with its tradition of nonviolence, is the perfect regional leader. Once the human rights questions are resolved by the new autonomy, the World Bank, the Asian Development Bank, and the International Monetary Fund, as well as private capital, would have the way cleared for participation in the Tibetan economy."

Finally, she is not at all subject to illusions about the probable reaction of China's present leaders to the realistic and potentially transformative roadmap she puts forward. She remains quite aware that, in addition to being competent executives and hard-working engineers of economic development, they are tough personalities who are still bound by their belief in authoritarian control as the way to security, enforced order, and continuation of their own power. Referring to them as the "Fourth Generation" of China's modern leadership, she wonders if we need to wait for a Gorbachev-type visionary to come forward in the "Fifth Generation," who will take the reins in 2012. I certainly join her in the hope that, however hard the present leaders may have had to be in order to assume and hold on to the power they currently enjoy, they may also have the insight and adaptability to realize the wisdom of a roadmap such as that Wolff puts forward. After all, Chinggis Khan was not exactly a softie, and the empire he and his heirs created without modern technology lasted for several centuries and demonstrated the prosperity and stability that a China—Inner Asian "loose-reins" federation could produce even back in the fourteenth century.

So I join with Ms. Wolff in hoping that pragmatic realism will replace ideology, denial, and reactive persistence in the ineffective policies of the past, and that the "Fourth Generation" will rise to the challenge of achieving a transformed twenty-first-century realpolitik in Inner Asia that will stand as their truly historic contribution to the emergence of Great China as a trusted and respected partner in the restoration of a prosperous and sustainable planet.

—ROBERT A. F. THURMAN
Jey Tsong Khapa Professor of
Indo-Tibetan Buddhist Studies,
Columbia University
New York
April 17, 2010

Introduction

History matters.
                —Simon Schama

Sacred though its real estate may be to Tibetan Buddhists, Tibet has the unfortunate fate of being a strategic state in a dangerous neighborhood at a momentous time in Asian history. For much of the last several centuries, Tibet remained isolated from the modern world. A Himalayan kingdom with a Buddhist population, Tibet had a traditional economy, based in part on animal husbandry and in part on agriculture, and a mixed clerical and secular government with a Buddhist monk as head of state, the Dalai Lama. It was located in one of the most forbidding terrains on earth, at the Roof of the World. It had unique art and architecture, and both aristocrats and common people had distinctive native dress. Its religion derived from the great intellectual tradition of Buddhism in India. Festivals of the Buddhist calendar marked the passage of the seasons.

South Asia has traditionally been a crossroads of culture and of trade and a highway for armies, from those of Alexander the Great to those of the British and Mongol Empires. Afghanistan has been called the "Graveyard of Empires" because of its formidable geography and the indomitable spirit of its tribal warriors. Because it was located high in the Himalayas, Tibet escaped being a battleground, but because it was at the fulcrum, the very center of Asia, it became a pawn on the colonial chessboard. Traditionally a center of trade, Tibet, for two centuries, was a prize, a strategic turning point in the Great Game, the competition for influence on the Asian landmass played out between Russia, China, and Britain.

Tibet was materially poor and backward. It had no roads, no telegraph, no electricity, no plumbing, no railroads, and no factories. Its principal treasure was the high scholastic tradition of India in the form of Tibetan Buddhism. Yet for more than a century, bigger states vying for power saw Tibet as a prize, as a critical buffer to protect their empires in Asia.

From the beginning of the Age of Exploration, Britain had the most extensive colonial empire in the world, extending from India to Burma and Malaysia. As the saying went, the sun never set on the Union Jack. The British expanded north to protect the jewel in the crown, India.

Russia expanded across North Asia. Under Peter the Great in the late seventeenth century, Russia was the largest land-based empire in the world, with borders extending across Eurasia from the Baltic Sea to the Pacific Ocean. The Romanov czars wished to protect their empire in the East, with the riches in natural resources and the Pacific ports. The early twentieth century saw the building of the Trans-Siberian railroad to connect Moscow with the east.

Qing China was militarily strong. When the dynasty still had vigor, the imperial government watched the colonial competition from its capital several thousand miles away. Qing China, by the request of the Tibetan government, entered Tibet to repel invasions from Nepalese Ghurka forces twice in the eighteenth century. Afterward, the Qing emperor placed a Chinese official, an *amban*, and a small garrison in the Tibetan capital. Tibet had no modern defense forces of its own and instead relied upon its neighbor for protection. The Chinese expanded west and south.

The dependence on Qing China was to prove disastrous for Tibet. By the early nineteenth century, the government of Tibet had closed its borders to foreigners. China was also isolationist, and closed itself to what it perceived as unwelcome Western influences. Modernization, a response to the science and technology of the West, was perceived as Westernization, and Qing China rejected it.

The twenty-first century has seen the South Asian region change from a backwater to a global hotspot: The region is poor, with a lack of material development, but it is home to a shooting war in Afghanistan that includes the United States and its coalition as combatants. The subcontinent also is host to an insurgency in Kashmir, whose combatants include extremist Islamists attempting to wrest control of disputed Muslim majority territory from majority Hindu India. The Muslim side is backed by Pakistan, India's bitter antagonist since partition, when the British quit its colonial empire in India after the end of World War II.

The region has known natural disasters in the past decade, from the devastating earthquake in Pakistan to the monster cyclones in Bangladesh. (The poor Muslim-majority country separated from Pakistan in the early 1970s, its birth as a nation the belated product of the partition of India.) The expansion and proliferation of the heroin trade threatens the region and the world. In Afghanistan, the narcotics trade finances insurgency and drives out sustainable agriculture. The trans-shipment of drugs is a critical problem for the region.

Before the age of aerial warfare, military advantage meant occupying the high ground. During the eighteenth and nineteenth centuries, the era of colonial expansion on the Asian continent, Tibet was traditionally the high ground of Inner Asia, a buffer zone between China and India. Modern warfare has rendered the security afforded by Himalayan geography obsolete.

In the twenty-first century, South Asia is the only place on earth where three nuclear powers—China, Pakistan, and India—live in uneasy balance. The CIA estimates that the most likely place on the globe for an outbreak of nuclear war is in South Asia, between India and Pakistan. China and India have gone to war twice over border disputes in the past fifty years. India and Pakistan have come to the brink of nuclear war twice in the past several decades.

At the beginning of the twentieth century, British opinion was divided between the romantics and the realists. Some thought Tibet a place of ineffable mystery whose treasure of spirituality would be destroyed by the arrival of the modern world. Others argued that Tibet was a filthy medieval backwater controlled by superstition that could only be improved by opening up.

Penetrating Tibet became an obsession with Lord Curzon, the British viceroy of India from 1898 to 1905. He decided to disregard Chinese suzerainty over Tibet. Observation and intelligence told him that czarist Russia intended to dominate Asia. Tibet was the high ground, a buffer state. Curzon sought reassurance that Tibet had not allied itself with Russia, and decided that it was in Britain's interest to establish commercial and diplomatic relations with Tibet. In 1904, Colonel Francis Younghusband shot his way into Tibet, slaughtering many Tibetan defenders. Some Tibetans were armed with antique weapons and others with amulets blessed by the Thirteenth Dalai Lama.

Yet the British mission entered Tibet based on a misapprehension. There were no Russian officials in residence in Lhasa, not even a Russian embassy or trading post. Shangri-la had been breached. In response to the British incursion, the Thirteenth Dalai Lama left Tibet and took up residence in India. He remained there until the fall of the Qing Dynasty, when he returned to Lhasa to oust the Chinese *amban,* and his tiny military retinue and proclaim Tibet's independence. The Great Thirteenth, as he was known, did not have a modern army to ensure Tibet's independence.

This would not be the last time that the Victorians set out for the magical mystery places of Asia. Later in the century, the reports of the Victorian explorer Sir Aurel Stein and his discovery of the lost Buddhist civilization in China's Taklimakan Desert (modern Xinjiang) would excite the public imagination in Great Britain. The newspapers were full of stories about the mysteries of the lost civilizations of the East.

The late Qing government could not exert control over its borders in the far west. Stein left China with five hundred carts laden with frescoes cut from the walls of caves, sculpture, ceramics, and manuscripts. These antiquities soon filled British museums, where the exhibitions created a sensation among the British public. Stein would later inspire adventure stories and become the model for popular novels and films; Indiana Jones is his cinematic heir. To the present day, China continues the pressure to have its antiquities returned.

When the Bolshevik Revolution brought down the czarist regime in Russia its leaders proclaimed themselves anti-imperialists, but the Soviet Union inherited czarist colonial ambitions in Asia. Lenin wanted the natural resources of Asia, especially the oil of Kazakhstan and the timber of Siberia. Dreaming that the East would be Red, he declared that he wanted to liberate the toiling masses of India from the yoke of industrialist Britain.

The Russian expansion into Asia continued with the incorporation of the five Central Asian republics into the USSR. These were the five "stans": Kazakhstan, Uzbekistan, Turkmenistan, Kirgizstan, and Tajikistan. This was Russian Turkestan, a Muslim and Turkic region bordering on Xinjiang, China's Far West, known then as Chinese Turkestan. Russian involvement began under the czars and continued under the commissars, who saw an opportunity to advance its interests. Chinese Turkestan was rich in natural resources, it was on the Russian-Chinese border, and the Chinese government was weak.

China's foreign policy was traditionally centered on the Inner Asian frontier, rather than the maritime coast. The Asian landmass was where the threats emerged, and Russia was a threat. Russia was mighty, and Qing China was weakening, decaying, dying. The fate of the Chinese border regions, including Tibet and Xinjiang, hung in the balance. Russia stepped up its spying activity in Xinjiang.

The imperial system had been ruling China for two millennia. When it fell as a result of the Republican Revolution of 1911, no central government replaced it. Reform and revolution had been in the air, but the Chinese center had not held. China entered a period of disunity and chaos. Control spun out to regional commanders known as warlords. The Nationalists failed in their attempt to assume control of the country.

The Japanese invaded China in 1937 and established Manchukuo, a puppet state in Manchuria; occupied Mongolia; and established a government at Nanjing. They remained in China until their defeat at the end of World War II in 1945. The Comintern of the Soviet Union helped the fledgling Chinese Communist party organize and offered it material assistance. The Communists were the only other contenders strong enough to compete with the Nationalists. After the defeat of the Japanese, Communists and Nationalists resumed the civil war, with the Communists prevailing in 1949. Mao Zedong went to the platform at the top of the Gate of Heavenly Peace and proclaimed the founding of the People's Republic of China.

In 1911 Tibet declared its independence and, until 1950, was in control of its own destiny. The end of World War II would change all that.

Unifying China had been a goal for both Nationalists and Communists. Both had accepted the Qing borders in the Far West and the Qing protectorate in Tibet. Within a year of gaining power, Mao announced his intention to liberate Tibet peacefully, but this proved to be rhetorical spin for an aggressive offensive. In October of 1950, three divisions of the battle-seasoned People's Liberation Army (PLA) invaded eastern Tibet and accepted the surrender of inferior Tibetan forces. A delegation (some Tibetans say an unauthorized delegation) went to Beijing and signed the infamous Seventeen Point Agreement for the Peaceful Liberation of Tibet. By treaty and by force of arms, Tibet had been incorporated into the People's Republic of China. The terms of the incorporation promised autonomy and the preservation of the traditional government.

The rise of communism as a viable political force in China began in the 1920s. China's fledgling Communist Party was under the influence of agents of the Soviet Union's Comintern, the association of communist parties of the world. China's concept of class struggle, revolution, governmental and bureaucratic organization, and minority policy all came from theorists in the Soviet Union—in particular, the writings of Lenin and Stalin. The Soviets considered communism to be modern and scientific, especially in applying the modern science of economics to politics. Their minority theory was derived from the nineteenth-century economic theory of Karl Marx, specifically on his observations of the Industrial Revolution in Britain.

Russia was key to the Allied victory in World War II, and Stalin thought that this made him the master of Asia. As the ruler of the world's first communist country and the holder of the lineage of revolution, Stalin saw himself as the senior partner and adviser to the new government in China. He considered Mao Zedong a junior partner, and China a backward country in comparison with Russia. The USSR was the great example of revolution.

Soviet influence in China was especially strong in the 1920s and 1930s, the formative early years, the period of revolutionary ferment surrounding the movement for modernization and reform in China.

During the 1950s, the relationship changed. Mao resented being treated as the junior partner, and his theories about the revolution in China differed from classic Russian revolutionary theory.

Mao adapted the ideology inherited from the communist founders to forge a new theory of revolution adapted to Chinese circumstances. Mao's theories of revolution differed from Stalin's—China had a peasantry not a proletariat, and its intellectual class, the Confucian literati, was not on the side of revolution but rather was part of the establishment. As the communists retreated, Mao traveled through China's southwest. There he had armed clashes with Tibetans residing in places incorporated into Chinese administrative areas under the Qing. Mao never forgot the experience.

As the newly opened Cold War archives of the PRC show, Stalin was the only man on earth of whom Mao was afraid. When Mao first visited Moscow in the early 1950s, Stalin kept Mao waiting for days before granting him an audience. Stalin considered the USSR to be the vanguard of revolution. He was the kingpin and treated Mao as the junior partner in revolution. The display of power rankled the Chinese leader.

The two giant communist states entered an era of competition. The Cold War had begun in Asia, with China and Russia vying for power, territory, and influence. As the newly opened archives of the Chinese Foreign Ministry show, Mao had good reason to mistrust Stalin.

The USSR brought Outer Mongolia, a traditional Chinese tribute state, into its sphere of influence. (Outer Mongolia thought it would fare better under the umbrella of autonomy, as a republic of the USSR, than if it became a province of China.) Stalin also attempted to take over the Chinese industrial heartland of Manchuria and wield influence in Xinjiang, the Muslim province bordering the Central Asian republics of the USSR. The West was preoccupied with the war against Germany and Japan during the 1940s, giving the Soviets a free hand in Central Asia.

The new government of the PRC sought to protect its western and southwestern borders, including Tibet and Xinjiang, out on the multiethnic frontiers. Chinese minorities are a very small percentage of the Chinese population as a whole, and they are concentrated on

China's borders. Stalin was greedy for Asian territory. Geopolitics gave Mao reason to fear Russia and led ultimately to the rapprochement with the United States. The historic meetings took place with President Nixon in 1972 through the diplomacy of Henry Kissinger and through back-channel connections with Pakistan. Mao had more to fear from the USSR than he did from the United States.

When Stalin died, Nikita Khrushchev succeeded him. Khrushchev reversed many of Stalin's economic policies and denounced the Stalin cult of personality. This accusation struck an uncomfortable chord in Chairman Mao, for Mao was at the center of his own personality cult. (See the Online Resources section, political cartoon, "Mao as a religious figure.")

Mao Zedong saw Khrushchev's economic policies as revisionism, accusing Khrushchev of being a "capitalist roader" and of betraying the revolution. Mao carved a role for himself as the spokesman for the revolutionary aspirations of Third World countries around the globe. By contrast, the USSR had become a member of the establishment, the post-WWII power structure, as a member of the UN Security Council's Big Five.

Mao's opposition to Khrushchev led to the Sino-Soviet split. The Chinese leadership was determined to unify a broken China and to protect itself on contested borders, especially those with Russia and India. Where Russia was concerned, on the Inner Asian frontier, China consolidated its hold on Xinjiang. Where India was concerned, China needed a buffer state. The geopolitics did not bode well for Tibet, but the context illuminates Chinese thinking.

In the early 1950s, the Cold War in Asia—the U.S. preoccupation with the Korean War and whether or not the Chinese would commit land forces in Korea—gave the PRC a free hand in Tibet. India did not want to antagonize China, for there were already frictions on their long border. Britain did not want to support Tibet's claim to independence in the U.N. because it deemed that its national interest ended with India's independence. Tibet was left without supporters in the international arena. It was a different time, and the geopolitics were against Tibet.

The struggle for political dominance—*hegemony* in the communist rhetoric of the 1950s and 1960s—in Asia continued until the fall of the Soviet Union. China was clearly the victor, a fact clearly recognizable from its rise as a regional and international power.

❧

By accident of history and geography, for centuries Tibet has been a pawn on the imperial chessboard, a small state caught up in the politics of powerful neighbors. China has become a global player and it has emerged as an Asian leader. The historical situation in South Asia demands new and creative solutions. The present moment offers a unique opportunity to reconfigure the structural relationship of China and Tibet—oddly enough the old system employed by Chinggis Khan, the "loose reins" approach, is very close to the modern network theory of the writer John Arquilla. China could also modernize minority theory, creating a win–win situation for China and Tibet. The question of political reform has been on the minds of the Chinese leadership for some time—ever since the much-studied demise of the Soviet Union. The road map described at the conclusion of this book is offered in the time-honored tradition of the scholar memorializing the throne. The old tradition survives in modern form. For millennia, intellectuals and scholars have been sending the throne their formalized communications concerning the state. They have been doing the same to the Chinese communist leadership since the Democracy Wall in Beijing became a forum at the end of 1978—at the outset of Deng Xiaoping's era of economic reform.

China's claim to Tibet dates to the Mongol Khans and the formation of their empire in the thirteenth century. Yet in the Mongol form of government—the "loose reins" approach designed by a half-Chinese courtier and modeled on the Chinese system, but adapted to local customs, institutions, and conditions—lies the beginning of a twenty-first century solution to the Tibet Question. For the rest of the solution one must examine history, and that is what this book seeks to do.

PART 1

Surging Storms

Tibet as the High Ground of Inner Asia

Six Tibets

The Dalai Lama says that there are six million Tibetans and that their fate is more important than his own fate. Whether or not he returns to Tibet, whether or not he has a role in the future of Tibet, is less important than the fate of the Tibetan people and Tibet's survival as a culture and homeland.

Inside Tibet and in diaspora, it is not difficult to find nationalist Tibetans who believe that the Chinese style of modernization and development is destroying their identity, their environment, and their way of life. The dredging of a sacred lake during construction of the newly completed Qinghai–Tibet railroad meant material progress to China, but to Tibet it meant desecration of holy land.

The character of the holy city of Lhasa has changed. Tibetans resent the diminishment of ethnically Tibetan Tibet in favor of a growing Han Chinese and Hui Muslim immigration. The good jobs and high pay that induce immigration stem from the government's promotion of a "Go West" policy. The influx of Han Chinese has had the effect of making Tibetans a devalued minority in their own land. The population influx is part of the general movement of poorer peasants from the interior to locations in China where jobs are more plentiful and salaries are better.

Tibetans resent that in their own country the material benefits of health care, education, and jobs go to Han Chinese and Hui immigrants, who have turned their holy capital into a Buddhist theme park. The proliferation of bad architecture, cheap hotels, and businesses that cater to Chinese and Western tourists is offensive to many Tibetans.

The Chinese invasion of Tibet occurred in October of 1950. For more than half a century since, China has attempted economic reform. The PRC has invested billions of yuan in the improvement of Tibet's infrastructure. They have also replaced Tibet's political system with a communist government and changed the class structure. Yet by China's own admission, the socialist dream of equality in a worker's paradise has not been realized. The application of force and the calling out of security forces, coupled with the official line that all problems in Tibet are the result of outside agitation, indicate that China has not addressed the root questions of unrest. If the PRC does not address the problem, new unrest is likely.[1] Neither China nor Tibet will benefit from renewed protest. The deadlock raises a number of questions.

Does Tibet's religion give its cultural heritage a special place among other countries? Would it be tragic if a multi-ethnic Tibet lost its unique identity? Is changing the composition and look of Tibet the necessary, justifiable, or inevitable cost of modernization? Is geography a part of the Tibetan identity? Does "genius of place" exist? Is it relevant?

Who decides how development is to take place? Should architects of new buildings design them to conform with the look and feel of old Lhasa or is this sentimentalism? Is strictly utilitarian architecture good enough as long as it improves living standards? Should these issues be handled in Beijing by the Chinese leadership rather than in Lhasa by those whose lives are affected?

Should Tibet be the Tibet of history? If so, then whose history is the correct version? Tibetans are not willing to trade a thousand years of culture for sixty years of modernization, some of it clumsy and misbegotten. These are philosophical questions, but they invoke passionate responses.

For the past century and a half, Tibet has been not only a place but also a state of mind, a projection of the imagination. The reader may count many Tibets—much like the smaller Buddhas that, in tangkha paintings, radiate from the consciousness of the central Buddha. First and foremost, Tibet exists in the Western imagination as a Shangri-la nestled in the high Himalayas, where a peaceful people lived among spiritually exalted Buddhist monks. An indigenous mountain people, materially poor but spiritually rich, Tibetans are seen to have lived an idyllic existence against the backdrop of the jagged peaks and the bluest of blue skies at "the Roof of the World." The major rivers of Asia originate in this landscape, the remote and forbidding habitat of the snow leopard.

In the 1937 film *Lost Horizon,* travelers reached Shangri-la as the result of a plane crash.[2] In the magical land, they were healed and found salvation. Because of its isolation from the modern world, Tibet is seen as a pure land—the custodian of a religion that offers a refuge from the Western materialism and even the new Chinese materialism.

In China today, spirituality has become a cultural fad. The materialism of the Chinese economic miracle has created a spiritual void in many of those who have succeeded. Han Chinese tourists number among the thousands who visit Tibet each year seeking spiritual renewal. Singers of Tibetan nationality have achieved pop-star status, and their melodies—with Buddhist mantras and nostalgic elegies for Lhasa—can be downloaded from the internet.

Remote and mysterious, Lhasa has proved to be irresistible and alluring to Westerners for some 150 years. Seekers, adventurers, merchants, officials, diplomats, spies, and soldiers have trekked across the passes of the high Himalayas, setting out from the colonial outposts of the British Empire to penetrate what was (before the age of jet travel) one of the most inaccessible places on earth. The vision of Potala Palace high above the city—a citadel of wisdom in a place of mystery and magic—has exerted a magnetic pull on the world's imagination. This is Hollywood's "magical mystery tour" vision of

Tibet, where one may find love, peace, happiness, and the answers to eternal questions.

A second Tibet is the vision projected by the Chinese. It derives from the ideology of communism, the dictatorship of the proletariat, with the party serving as the vanguard of the people's revolution. In this cosmology, Tibet is the socialist paradise represented on the Chinese flag as one of four small yellow stars on a red background. These little stars stand for the former tribute states of Mongolia, Manchuria, Tibet, and Xinjiang. The big star represents China proper.

In this worldview, China delivered Tibet from a feudal system that held the masses in serfdom. China was the heroic liberator delivering the benefits of modernity and material progress to a backward people. Tibetans should be grateful for what the Chinese Communist Party has done for them. Instead, they protest, their attitude resulting from ignorance and superstition. Tibetans want a return to feudalism, an exiled religious leader who is an anachronism, and a belief system that has kept them in servitude and poverty.

A third Tibet is virtual Tibet. It exists in cyberspace, almost like an ethereal projection of the future Buddha, Maitreya, floating in a tangkha painting's celestial realms. On the internet, Tibetans in diaspora have found a voice more powerful and far-reaching than at any time in their history. Those in China's Tibet have no such voice: The internet is heavily policed, and references to Tibet, websites about Tibet, and searches for Tibet are banned, blocked, and outlawed as criminal activity by the authorities.

In cyberspace, surfers beyond Chinese control access opinion journals such as the *Tibetan Review*. They glean information from the websites of authors and activists, and learn of the activities of pro-Tibet advocacy groups, such as Students for a Free Tibet. News services such as phayul.com keep the world informed of events inside Tibet. Human rights organizations, such as the International Campaign for Tibet and Amnesty International, pressure the international community to respond to Chinese violations of the human rights of monks and nuns in Tibet.

Academic websites, such as that of Australian National University, publish work by the global community of Tibet scholars and keep followers informed with a calendar of events relating to Tibet. Exile Tibetans, together with dissident Chinese in the West, organize conferences where experts in the many disciplines of Asian Studies discuss the Tibet Question. The records of these conferences are subsequently published on the internet for use by the international scholarly community.

The Voice of America has a Tibetan language channel on the web. Exile journals of diaspora Tibetans, including the *Tibetan Review,* publish a wide variety of opinion. A Colorado art gallery exhibits the paintings of diaspora Tibetan artists, whose artistic output is not the classic tangkha painting of Tibet, but modern work in keeping with trends in the international art world.

Cyberspace has also provided a home for organizations dedicated to Tibetan culture, including Tibet House and the American Himalayan Foundation (which has developed micro-enterprise and health projects in central and eastern Tibet). The Mechak Center for Tibetan Art promotes contemporary art from a traditional society, no matter where in the world it is created.[3]

Cyberspace is cheap and it is hip; it is messy and unruly, but in its variety and availability it gives David, the small state out on the multi-ethnic frontier, some traction against Goliath, the power in the capital. Although the public security watchdogs of Beijing censor internet material related to Tibet, the young and the technologically savvy have ways of getting around the firewalls.

A fourth Tibet, the Tibetan Government in Exile (TGIE), was established in Dharamsala, India, after the Dalai Lama fled Tibet in 1959. In exile, the modernization of the old system has progressed along democratic lines, although the Dharamsala government is not a perfect democracy. The Dalai Lama has expressed his wish that it should be a complete democracy, without himself as an unelected head of government. The TGIE has a global media presence and uses the web to maintain contacts among the fifty or so communities of Tibetans spread all over the globe.

A fifth Tibet is that of the Tibetan independence movement, various groups that see their homeland as illegally invaded and occupied. The Tibetan Youth Congress and the Young Tigers oppose the Dalai Lama's Middle Way of autonomy, are willing to consider violence as a tactic, and do not wish Tibetans to be seen as (in the words of Professor Robert Thurman) the baby seals of the human rights movement—pathetic victims clobbered by a bully's club. For members of the independence movement, the Tibet Question is a political issue of self-determination, not an issue of cultural preservation or religious freedom.

The sixth Tibet is that of the global community of Buddhist practitioners. It is estimated that this community numbers in the millions. Until the recent fad for pop Kabbalah, Tibetan Buddhism was the spiritual path favored even by seekers among the Hollywood glitterati. Through his writings and personal appearances, the Dalai Lama has become a charismatic and popular spiritual mentor for the world.

The diaspora of Tibetan monks has made Buddhist teachings available to more people than at any time in the religion's history. Tibetan Buddhism is now a world religion. A vast array of Tibetan Buddhist websites and magazines inform practitioners of where they may receive teachings, go on retreats, and avail themselves of the vast canon of Tibetan Buddhist literature.

❧

At the heart of the Tibet Question is the rivalry of ethnicity and nationality, the clash of cultures, the slippage of the tectonic plates joining two civilizations.

Tibet's Backstory

Tibet is a Central or South Asian culture, falling within the Indian sphere of historical influence. East Asian societies such as those of Japan and Korea are similar to China, influenced by Confucianism and later forms of Buddhism, more authoritarian and centralized than non-Confucian Asian societies. These countries came within China's cultural sphere and absorbed China's historical influence. They fall within the East Asian tradition.

Traditional Tibetan society was different from traditional Chinese society. It was not a rice-based culture and did not feature the centralization and organization that rice cultivation requires. Tibet was more decentralized, with local lords and monasteries establishing their own local chieftains and internal power structures.

In the seventh century, Tibet was unified under the warrior King Songtsen Gampo. This was Tibet's imperial period, and the dynasty lasted for two centuries. During this time, Tibet's borders expanded to include Xinjiang province in the north, parts of modern Ladakh and Kashmir in the west, and in the east, Amdo and Kham (parts of today's Gansu, Qinghai, Sichuan, and Yunnan provinces). This accounts for Tibetan populations throughout the vast expanse of territory in southwest China and northern India.

This era marked the beginning of diplomatic relations between China and Tibet. Before the Tibetan imperial expansion, parts of the territories were subordinate to Tang China. In the Asian manner of making political alliances, the Tibetan king wed a Chinese princess, and Tang China was required to pay tribute to Tibet. After the Tang failed to pay its tribute, Tibetan armed forces seized Ch'ang-an (modern Xi'an), the cosmopolitan Tang capital.

These conflicts were put to rest by 822, when China and Tibet signed treaties and fixed borders. A stone pillar in Lhasa memorialized these events. In the imperial period, China and Tibet were separate states. Buddhism came to Tibet in the ninth century and found itself in conflict with the native Bon religion, a shamanist faith. Religious conflict caused the Tibetan dynasty to come to an end. In the 10th century, the Tang Dynasty ended. Because of the internal politics in both countries, formal political relations between China and Tibet were nonexistent from the ninth century onward.

In the thirteenth century, a new and formidable power arose in the steppes north of the Great Wall of China: Chinggis Khan unified the warring tribes of Mongolia and led his army to victory in a war of national revenge against the Chin Dynasty. Chinggis Khan was the new political master of East Asia. His empire was the largest land-based empire in world history and ushered in a new historical era.

In 1207, Tibet submitted to the Mongol Empire without a war of conquest. As with all the states that submitted and became his vassals, Tibet saved Chinggis Khan the trouble of going to war, so he was lenient. The Mongol Army did not invade Tibet; neither did it place a military governor or garrison there, as it did throughout the rest of its empire. Chinggis Khan's aim was not to acquire territory, but to extract wealth from it. He instituted indirect rule in Tibet, choosing the Sakya branch of Tibetan Buddhism as rulers and administrators of the country. As long as Tibet paid its tribute, it enjoyed local rule. Tibet paid tribute. On the occasions it failed to pay, the Mongol imperial government dispatched troops to collect the missing remittance.

The man known as The Conqueror revered those whom he termed Speakers to Heaven, his term for holy men of all faiths in his empire. The Mongols practiced religious toleration throughout their empire.

❧

The southernmost part of Tibet was mainly agrarian. The principle crop was barley, a staple of the Tibetan diet. Buddhism had its own system of ecological protection that arose from its philosophy of compassion toward sentient and nonsentient beings, and famine was unknown in traditional Tibet. In the northern areas of Tibet, the principle means of livelihood was mixed herding. The majority of peasant families produced their own food and clothing. Tibet did not develop an internal market economy. As Tsering Shakya states, "Before the 1950s, it was unheard of for *tsampa,* barley flour, the staple diet—to be bought and sold in the marketplace. Even in a city like Lhasa, families relied on relatives from the countryside to supply their basic needs."[4] A few hundred noble families staffed offices of the government, and a fourth of the adult male population resided in monasteries. The rest of the population lived as farmers, serfs, or nomads. The Tibetan political system was not a modern democracy, but its monastic and civil branches of government did provide some checks and balances.

At the time of the Chinese invasion in 1950, Tibet had neither elections nor a popular vote. Much as was the case in pre-modern Europe, the church played a crucial role in running the state. Control rested in the hands of a few hundred landowning families. The government body, the Kashag, was similar to the English House of Lords and was composed of representatives from the landed nobility.

Tibet was the only country to inherit the high scholastic tradition of Indian Buddhism, and while the Muslim conquerors destroyed the Buddhist institutions of higher learning in India during the Arab conquests of the eighth century, they were preserved in Tibet. The monasteries functioned as Buddhist universities and as an educational system for many boys. In a Buddhist form of affirmative action, the poorest peasant boy from the most remote part of Tibet could acquire an education if he could demonstrate ability. Through merit and achievement, these youths from humble beginnings advanced to monastic centers of power. The education of a young monk included scholarly study, memorization, a lively and vivid form of debate, and the mastery of meditation practices. Tibetan Buddhism involves a sophisticated understanding of the human mind; the goal of years of meditation practices is to gain illumination, wisdom, and insight.

One point seems particularly important to many exiled Tibetan intellectuals: Traditional Tibet did not disdain poverty, perhaps because of the pervasive influence of Buddhist spirituality. The Dalai Lama could be selected from a poor family. Indeed, the present, Fourteenth Dalai Lama, Tenzin Gyatso, came from humble beginnings. Traditional China, with its pragmatic Confucian influence, valued prosperity and disdained poverty. Buddhism in general fosters a respect for all human beings. There was no disdain for the masses in Buddhism as there was in traditional China. Attaining political position and power was feasible even for ordinary people. For them, monasteries were the route to advancement. Lamas (religious clerics) selected the abbots, whose sole requirement for selection was human development. From the beginning, the Chinese understood that an entrenched, educated, scholarly elite posed a threat to their system of political education and control.

The three great traditions of medicine in Asia are Chinese traditional medicine, with its offshoots in Japan and Korea; Tibetan medicine; and Indian Ayurvedic medicine. These Asian systems have enjoyed increased popularity in the West in recent years. The

Tibetan system of medicine was regarded as one of the most advanced in Asia, and it may have had a significant influence on Chinese traditional medicine. With the advent of globalization, major Western medical schools have begun to study these indigenous medical traditions and the botanical medicine that is integral to them. One reason why conservations view the preservation of the fragile ecosystem of Tibet as important is the protection of endangered plant species with medicinal value. In traditional times, Buddhism provided the medical system of Tibet. Lhasa was home to a huge medical college under religious auspices. The Buddhist medical tradition was of great benefit to the populace, and compared favorably to the "barefoot doctor" type of medicine brought to Tibet by the Chinese before they built hospitals in the country.

∽

Positive portrayals of pre-1950 Tibet have been criticized by some scholars as being too idealistic, too benign a view of the system of manorial estates owned by the aristocracy and the monastic elites. Some Western academics, many of them experts on Buddhism, support this rendering of Tibetan history. Yet there are other Tibetans, intellectuals and activists both, who level criticism against Old Tibet and argue that it was slow to modernize and ineffectual at arranging for its own defense. In this narrative, the governing class brought about its own demise during the period of Tibet's independence from 1912 to 1950. Tibet did not have a modernized army to back up its definition of nationhood, nor did it gain the recognition of any members of the international community.

Whatever the social system—and many in Tibet had come to see the need for reforming it before the Chinese invasion of 1950— Tibet had been functioning as independent state for forty years. When the People's Republic of China (PRC) came to power, Mao announced his intention to reunite Tibet with the motherland. This was not a humanitarian project. Mao was a strategic thinker with geopolitical concerns. China was closing its "back door."

Whatever the Chinese view of history, Tibetans recall a past that is not Han Chinese.

China's Backstory

China has traditionally viewed itself as the most exalted civilization of East Asia. The Australian China watcher Ross Terrill makes the argument that China is not merely a civilization, but an empire and a state of mind.[5] Dynasties came and went but somehow preserved the same form and content. Dynasties lost the Mandate of Heaven—the right to rule—and passed from the scene, but new dynasties arose, phoenix-like, from the ashes. The archetype, with the same forms and rituals, came from a template, a collection of texts, those of Confucianism and the philosophical school known as Legalism. Confucianism was benevolent, the basis of moral rule. Legalism provided the full authority of the Emperor to assert his will by use of force if necessary. The Emperor was above the law, but he was benevolent, unless he required the use of killing to remove his opponents.[6]

From the sixth to the ninth centuries, Tang China was the most advanced and richest civilization on earth. Ch'ang-an, the capital, was situated in the old feudal and agricultural heartland of China's northwest and was laid out in the form of a mandala—a diagram of the cosmos—with gates opening to the four directions and the imperial palace at the center. The Emperor of China resided at the heart of the world. All nationalities and faiths were represented in Ch'ang-an. It was also the eastern gate to the Silk Road, the caravan trail where China's foreign trade began with the Inner Asia, Persia, and Europe.

This was the old China, with its military feudal culture and its capital in the northwest, reaching out to the old khanates of the Asian landmass where the tribal peoples, the womb of nations, lived. This was the millet-eating culture of the north, not the rice-eating culture of the south. The old stone portal at the beginning of the Silk Road was the gateway where cultural influences of all types entered China. The oasis towns of the Silk Road (Kashgar, Khotan, Yarkand, and others) were a mix of languages and nationalities, a melting pot of adventurers, traders, missionaries, and scholars where culture and religion mingled: Buddhist, Christian, Confucian, Daoist. Sufi Islam came to China's west in the tenth century, brought by Turkic Muslims who had their roots in Central Asia.

The northern and southern branches of the Silk Road surround the Tarim Basin and the vast and forbidding Taklimakan Desert. Western explorers and archaeologists of the Victorian era recorded that the Taklimakan had dunes as high as a many-storied building. The whistling sands frightened many an explorer, archaeologist, and missionary. As far back as the thirteenth century even Marco Polo commented on the "singing sands," reputed to be inhabited by demons. Ghost stories abound in the travel literature.

A challenge to man and beast, the Taklimakan was far more dangerous and fearful than the Sahara, the great Rub' al Khali (Empty Quarter) desert of Saudi Arabia, or the vast and inhospitable Gobi Desert. Many an explorer, together with his caravan train of Europeans and local guides, perished there. This did not dissuade others from following in the footsteps of the discovery of the old lost civilizations, such as that at Dunhuang. The traffic in antiquities was highly profitable.

The late Qing Dynasty was weak and could not spare the troops to control its far western borders. Victorian explorer-adventurers looted the Buddhist sites and carried hundreds of cartloads of antiquities off to European museums. This remains a sore point with the Chinese to the present day, as they continue to press for the return of their artistic treasures.

Surrounding Xinjiang are the mountain ranges that form the Roof of the World, the Kunlun, the Pamirs, and the Tien Shan, or Heavenly Mountains. In what must be one of the greatest military feats in history, Chinggis Khan took his armies through these high mountain passes on his way to making war in the Muslim lands. He returned as a victor, bringing his army and his captives back to settle in the Inner Mongolian capital of Khara Khorum. He was the only nomad general ever to have conquered so vast a land-based empire, and his heirs were the only nomads ever to rule all of China.

It is not difficult to see how the Sinocentric view of Asia began. China's geography defined it as the Middle Kingdom and placed it at the center of Asian politics (see map, page vi–vii). To the north, beyond the Great Wall, lived nomad tribes of the steppes, pastoral peoples of Mongol and Turkic extraction. To the northeast, Khitan and Manchu tribes lived on the Liaotung Peninsula and in Manchuria. To the east, the civilizations of Korea and Japan were influenced by Chinese culture. Vietnam and Burma lay to the southeast.

To the far west lay the oasis towns of the Silk Road, centers of commerce for millennia. Beyond the mountain passes lay the great centers of Islamic civilization in Inner Asia, including the fabled cities of Samarkand and Bukhara, with their universities (centers of Islamic learning), markets, and caravanserais (Marco Polo describes these as inns for caravan merchants built around courts where animals and valuable cargo remained under the watchful eye of their owners). Beyond lay Baghdad, where the armies of Chinggis Khan's descendants destroyed the Abbasid caliphate and replaced it with a Mongol regional government whose headquarters lay in China proper. In fact, the Mongol destruction of the caliphate is lamented down to the present, and is at the center of the call for its return among the radical Islamists of today. Far to the southwest are the Himalayan civilizations of Tibet and Nepal, which fell within the cultural orbit of India. Tibet was called Xizang, the Western Treasure House.

China was the Rome of Asia. All roads led to the Middle Kingdom.

❧

In early Tang, the military feudal families of the northwest dominated the government. The loneliness of the frontier and the valor of the forlorn soldier assigned there—longing for his family, his sweetheart, the Chinese countryside, Chinese seasons, his village—has been the subject of thousands of classical Chinese poems, so many that they constitute an entire category of Tang literary activity. By late Tang, in the tenth century, the center had weakened and the Chinese state imploded. Foreign invaders brought down the dynasty that had created China's golden age, the most cosmopolitan era in Chinese history.

For the next four centuries, China was like a modern European state, one country among many equals rather than the sun in the center of the solar system with planets revolving around it. China remained divided for 400 years. Foreign khans ruled North China. A Han Chinese dynasty, Southern Song, controlled the country south of the Yangzi River.

China's unique system of foreign relations is necessary context for understanding the relationship between China and Tibet today. In *China among Equals,* Morris Rossabi observes that the Chinese "devised a scheme which demanded acknowledgement of their superiority."[7] Tibet, Mongolia, Manchuria, and Xinjiang were tribute nations in traditional times. Incorporated into the Chinese system of diplomacy, they and had a role to play in court ritual, including symbolic submission to the Dragon Throne. (Today these states are Autonomous Regions of the PRC.)

Traditional Chinese foreign policy admitted foreign dignitaries into China at certain times of the year, at imperial expense, where they were guided by Chinese officials who instructed the "barbarians" in Chinese court etiquette. The visitors were completely under Chinese control. This system was a defense mechanism against the threat of the mounted warriors of the Asian steppes—the greatest cavalry in the medieval world. These were the tribal peoples who brought Chinese dynasties down: the Huns,[8] the Turks,[9] and, most dangerous of all, the Mongols. China's relationship with the wild men of the north has often been described as "trade or raid." In peaceful times, the Mongols engaged in commerce, trading their horses and tanned hides for tea and silk and other types of manufactured goods and foodstuffs produced by China. At other times, the nomads challenged the Chinese imperial governments of Han, Tang, and Song.

Mongol cavalry was capable of penetrating Chinese defenses and mounting attacks on Chinese soil. The Chinese may have bought horses at the horse fairs of the nomads and received many as tribute, but they were still at a disadvantage. If attacked, they could not pursue the offenders and punish them because the terrain was against them: they had no supply lines.[10]

The Mongols did what the Chinese were unable to do for themselves: recover the north and unify the country for the first time in 400 years—since the fall of the Tang Dynasty.

A number of foreign dynasties ruled North China, among them were the Jurchen, semi-nomads with origins in the forest areas of Manchuria. In 1115, they took the Dragon Throne and founded the Chin (or Golden) Dynasty. The Chin espoused the strategy of divide and conquer. Chinese foreign policy against the nomad tribes was called *i-i-zi-i,* using barbarians to check barbarians. They fomented warfare in the steppes, pitting the tribes against one another, backing first the Tatar and then the Mongols. Chinese interference in steppe affairs was responsible also for the young Chinggis Khan's loss of his birthright, stature and inheritance.

Chinggis Khan had been a vassal of the Chin Emperor, but after he unified the warring tribes of Mongolia, he declared a war of national revenge against the Chin. They were responsible for the death of Mongol kings and for the murder of his father. In a series of brilliant campaigns, he conquered North China in the year 1215. He appointed a Viceroy to rule North China when a Muslim ruler defied his authority and gave him cause to ride west and make war in the Muslim lands. Mongol control over North China was consolidated under the reign of Chinggis Khan's son and successor, Ogodei.

Tibet submitted to Chinggis Khan and attained privileged status. A hallmark of the Mongol *imperium* was that it never attempted direct rule; instead it used local forms of rule under the watchful eye of a *darugachi* (military governor) and a garrison of troops to keep the peace, guard the roads, protect the caravan traffic, and to collect taxes and take a census that set levels of corvée (unpaid labor) and military service. So effective was the Mongol system of government that it was said that a virgin could walk from one end of the Mongol Empire to the other with a sack of gold on her head and remain unharmed.

Chinggis Khan appointed the Sakya branch of Tibetan Buddhism to be the rulers of Tibet. The Sakya Pandit and his nephew the Phagpa Lama took up residence in the Chinese capital, where they met Khubilai Khan (grandson of Chinggis Khan).

In a bloodless coup, the throne had passed to Tolui's branch of the Mongol imperial family. Tolui was Chinggis Khan's youngest son and his military chief of staff. He had fought alongside his father in all the major campaigns and inherited his army. His wife, Sorghagtani Beki, was Chinggis Khan's favorite daughter-in-law, and his sons were the most able of Chinggis Khan's descendants.

The most brilliant of Chinggis Khan's successors, Mongke Khan, began the conquest of Southern China. Mongke was Khubilai's older brother and delegated Khubilai to be the Khan of China, where his assignment was to protect the interests of the Mongol imperial family. After twenty-five years of constant warfare, North China was chaotic—Mongol generals taxed at will and requisitioned crops. Chinese peasants were abandoning their farms to move below the Yangzi River, where a Han Chinese emperor ruled. As a result, tax revenues were down. Khubilai soon assembled a team of advisors and established order in North China and on the advice of Confucian scholars, levied the traditional Chinese taxes, which the peasants were used to paying. Order returned, the peasants paid up, and Khubilai restored the tax base in the North.

Mongke Khan began the conquest of Southern China. Mongke had been a hero of the Russian Campaign and entered the field against China with confidence and enthusiasm. He would not live to see victory against the South because he died of a disease contracted on the battlefield. Khubilai succeeded his elder brother as the Supreme Khan of the Mongol Empire. The conquest of Southern China was completed under Khubilai Khan in a five-year campaign headed by the brilliant General Bayan. The unification of China was accomplished in the year 1279.

Over the opposition of the traditional Mongol aristocracy and the Confucian ruling elite, Khubilai converted to Tibetan Buddhism and made it the state religion of China. His patron deity was the fire-breathing Mahakala, the wrathful emanation of Avalokiteshvara, the Buddha of Infinite Compassion. The unique priest–patron relationship began under Khubilai Khan, between the Emperor of China and his imperial tutor, the Phagpa Lama, and Khubilai Khan. To the horror of Confucians and Chinese Buddhists alike, the Phagpa Lama performed the dedication ceremony for the new capital of Shangdu (Xanadu). The Mongols believed in religious toleration and permitted the practice of all religions within their empire. This even extended to Christians, papal envoys, who had come from Europe to the court of the Great Khans, such as William of Rubruck and John of Plano Carpini.

Khubilai did not trust the Confucians because he knew that they could rule China without an army. He wanted to diminish their power. He gave the control of the treasury to a succession of Central Asian Muslims and control of the religious establishment to the Tibetans. His was a conquest dynasty and he wanted to deflect popular resentment away from the Mongols.

Both North and South China were conquered by force of arms. Tibet submitted without a conflict. Both were part of the Mongol multi-ethnic state. After a century, the Mongol dynasty weakened under the rule of a series of less than competent emperors. In 1368, the Yuan fell and the Ming Dynasty took its place. The last of the Mongol emperors got on his horse and rode back to the steppes.

For almost a millennium China experienced foreign rule by Asian conquerors from the former tribute states. The Ming (1368 to 1644) was the only Han Chinese dynasty to preside over China until the fall of the dynastic system in 1911, a period of 277 years. This is a short amount of time by the standards of Chinese history. It is no small wonder that both Chinese Nationalists and Chinese Communists had Chinese unity as a primary goal of their regimes.

The Ming Dynasty presided over a period of cultural glory and economic prosperity. Historian Jonathan Spence describes it as follows: "In the year A.D. 1600, the empire of China was the largest and most sophisticated of all the unified realms on earth."[11] The Ming expanded urban society, presided over a burgeoning commercial expansion, was justly proud of a flowering culture, and waged several hundred wars over its nearly three centuries of rule. Its territory was smaller, about half the size of that later conquered by Qing.

The Ming Dynasty came to an abrupt and violent end brought about by a series of political miscalculations and failed policies. Most importantly, diminishing tax revenues meant that the army was not paid. This led to borders whose security was compromised by troop desertions and hostilities with border tribes. Poor management of government granaries led to malnutrition and disease in the countryside, which eventually led to peasant rebellion. Jurchen tribesmen from the area of Manchuria, in China's northeast, swept down into China proper and conquered the country. As with previous barbarian conquerors, the Manchus were militarily strong. They also entered China with an infrastructure that was ready to govern, ready to impose order on the chaos that accompanied the loss of the Mandate of Heaven. The Manchus founded the last dynasty, the Qing.

The most important of the early Qing emperors was Kangxi. Upon his accession to the Dragon Throne, he set about the task of consolidating China's territory. One of his first moves was to militarize China's borders to the northwest, south, and north. The Russians were a problem in Manchu lands in the northeast; the Mongols were militarily powerful in the north; and the Tibetans presented a problem because of Mongol support for various factions in what amounted to a civil war among warlords, each of them backing a different faction of Tibetan Buddhism. Kangxi also launched a military expedition that incorporated the Muslim region of Xinjiang into the Chinese empire. By militarily defeating former tribute states, Kangxi strengthened his borders. His consolidation of empire set the precedent for the Nationalists and the Communists after the fall of the Qing Dynasty in 1911.

The Nationalists leaders—Sun Yatsen and Chiang Kaishek—attempted without success to control territories that Qing had won by force of arms. The Nationalist Army proved unequal to the task, and the Communists prevailed in the Chinese civil war. The People's Liberation Army was battle-hardened, and it was successful in consolidating Chinese borders. The communist central government was organized and received the support and advice of the USSR. Mao succeeded where the Nationalists failed: in establishing control over the border territories of Tibet, Inner Mongolia, Manchuria, and Xinjiang.

Throughout its history, the Chinese empire never occupied a fixed territory: The fluctuation of borders and territory over the course of 2,500 years is a feature of the Chinese empire, described as a yin and yang pattern. When the Chinese center was strong, China expanded her borders. When it was weak, as in Ming, the size of the empire contracted (see the maps referred to in Online Resources, page 217). The fear of the present leadership and that China might split apart is deep-seated and grounded in history. It has happened before, so it could happen again.

Seeds of the Present Problem

The modern era of Chinese state building began in the seventeenth century during the Qing Dynasty. China competed with Britain and Russia for influence on the Asian landmass during the era known as the Great Game. Russia expanded its influence into Central and East Asia. Under the czars, Russia expanded its empire from the Baltic Sea in the West to the Pacific coast, through its conquest of Siberia. The Russian Empire extended from the Arctic Ocean in the north to the Black Sea in the south, making it the second-largest land-based empire in world history (only the Mongol Empire was larger).

After the Russian Revolution of 1917, Vladimir Ilyich Lenin, the leader of the communist party, did not repudiate the colonial ambitions but continued Russian expansion into East Asia. The Communists struggled to gain a foothold in the old czarist possessions, the predominantly Muslim lands in Central Asia.

Lenin dreamed that the East would be red. If Europe were not open to revolution, then Asia would still be fertile ground for communism. Lenin envisioned an international proletariat destroying the British Empire by co-opting its workers into a communist revolution.[12] He hoped that the Russian presence in Asia would influence the workers and peasants of India.

As part of the game for power and influence in Asia, Russia and Britain spied on each other. The British established the Raj in India and expanded their reach into the southern Himalayan kingdoms of Sikkim, Bhutan, and Nepal. Britain was especially keen on preventing Russian soldiers from gaining any foothold that might rob the Empire of India. Before he invaded Tibet on orders of the viceroy of India, the British colonel Francis Younghusband was given an intelligence assignment: Travel to the far west of China and determine the extent of Russian advancement there.[13] In colonial parlance, Tibet was considered a protectorate of China, an off-and-on arrangement that lasted until the fall of Qing.

Deeply isolationist, the Qing rulers paid little attention to their long eastern maritime coast. The Manchus were unaware of what was happening in the wider world. The Qing Dynasty exerted reach in its traditional sphere of influence—on the Asian landmass. Although decaying at its center, the Qing Dynasty attempted (with varying degrees of success) to exert influence in Tibet and thereby protect itself from British and Russian competition. Having been forced to intervene in Tibet on several occasions, the Chinese wanted Tibet firmly under the protection of the Dragon Throne. They did not want a European power at China's back door. Britain sought to protect the crown jewel of its colonial empire, India, by expanding its own influence northward into the Himalayan region. China watched the expansion of both powers. Extending its borders was a way for China to protect its sphere of influence.[14]

The early Qing emperors were militarily strong. State building consisted of incorporating the border regions into China proper. The Kangxi Emperor waged a military campaign that resulted in the incorporation of the New Territories (Xinjiang) into the empire. The inhabitants were mostly Muslim and of Turkish descent. This included the Muslim regions around the Tarim Basin (modern Xinjiang) and Tibet. Chinese influence in Tibet was not constant; Qing were only occasionally able to post a Chinese bureaucrat, called an *amban,* such as when Tibet called for help to ward off foreign invaders.

In the late eighteenth century, Tibet requested Qing military assistance to fend off the Ghurkas, Nepalese troops that invaded in 1788 and 1792. The Qing dispatched troops to protect a militarily weak Tibet. The Qing feared further military incursions into this sensitive region, and the Manchu general Fu Kangan recommended the establishment of a Qing bureaucratic office and an *amban* in Lhasa. The Emperor agreed with this recommendation, and the *amban* was dispatched to Tibet with a small retinue of about a hundred soldiers. This was the first attempt at direct rule by China, and it was also the first formal acknowledgement of

Tibet as a Chinese protectorate. From this time on, both Britain and Russia recognized that, with regard to Tibet, they had to deal with the Chinese.

In the north, the Qing had problems with marauding Mongols. The dynasty's goal was to prevent troublesome barbarians from making war at the borders or taking Qing territory. The solution was military and political. When its capital was invaded and captured by Mongols, the Qing sent troops. The Mongols had converted to Tibetan Buddhism, and the Qing believed they could gain leverage against the Mongols if the Dalai Lama was part of the Qing imperial system.

❦

The Industrial Revolution created wealth in Britain. Fashionable taste created demand for Chinese imports, with tea, porcelain, silk, and handicrafts being the most desirable items of trade. Europe had no indigenous porcelain industry—the Chinese had traditionally kept the manufacturing process (as it had with silk) a closely guarded secret. The Qing restricted trade to the coastal port of Canton (present-day Guangzhou), which reflected the Qing policy of keeping foreigners away from the capital.

By the late eighteenth century, Great Britain had become dissatisfied with these trade arrangements. Local disputes had grown up between the British and Chinese trade officials, licensed Chinese Hong merchants who sometimes engaged in dishonorable business practices. The only recourse for Westerners was to complain to the Chinese court-appointed official, who would then communicate with the provincial governor or the capital. This was not the sort of trade relationship the British wanted.

In 1793, King George III dispatched a hundred-member trade mission of the British East India Company, a corporation licensed by the British Crown. The purpose of the mission was to negotiate directly with Emperor Qianlong, who by this time had occupied the throne for more than thirty years. The British trade mission consisted of a convoy of ships: a man of war with 66 guns and two support vessels loaded with gifts and examples of British

technology. The British claimed to be bringing birthday greet
ings to Qianlong on his eightieth birthday. The Qing government
allowed the convoy to proceed from Canton to Tianjin. The trade
mission was received at Peking, described in court documents as
"tribute emissaries."

By way of response, Qianlong sent an edict to King George
refusing to grant Lord Macartney's requests and stating that China
had not the slightest need of British articles of manufacture. The
British were ordered to continue doing business at the Canton trading establishment as they had done previously. The Emperor's decision made sense in Chinese terms: How could the British attend the
Chinese court? They were ignorant of the Chinese language and
did not understand court ritual. The trade mission cost the British
East India Company a vast amount of money and was a complete
failure.

The British had begun shipping opium from India to China,
using it as the exchange medium in payment for Chinese goods. The
Chinese wanted to ban the practice, and Britain ultimately went to
war against China over the issue, a low point in the annals of British
diplomacy. The result of two Opium Wars (1840 and 1856) was that
British force of arms imposed the trade. The British induced the
Emperor to sign the Unequal Treaties, which led to the establishment of foreign trading enclaves on Chinese soil.

The Qing response to the modern world's knocking on its
door is described by Ross Terrill as a combination of superiority
and defensiveness—the classic Chinese imperial attitude. In hind-
sight, this rejection of the advances of Western technology and
science seems a mistake of the greatest magnitude. Qing power
and range of authority were at their high points, and China could
defend its imperial tradition only as long as its vision—of China
as the fount of civilization—remained unsullied by Western
influences.

As a consequence of their defeat in the two Opium Wars, the
Qing granted trading concessions to foreign states. The Century of
Humiliation had begun.[15] The Qing had made a fatal error in not
opening to the West. In little more than a century, the dynasty and
the dynastic system would no longer exist.

The twin issues of Westernization and modernization stirred debate among Qing intellectuals about the necessity for reform. Many recognized the problem and knew what had to be done, but overall the Qing response was inadequate. The dynasty, beset by internal rebellion and outside challenges, faltered and failed. The Republican Revolution of 1911 ended the imperial system that had governed China for 2,500 years. Qing China had responded to the modern era by settling into isolation. Had it opened, China might have had an easier passage into the modern era.

With the Republican Revolution, China began its transition into the modern world.[16] Two systems imported from the West had captured the imaginations of the Chinese revolutionaries. The Nationalists represented the liberal democratic tradition, and the Communists represented the progressive, radical tradition. The Nationalists were the heirs of Sun Yatsen, father of the Republican Revolution. They established a capital at Nanjing but never extended control to the whole country.

Reform movements abounded. Some worked within the imperial framework while others imported ideas from the West.[17] One of the first, the May Fourth Movement, was composed of students whose slogan was "Democracy and Science." Clearly, the desire for modernization was there. (In fact, this movement inspired the students who called for political reform at Tiananmen in 1989.)

China's second humiliation came at the hands of an Asian power. Meiji Japan faced the challenge of modernization by opening up to the West. In a grand experiment, Japan sent representatives to the West to learn and adapt Western advances to the Japanese situation. Japanese delegations studied everything from rail systems to the military to Western institutions. Meiji reforms succeeded. Without compromising its own culture, Japan adapted and refined what it needed while rejecting the rest. Having navigated the passage to modernity so successfully, by the early part of the twentieth century, Japan became nationalist and expansionist. It began to seek Asian colonies and conceived of itself as the dominant power in Asia in the Greater Asian Co-Prosperity Sphere. Japan wanted the natural resources of the Dutch West Indies and Malaysia. In addition, Japan sought to acquire territory in China.

The contenders in the Chinese civil war, Nationalists and Communists, formed a temporary alliance for the purpose of ousting the Japanese invaders in the years leading up to World War II. Following the Japanese surrender in 1945, the combatants resumed the civil war. The Communists ultimately won and established the People's Republic of China in 1949.

❧

In Tibet, the twentieth century brought confusion, discord, and factionalism over the issue of modernization. Some reformers ran up against the conservatism of the monastic establishment, which resented any change that would diminish their power and influence.

The last will and testament of the Thirteenth Dalai Lama, "the Great Thirteenth," exhorted the Tibetan government to maintain good relations with both India and China, yet to beware the influence of communism. He was appalled at how the communists had desecrated the religion in Mongolia, and he admonished Tibet to strengthen itself against the Red anti-religion.[18] Tibet attempted to modernize its military but failed to do so.

Tibet was strong enough to resist the Nationalists' attempts to incorporate them into their new government, but they were no match for the Communists. After almost a century of maneuvering among competing powers and forty years of independence, Tibet surrendered to the PLA. The Tibetan forces were weak. Communist forces were battle-hardened, they had revolutionary zeal and nationalist pride, and it was an article of faith among Communists that Tibet had once been a possession of Qing and was going to be a possession of the People's Republic. To this day, the unification of China remains one of the PRC's most prized accomplishments. The new rulers of China could not allow a weak and underdeveloped state, such as Tibet, to be on their border in South Asia.

The Ice of the Cold War and the Thaw of Globalization

As early as the 1920s, the newly established Soviet Union had agents in China working at recruiting Chinese into the Communist Party.

Thus Soviet Russia became the all-important influence on the Chinese revolution.

Communist ideology as developed in the Soviet Union became the major influence on Chinese communist thought until Mao Zedong, rising through the ranks, realized that the Soviet experience did not apply to China. While still a young man, Mao realized that Soviet political theory had to be adapted to Chinese conditions. The Soviet agents in China conceived of revolution in terms of an urban proletariat, but China was not industrialized and had almost no proletariat. What it had was a vast peasantry.

Mao also rejected the Soviet model of minority theory. In its early days, the Party had promised to preserve minority areas as ethnic regions. During the Long March, the Communists fought minority peoples in China's southwest. Mao came to realize that many of these peoples had previously suffered Chinese invasion of their lands. The minorities resented Han chauvinism. Given the right, they would prefer to secede. Minorities in some locations complained that the Chinese cadres—sent in to implement the socialist transformation of society—refused to use local language or observe local customs.

The Han Chinese saw Tibetan civilization as inferior. Even though cadres working in minority areas were instructed to be sensitive, they had difficulty understanding why Tibet would resist being transformed by China's superior civilization. Anger and frustration built up among the Tibetan populace. In a top-down system, there is no steam valve to let off pressure.

Many Tibetans welcomed the changes brought by the Chinese. The modernizations were popular in the beginning: new roads, modern telegraph and telephone communications, a new postal service, electricity generating plants, hospitals and schools, newspapers, and radio stations. As June Teufel Dreyer put it: "Acquiescence toward the presence of the Han and the broad principles of socialism rather than wholehearted enthusiasm for either was deemed sufficient" for minority areas.[19]

In the northwest, geography was the determining factor. By the 1930s, Mao realized that Stalin had expansionist ambitions in Xinjiang. The region was rich in natural resources and Stalin wanted them. Stalin had proved to be a faithless ally and had already engineered the secession of Outer Mongolia. Mao realized that the Turkic Muslims of Xinjiang might want to reunite with their fellow Turkic Muslims in the USSR's Asian republics. The region would thus be divided along ethnic lines.

After the Long March, Mao scrapped the Soviet model. By 1945, Mao was referring to any minority call for independence as "narrow nationalism." Mao had begun his military career as a guerrilla warrior among the non-Han peoples. He never again promised minority peoples the right to secede. He began to see any aspiration of minorities as an imperialist plot against the unity of China.

At the birth of the PRC in 1949, Chairman Mao decided to reassert Qing borders and incorporate the regions of the "national minorities." Mao had important strategic concerns on his mind: He feared encroachments on the Asian mainland from India and the USSR.[20]

India shared a long border with China. The country was independent, but it had drawn closer to the Soviets. China also shared a long border with the USSR. Mao, the Great Helmsman, feared that together India and the USSR could encircle China (see map, page vi–vii).

Mao's instincts proved to be accurate. In 1962, China and India fought a five-month war over a border dispute in the Himalayan region known as the Northeast Frontier Agency, or NEFA (the area consisted of southern Xinjiang and southern Tibet). The exact demarcation of the border was an unresolved issue left over from the British Empire.

In the 1950s, Mao began integrating minority areas (other than Tibet) into the Chinese political structure. During the Hundred Flowers campaign, a brief experiment in which artists and intellectuals were encouraged to criticize the Party, Mao discovered that criticism from minority areas exposed separatist inclinations. In Xinjiang, Uighurs wished to set up an independent republic, and Kazakhs wanted to create an Islamic state that ignored the existing Sino-Soviet border.

Mao distrusted the USSR and feared Stalin's treachery. After World War II, Stalin had put troops in Manchuria, China's industrial heartland. He had lured Outer Mongolia into the Soviet fold, and was meddling in Xinjiang on the long Sino-Soviet border. Stalin felt that his participation in World War II guaranteed that the USSR would be the dominant power in Asia. China was to be the junior partner. Stalin treated Mao in a patronizing fashion, and Mao resented the disrespect. The battle between Russia and China for supremacy in Asia amounted to a Cold War in the communist world.

Mao's analysis of Russian motives and designs also proved to be correct. The Sino-Soviet split erupted in the years after Khrushchev was purged. The rift between the communist "brothers" began with heated rhetoric, but ended in a border war. The United States stood to gain from a split between Moscow and Beijing. At the end of the 1950s, China saw the United States as its greatest enemy. The principal reason for this was the 1958 confrontation with the United States over Taiwan. China believed that the United States might be fomenting a regional or a world war.[21]

By the 1960s, the Sino-Soviet split had caused the communist states of Asia to choose sides. North Vietnam and North Korea sided with China. Mongolia sided with the USSR. Beijing promoted itself as the vanguard of communism, and accused the Soviets of "revisionism."[22]

In 1969, a series of border clashes erupted on the Ussuri River, along the almost 3,000-mile border between the PRC and the Soviet Union. Leonid Brezhnev placed six Soviet divisions on the Sino-Soviet border in Xinjiang, a move that he described as "the gun upon the table." Tensions were high, and it was feared that the two communist giants might engage in nuclear war. The issue was resolved when they agreed to return to the negotiating table.

Mao felt that he had less to fear from the United States than from Soviet Russia. In 1972, he accepted Richard Nixon's proposal that China and the United States have a rapprochement. After a number of secret meetings conducted by Henry Kissinger, the historic Nixon trip to China took place in front of the cameras of the world.

❦

In the 1940s, the West was preoccupied with the war against Hitler and Hirohito. This gave the Soviets free rein to establish themselves in Central Asia. Likewise, America's preoccupation with the Cold War gave the PRC a free hand in Tibet in the early 1950s. The post-World War II era witnessed the old European colonial empires in Asia (and elsewhere) breaking apart. This was the time of wars of national liberation. Neither America nor Britain protested the Chinese invasion. The United States was sympathetic to Tibet but feared that supporting Tibet at the United Nations would drag the region into the Cold War. The Soviet Union had made an ally of India, and the United States had made an ally of Pakistan.

India had gained its independence from British rule in 1947. After three centuries, the British had just quit India. Britain no longer had any national interest in the South Asian region and felt they could not interfere. As far as the British were concerned, Tibet was now in India's sphere of influence.

The first prime minister of India, Jawaharlal Nehru, did not want to antagonize its neighbor. The USSR had vast territory in the Far East as well as a long border with China that was a subject of dispute.

The United States was focused on the threats posed by the Soviets as far as the proliferation of nuclear weapons. In fact, as the recently opened Soviet Cold War archives show, the desire of the USSR to pursue détente with the West in the 1950s caused them to renege on promises of help with the development of the PRC's nuclear program. This was to be a factor in the Sino-Soviet split.

The United States privately offered aid and assistance to the Dalai Lama. India was initially uncertain about granting the Dalai Lama exile status but offered him asylum. Off the colonial chessboard, Tibet was caught between superpowers, frozen in the ice of the Cold War.

During the early 1950s, a number of rebellions took place in eastern Tibet, especially when the Chinese attempted to introduce socialist economic reforms by establishing cooperatives in Kham. During 1956 and 1957, resistance spread into the rest of Tibet. Eventually, the appearance of refugees in Lhasa—bringing news of what the communists had in store for central Tibet—led to the Uprising of 1959.[23] The Chinese called out the military, and the Dalai Lama went into exile in India.

Although unwilling to bring the issue of Tibetan independence before the United Nations, the United States wanted to promote its own interest in the region within the Cold War framework. Through the CIA, the United States began giving covert support in the form of arms and money to a Tibetan insurgency. The CIA also trained guerrillas in Camp Hale, Colorado, for insertion inside Tibet. The Khampas retained leadership and eventually established a base in Nepal in a place called Mustang.

By 1958, the several bands of Tibetan rebels formed one resistance army. Its purpose was to oust the Chinese, though the insurgents had no organized political structure to replace the communists. The guerrillas were greatly outnumbered by the PLA but enjoyed popular support. As Tibet watcher Jane Ardley states: "The monastic community had been inextricably linked with the guerrilla movement from its inception, and monks not only offered their spiritual support but in many cases fought alongside the guerrillas."

By the 1960s, the CIA had abandoned its Tibetan project. In 1972, with the U.S.-China rapprochement initiated by Richard Nixon and Henry Kissinger, U.S. support for Tibetan independence ended. Since the end of the Cold War, major protests in Tibet have turned violent on at least three occasions. Having emerged from the Cold War into the thaw of globalization, Tibet is now on the international media's radar screen. The South Asian region has changed since the days of imperialism and the Cold War. This points the way to a new conception of the region and of Tibet's role in it.

Many of today's geopolitical hotspots can be traced back to the legacy of British colonialism with a map and a pen. At the height of Empire, the sun never set on the Union Jack. In its aftermath, the sun never sets on the many local wars it spawned. Some of the most troublesome hotspots continue to be in South Asia. Afghanistan has been at war since the late 1970s, first with the Soviet Union, then in a civil war, now with the United States seeking to eliminate a terror base for Al Qaeda. The Northwest Frontier Region on the Pakistan-Afghan border is a refuge for Islamist extremists, Al Qaeda, and the Taliban. The southern Himalayas are also problematic—Nepal has grappled with Maoist-inspired revolutionaries in the recent past. India's indeterminate border with China has been the cause of two wars, yet, as a hopeful sign, recently both countries have made progress toward resolving their differences.

The once idyllic Kashmir has been the site of an Islamist insurgency fomented by Pakistan in an attempt to wrest the Muslim majority territory away from India by force of arms. (Kashmir went to India as the result of Partition as the British quit India.) By way of rounding out the region, one could add the war in the 1970s that separated Bangladesh, formerly East Pakistan, from West Pakistan. Also, in the former British colony of Ceylon, now Sri Lanka, a Tamil separatist insurgency has devastated the island for many years and has only come to an end recently. The Tamils are ethnically connected to their fellow Tamils on the Indian mainland, while the majority population of Ceylon is Sinhalese. The Tamils fall within the Indian cultural sphere. All these fit squarely into the category of post-colonial quandaries. Many of these decades-old problems have only recently found resolution, after much tragedy and bloodshed.

China has made its influence felt in South Asia as the most important regional player in recent years. With the U.S. government announcing a troop drawdown beginning in 2011, China has increased its regional role, particularly in drawing closer to the Kabul government in Afghanistan.

Tibet is no longer the isolated and mysterious Shangri-la. Travel is easy and communication instantaneous, as words and images speed through the air via modern technological devices. China cares how the world perceives it. The Tibet Question is among the top priorities of the Chinese leadership because it has the potential to destabilize China. Most of the Chinese leadership believe in what can best be described as the domino theory: If one autonomous region gains true political autonomy, then all the regions will seek independence. If one goes then they all will go.

Hu Jintao, the president of China, is a member of the fourth generation of Chinese leadership. These men are technocrats who were educated abroad with an internationalist point of view. Yet behind the plum-colored walls of Zhongnanhai, headquarters of the Beijing leadership, the leadership may be stymied as to what to do about Tibet. The policies of investment and immigration have clearly failed, as the 2008 unrest in Tibet and the 2009 unrest in

Xinjiang show. Reformers wish to return to the ethnically sensitive policies of the 1980s. Hardliners value social stability and unity at all costs while pursuing economic development.

The hard-line policy that focuses on assimilation, Han immigration, and economic development has been in place since the late 1980s, but does not address the root cause of unrest, ethnicity. The time is ripe to make a change that would be beneficial to both China and Tibet.

With the political dynamics of the region changing, the conservative leadership in Tibet could update policy in its western regions to forestall further unrest and become part of a wider solution for the region. This would accrue to the benefit of China as well as Tibet. The historical moment is perhaps the most propitious in the sixty years since the "peaceful liberation" of Tibet. A new approach by Beijing could bring closure to the old era of imperialist interference and usher in a new era for the region.

For some time now, the Chinese leadership has been investigating federal models from all over the world. Perhaps a new political structure for Tibet already exists. Included within Deng's reforms are the Special Administrative Regions, or SARs. SARs have already been employed with success in Hong Kong and Macau. The legal framework of a SAR permits autonomy with executive, legislative, and independent judicial power. The arrangement "requires security forces to be comprised of local citizens, while residents inside SARs are granted protections covering freedom of speech, press, assembly, privacy and perhaps most significant... religion."[24] The SAR arrangement contains checks and balances that may be implemented more effectively than those in the Chinese constitution. The SAR charter also has an immigration provision, requiring citizens from outside the SAR to apply for approval from local authorities for entry. This would solve the imbalance that immigration has created, while it grants a waiver to anyone who has been living in the SARs for more than seven years.

Could the deal be consummated? The solution would most likely meet with acceptance from the Dalai Lama. It resembles his solution, but with some differences that would mean compromise on his side. On the Tibetan side, it would provide for the major issues regarding ethnicity and freedom of religion. This solution would solve China's major headache in terms of its domestic politics and also be a bonus for China on the international scene, for it would remove a horrendous public relations problem at the time of China's emergence on the world stage. As Christian LeMiere states, "Such a solution would allow for linguistic and cultural—but not full political—independence. The provinces would remain within China's borders, their resources would be national possessions, and the cost savings would be enormous. Estimates suggest that the Chinese government spends more than a billion yuan a month to maintain security forces in the region."[25]

The diversification of the Tibetan economy along the lines suggested in my conclusion and the opening of trade along the southern Himalayan border would enable more exports from Tibet to the region and initiate a new era of regional trading patterns. This would be of economic benefit to China.

The concept of the SAR could even be expanded into an innovative version, with special characteristics created for Tibet: the Special Ethnic Trade and Environmental Zone, or SETEZ, as outlined in the conclusion to this book.

❧

As a non-Western model, India employs a federal system successfully, even though the country is vast and contains many different languages, ethnicities, and religions. Protests in India sometimes turn violent, but ten thousand people demonstrating in the streets of India signifies nothing so much as a challenge for law enforcement to guarantee public safety. By contrast, ten thousand people taking to the streets of China creates a crisis of legitimacy for the PRC leadership. India has a mechanism for allowing the populace to protest and let off steam.

Clearly the old thinking on Tibet has arrived at a dead end. Assimilation has not worked, and renewed violence is in no one's interest. Will this generation of Chinese leadership be able to undertake a radical but necessary restructuring of its system? Those who see the need for reform may not have the clout. The leadership may leave the problem to the Fifth Generation, but at some point it is clear that they will have to deal with the real roots of the problem of ethnic unrest in Tibet. The world is undergoing a unique historical moment with a rare opportunity for China to adapt to new circumstances as part of a regional projection of influence and power that is already underway. The solution to the Tibet Question might become part of a natural process of growth and development in the region.

PART 2

The Mongol Khans

China's Claim to Tibet

Chinggis Khan and the Conquest of North China

China's claim to Tibet originates with the Mongol khans. In the thirteenth century, some eight hundred years ago, China was the richest and most advanced civilization on earth. Though the Mongol Empire eventually extended from the Pacific to the Mediterranean, China was always the ultimate object of Mongol warfare. Chinggis Khan began the conquest and his successors completed it. The conquest of China took sixty-eight years from Chinggis to his son Ogodei, to his grandson Mongke and finally, his grandson Khubilai.

The Chin, or Golden Dynasty, occupied the Dragon Throne. They were a conquest dynasty: they were Jurchen, from Manchuria, and they had taken the capital in the twelfth-century. Even before, they had been meddling in the politics of the steppe tribes, backing first one tribe and then another. They were responsible for the death of Mongol kings and for the death of Chinggis Khan's father. After he unified the tribes of the steppes into a nation, he declared a war of revenge against China.

Ultimately the nomad warriors of the steppes succeeded in ruling all of China. Although Turks, Huns, Khitan, and Jurchen conquered parts of China, the conquest of the whole country by force of arms had never been accomplished by any other foreign invader.

In the year 1211, Chinggis Khan raised his standard of nine white horse tails and led the Mongol Army across the Gobi Desert. A military genius, he rode at the head of his mounted horsemen, slept in the same tents as they did, wore the same uniform, and ate the same food. He fought almost a hundred battles and never lost one. His battles were not equaled in scale or scope until the Napoleonic Wars of the nineteenth century. They were not exceeded until the Second World War.

The Mongol cavalry was trained to a high standard of warfare and was superior in horsemanship to the Chin Imperial Army. Chinggis Khan modeled his tactics on that of the Mongol Grand Hunt, the most fantastic display of horsemanship and weaponry in Asia. His was not the warfare of the samurai, the display of individual acts of valor. It was a display of warfare as a team sport: the wings of his army moved as one, thought as one, attacked as one.

For his campaign in China, The Conqueror planned a stunning crossing of the Gobi Desert in winter with 120,000 troops divided among two armies, one led by him and one led by his sons and his most talented general. In one of the most brilliant military campaigns of all time, the Mongols entered China and ousted the Jurchen. The wild horsemen of the north now ruled North China. It would take a generation for the grandson of Chinggis Khan to conquer the south.

Chinggis Khan began by unifying the warring tribes of the Mongolian steppes. For generations, tribal warfare had made the steppes a boiling cauldron of conflict, with feuding and revenge fueled by the crimes of horse theft, bride theft, and murder.

Chinggis Khan founded the Yesse Mongol Ulus, the Great Mongol Nation, created a system of laws, gave his people a written language, and created a rudimentary government. Soldiers no longer owed their allegiance to the tribe but to the nation. He destroyed the tribal structure, transferring the loyalty of the nomads who lived in white felt tents to the new nation. He incorporated the tribes into his army, assigning conquered Khitan, Tatar, Mergid, and Naiman, to serve under Mongol commanders loyal to him.

He created and trained an imperial guard so that he knew the characters of his commanders from personal experience. Perhaps his greatest talent was choosing a peerless group of generals to lead his army. A little known fact is that when he went to war in China, Chinggis Khan ordered his generals to give good treatment to any Chinese officers who defected to the Mongol side, and gave them a command under Mongol generals. This gave him intelligence about Chinese methods of warfare, including expertise in siege warfare, a new technique. The Mongol Army had never made war against walled cities until it entered China and this was valuable expertise.

Chinggis Khan trained his cavalry to a high standard of performance using exercises of his own devising. He modeled their battle formations—thorny bush, chisel, wedge—on the maneuvers of the Mongol Grand Hunt: thousands of mounted archers spread out in a hunting circle that extended for miles. Beaters went forward rousing the game as the riders closed the circle. The khan shot first, then the members of the clans shot, and all the tents were provisioned. This was the occasion for a grand and drunken feast. The music, dancing, and merriment went on for weeks, with food killed in the hunt cooked over pits and spits. The Mongols were voracious eaters, and the great Mongol vice was alcohol.

❧

The Chinese had employed their classic foreign policy among the steppe tribes, with the Chin Emperor backing the Mongols. These old Mongol kings were Chinggis Khan's relatives. After a time, when the Mongols grew too powerful, the Chinese switched allegiance and backed the Tatar in the tenth-century. The Chinese called this form of diplomacy *i-i-zi-i* (using barbarians to check barbarians). The strategy may have been effective in managing China's northern border, but it had a tragic consequence for the young man Temujin (as Ching+gis Khan was called in his youth). In an act of revenge, the Tatar murdered his father and mother, and small children and family retainers were abandoned by relatives who wanted control of the tribes and the wealth that came from them. The family was left to die in the brutal steppe winter. The young khan's father had been poisoned by Tatar tribesmen when returning to his native pastures after betrothing his son to a beautiful young Khongirad girl. The Khongirad were the marrying clan of the Blue Mongols, Chinggis Khan's tribe. They were renowned for the beauty of their women and were literate and semi-agricultural, semi-nomadic. Located to the northeast of China in the steppe country, they were prosperous from their long association of cross-border trade with China. Chinggis Khan's mother was from this clan.

The loss of his father was probably the most significant event in Chinggis Khan's early life, and he blamed it on the Chinese. As a youth of perhaps 14, he was too young to take command of the tents living under the rulership of his father. Nomad wealth was based on the tithe—10 percent of the herds—of those receiving the khan's protection. The tribes abandoned him, and he lost the herds and the wealth that came from providing good governance to the clans living in the white felt *ger* tents of the steppes.

As a young aristocrat of the steppe nobility, he would have inherited tens of thousands of commoners, as well as vast animal herds consisting of the "five snouts" (horses, camels, sheep, goats, and yak). Instead, he inherited nothing. He was poverty-stricken and he and his family almost perished in the brutal steppe winter. His jealous kinsmen captured him and took him into slavery, but with the help of commoners, he escaped with barely the clothes on his back.

Chinggis Khan survived abandonment, betrayal, and attack. He married a bride who brought him a rich dowry and he found a patron who was the legacy of his father, the most powerful lord in southern Mongolia. He attracted followers, young men of the steppe nobility, who agreed to be his vassals. Soon he had reestablished himself as a young khan of the steppes. The young Temujin defeated his rivals for power in the steppes and unified the warring elements into a new political entity. This occurred over a period of years, after which he was left with a battle-seasoned army.

The Mongol tribe was rising to prominence again, a fact that was not lost upon the Golden Emperor. When young Temujin unified eastern Mongolia under his banner with the nine white horse-tails and proclaimed the founding of a nation, the Emperor of China sent an emissary to his camp.

A new power had arisen in the steppes, and the Chinese Emperor had good reason to fear it. The Chin Emperor invited Chinggis Khan to become his vassal. The new Khan of Mongolia accepted, performing the *ke-tou* (the knocking of the head on the ground, a sign of submission to the Chinese emperor), and paid an annual tribute. His diplomatic relations with Chin continued for years.

The Chin had previously backed the Tatar tribe, but in the twelfth century switched their patronage to the Mongols. The Mongol khan could not wage war against a Chinese vassal without inviting the imperial army into the steppes to attack the Mongols. The Chin emissary asked for Chinggis Khan's help in waging war against the Tatar. As a loyal vassal, he was only too glad to make war on his old enemies, the tribe responsible for the murder of his father. Once he had the permission of the Chinese Emperor to make war on the Tatar, he annihilated them.

Next he gathered a great confederation of tribes and made war on the Naiman, the most powerful tribe in western Mongolia. The Naiman were more civilized than the Mongols and looked down upon them. This campaign marked the defeat of Chinggis Khan's only other rivals for supremacy in the steppes. He returned to his native campgrounds as the most powerful ruler in East Asia. Next, the Supreme Khan announced a war of personal and national revenge against the Chin Emperor. He declared that the Chinese had been meddling in the politics of the steppes for generations, and he held them ultimately responsible for the murder of his father.

What better way to employ the army than to lead it to a foreign war? The Mongol Army would follow him to glory and riches. The Conqueror was a meticulous planner. No detail of a campaign was left to chance. The planning of the invasion went on for years. As plans progressed, merchants, spies, and defectors kept the Supreme Khan continually informed of the situation at the Chinese Court.

The conquest of North China took four years. It began in 1211 and ended with the ten-month siege of Qungdu in 1215. Chinggis

Khan galloped into China like a lightning bolt from the north, waging a swift campaign on difficult terrain. After only four months, he had fought his way down through the mountain grille in the Chinese northeast—this is the region where the Great Wall ends. Coming down the mountains with his army, he conquered the mountain fortresses that protected the passes. At the foot of the mountains lay a double wall that protected the plain of North China. He defeated the imperial forces sent to keep the barbarian invaders out, and the road to the capital lay open. The Mongol Army was inside northern China, in command of the road that led to Qungdu.

The Supreme Khan did not understand civilization, continuous settlements. He did understand warfare, and in China he modified his battle tactics. He unleashed his army and let them plunder North China for six months, giving them what he had promised: vast amounts of booty.

He rode around the perimeter of the capital city. The walls were eighteen feet thick and thirty feet high. He was at the point of giving up, thinking that he could never breach the walls. A Chinese general came to his camp and told him of the disorder within the city walls. Chinggis Khan decided to surround the capital and blockade it. He did so for ten months until he starved the city into submission. He then unleashed his army. They plundered the city, setting one-quarter of it on fire. Women threw themselves off the battlements rather than allow themselves to fall into the hands of the rude horsemen from the steppes. Chinggis Khan's adopted brother supervised the removal of the treasury of Chin onto the big black Mongol carts—gold, silver, silk, porcelain, art treasures, all of it rumbled across the Gobi in five hundred carts. Every Mongol was rich. By the time the army departed the city, there were no bells left to toll in celebration. They had all been loaded onto carts. Northern China was a smoking ruin. A Chinese chronicler who had joined the Mongol camp wrote: "Everywhere north of the Yellow River could be seen dust and smoke and the sound of drums rose to heaven."

Chinggis Khan never intended to occupy China and rule it from the Dragon Throne. He was a son of the steppes, and he wished to return to the steppes and live the grand life of a nomad khan.

The Supreme Khan's motive was not the acquisition of territory but rather prestige: He had been intent on becoming the most important political and military power in Asia and he achieved his goal. In the end, the Chin Dynasty was no more. North China had fallen to invaders, and Chinggis Khan was the new political master of East Asia.

This history establishes a simple but crucial point: Both China and Tibet were states ruled by the Mongols. Because the Mongols were not Chinese, any Chinese claim to Tibet that is based on the Mongol conquest is tenuous at best. Such claims make sense only if one accepts the old theory (promulgated during the Nationalist era) that the "five races" are but branches of a single Chinese "race." The small stars on the Chinese flag are said to represent the four races—Tibetans, Mongolians, Manchurians, and Muslims—while the big star represents the Han Chinese. Mongols do not consider themselves a branch of the Chinese, and neither do the Tibetans. (Modern science likewise casts doubt on the Chinese "race" claim, but such scientific arguments are a topic for another book.)

A Literary Man Joins a Military Government

Chinggis Khan understood nothing of sedentary civilization—that is, of agricultural and urban civilization. He was proud of being a nomad who owned vast herds, and he loved the free, open life of the steppes. He loved being a soldier. He wore the same rags as his men and ate the same greasy broth. He rode into battle at the head of his army and was always victorious. Only at the end of his life did Chinggis Khan allow himself to grow accustomed to the luxuries he had plundered in China.

Under the vast blue sky of Mongolia, the land was empty as far as the eye could see. Populations were small, and nothing was grown or manufactured. The method of warfare Chinggis Khan used during his rise to power in the steppes was the total slaughter of enemy populations. This seemingly bloodthirsty tactic reflected an elementary logic: The Conqueror could never leave an enemy population behind the advancing front line of his army. Once an enemy was wiped off the face of the earth, they were annihilated for all time.

Chinggis Khan was a man born to the horse. He knew nothing of walls, gates, battlements, fortifications, or citadels. The old tactics of steppe warfare were useless against walled cities. It took several years, but the Supreme Khan adapted his battle tactics and mastered the art of siege warfare. Chinggis Khan had to learn to leave a garrison behind in the mountain fortresses, for after he conquered them and rode on, new inhabitants came and took them over. They had to be reconquered again or the Mongols would have enemy troops at their rear.

In the aftermath of his conquest of northern China, Mongol generals wanted to raze the entire region and turn it into pasture for their horses. This, too, made a certain sort of sense. Epidemics of battlefield diseases—typhus, dysentery, cholera—ravaged the Mongol Army during its Chinese campaign. In the end, the courtier Yeh-lu Chu-tsai dissuaded him from this course of action. The man who was to become Chinggis Khan's chancellor appealed not to the Supreme Khan's compassion, for he had none. Instead he appealed to greed, which the Mongols had in abundance. "You would gain more from taxing the population than from annihilating it," Yeh-lu argued. He taught Chinggis Khan the system of regular taxation that the Chinese populace had been accustomed to paying for more than a millennium.

Yeh-lu was half Chinese and half Khitan, a descendant of the royal family of the Liao Dynasty. He had been a senior official at the Chin court. His mother had seen to his classical Chinese education. He was a Confucian in his public life and a Buddhist in his private life. (The Supreme Khan was a shamanist, adhering to the old religion of the steppe nobility, but he had a lifelong curiosity about men whom he called Speakers to Heaven.) Yeh-lu was the perfect intermediary as well as a highly skilled diplomat. He spoke Chinese and also the languages of the steppes. He, his father, and his grandfather had all served the Chin. Yeh-lu knew administration and the keeping of records, skills that the Mongols did not possess.

Many of Yeh-lu's fellow literati fled to Southern China to become subjects of a Han Chinese emperor. Yeh-lu wanted to save northern

China from the harsher aspects of Mongol rule. Summoned from a Buddhist monastery where he had gone to heal himself from the horrors he had witnessed during the siege of the Chinese capital, Yeh-lu traveled to Chinggis Khan's capital of Khara Khorum, in Inner Mongolia, and accepted the job offer from China's new conqueror. He had come to appreciate many things about nomad culture. He served Chinggis Khan as the senior statesman of the empire for thirty years and remained a literary man serving in a military government.

Yeh-lu became Chinggis Khan's astrologer and personal physician, secretary, and a principal advisor. Yeh-lu invented the Mongol system of government based on the Chinese model of administration working through local rule. All the khanates (Chinese, Inner Asian, Russian, and Persian) were incorporated into a federal system headquartered in Khara Khorum, but employing a Mongol governor and a garrison under his command. Yeh-lu, the half-Chinese courtier, invented this "loose reins" system of government, a highly successful system that lasted for a century.

Local officials could employ local forms of administration, justice, and taxation as long as they met their responsibilities to the Khara Khorum government: these were an annual tax and an annual census that served as the basis of levying corvée (unpaid labor) and service in the army. The khanates functioned as provinces in a federal system. Securing these revenues and conscriptions was the duty of the appointed military governor (*darugachi*), who also commanded a military garrison that kept the peace.

Tibet was an exception. Because Tibet accepted Chinggis Khan's rule, it was never garrisoned nor was it subject to rule by a Mongol military governor. Chinggis Khan designated the Sakya branch of the Tibetan Buddhist faith to rule as his surrogates. Tibet was not assigned a Mongol *darugachi*. It fell under the authority of the regional khan who made his military camp in southwest China adjacent to Tibet (in Ogodei's time, this was Godan), but a member of the Sakya sect ruled it internally. As has been noted, Chinggis Khan revered Speakers to Heaven and recognized Tibetan Buddhist clerics as holy men. Only in cases where taxes were not remitted did Mongol troops enter Tibet.

As Chinggis Khan announced the formation of his empire and began to pacify tribes in the west, the Uighurs submitted to him. He accepted them and treated them well, and used them as administrators, clerks, and translators in his government. This was because they were literate and the Mongols were not. Chinggis Khan even took a Uighur as his personal scribe and adapted the Uighur alphabet for the writing of Mongolian.

Tibetan Buddhism as the State Religion of China

The Mongol nobility ratified the choice of Chinggis Khan, and after his death elected his third son, Ogodei, as his chosen successor. Ogodei was a wise prince but not a practical one. Famous for his intelligence and ability, his counsel and firmness, his dignity, justice, and generosity, he was pleasure-loving in the extreme and too fond of alcohol. The merchants who visited his palace in Khara Khorum said that he was generous to a fault and constantly overpaid by as much as the price again. From his treasury, he gave vast sums to the needy so that his name would live forever in the hearts of men. His reputation increased among the common people to the exact degree that the contents of his treasury decreased. The business of state bored him. Ogodei maintained a harem of moon-faced mistresses, a retinue of "lewd women" as he liked to call them—Mongol, Chinese, and Muslim. He spent the year traveling from one hunting lodge to another, indulging in his favorite pastime.

His favorite brother's widow was Sorghagtani, a woman famous throughout the kingdom. She was Christian, of the Nestorian or eastern rite. Her sons were also raised as Christians and were the first of the Mongol princes who were able to read and write. Ogodei wanted to make a royal marriage for Sorghagtani and suggested his own son Guyug, but Sorghagtani said that she wished to devote herself to the careers of her sons and asked for estates in China for herself and Khubilai. He was living the carefree life of a young aristocrat of the steppes in Khara Khorum and she wished him to settle down. Ogodei missed his brother so much that he felt that could not do without the company of Sorghagtani, but he granted her wish and in 1236 allowed her and Khubilai to move to estates in China that had been confiscated from provincial governors.

The Emperor had a need for revenues, and the peasants were leaving the chaos of North China and moving to the south, where a Han Chinese ruled as the Southern Song Emperor. At his mother's urging, Khubilai began studying governance from the Confucians and restored order to lands under his control. Soon the land was productive again because Khubilai forbade the Mongol generals from requisitioning food at will, and regular taxes brought revenues to the imperial treasury. The traffic in refugees, the endless trains of wagons and animals moving south, stopped. The peasantry began to return to the north. Khubilai's reforms were a success. He became the family expert on China.

By the time of Ogodei's accession to the throne, North China had been at war for several decades. After his election, Ogodei was faced with two sets of goals there: to vanquish Chin and to pacify the countryside and bring it into regular administration. He ordered the armies left to him by his father to consolidate the conquest. This they did.

In 1240, Ogodei sent his second son, Godan, to live in the Minag country northeast of Tibet, in the region of Kokonor (present-day Qinghai province). There had been no contact between Central Tibet and the Mongols before 1240, but the Mongol rulers exerted their political influence in Tibet through the lamaist clergy. Godan, suffering from leprosy, summoned a Tibetan grand lama to his residence. Legend has it that the Sakya Pandit, head of the Sakya lineage, cured him. (The lama had the honorific title *pandit* in the Indian styling because of his great knowledge.) The lama also convinced Godan to stop drowning his prisoners of war in the river and instead to spare their lives.

Most of Tibet lay outside the direct control of the Sino-Mongol bureaucracy, and the borderlands were an unruly and troubled region. From time to time, princes of the imperial family were ordered to stabilize Tibet. During the early reign of Khubilai Khan, the Tibetans rebelled and attacked Mongol-held garrisons. There were numerous punitive campaigns. Whenever Tibet failed to remit its tax burden or created some other disturbance, Mongol officers had to chastise (or threaten to chastise) Tibet, but these incidents were few and never changed the arrangement of indirect rule.

Godan initiated the contact with Tibet by writing to the head of the Sakya sect and asking for teaching. This was, in effect, a request for Tibet to surrender and become a vassal state. Two nephews of the Pandit, Phagpa and Phyagna, accompanied him to Godan's court in 1247. Sakya Pandit performed an initiation ceremony for the Mongol prince. In return, the Sakya Pandit received a "Golden Patent," which made him viceroy of Tibet.

❧

During his youth, Khubilai Khan was a minor prince in a minor branch of the Mongol imperial family. He was the second son of Chinggis Khan's youngest son, Tolui, who had served his father as military chief of staff in all the campaigns. An aging Chancellor Yeh-lu, the most important statesman of the Mongol Empire, also advised Khubilai.

As Khan of China, Khubilai established a coterie of Confucian advisors on his estate and he implemented many of their reforms and suggestions. Khubilai and his principal wife, Chabi, were sophisticated members of the younger generation of Mongol nobility. Khubilai and Chabi considered the traditional Mongol religion, a form of Altaic shamanism influenced by Chinese religion, to be insufficient for their spiritual needs. Emperor Ogodei dispatched the renowned Abbot Hai Yun, the head of one of North China's most famous monasteries, to give Khubilai religious instruction. Khubilai had a philosophical turn of mind and began to explore Buddhism, but he found the Chan sect too difficult for him. Chan (*Zen* in Japanese) is a difficult practice with less support in the way of ritual for the beginner. It is not difficult to imagine that Khubilai could make nothing of the koans (riddles), which are a feature of the school and are designed to circumvent rational thought and promote insight. The sparseness of the Chan practice—although appealing to the Chinese scholarly elite—was less appealing to the Mongol nobility.

Upon his accession to the throne, his brother, Mongke, revealed to his inner circle his plans for the commencement of the conquest of southern China. Mongke had been a hero of the Russian Campaign and had earned the respect of the Mongol nobility in the time-honored way. By contrast, Khubilai had never had a military assignment, which was essential to earn the respect of the Mongol nobility. Mongke gave Khubilai his first command, a campaign in the wild country of present-day Yunnan, where his assignment was to attack the small state of Da-li. Mongke was clearing his flank in preparation for his assault on Southern Song.

Khubilai and his army made a passage across eastern Tibet. Khubilai wanted peaceful relations with the Tibetans. He invited the Phagpa Lama, who had the reputation of being a brilliant young scholar, to his camp. Khubilai built up an affinity with Phagpa. The young lama subsequently moved to Qungdu, the Chinese capital, with his uncle and took up residence in a monastery, where he continued his scholarly studies.

❧

Mongol princes traditionally had four wives, one of whom was considered the principal wife and mother of the heirs to the empire. The imperial princes also usually had numbers of concubines gained as the result of conquest. Khubilai's relationship with his principal wife, Chabi, appears to have been a real love match, certainly a match that had Sorghagtani's approval. Chabi was one of Khubilai's principal advisors. The Confucians were not used to having women at court, and Khubilai used Chabi's presence to keep them off balance.

In the Mongol world, the women exerted tremendous power and authority when their men were away making war. They served as rulers in the absence of their husbands, and this was the significance of being designated as principal wife: She held the reins of power, at least in the early years of empire before the foundation of a Chinese-style dynasty.

Khubilai and Chabi were comfortable with the ceremonies and teachings of Tibetan Buddhism. The couple converted, and it seems to have been a sincere conversion. The Phagpa Lama became their teacher and spiritual advisor. Mahakala, the wrathful emanation of

Avalokiteshvara (the Buddha of Infinite Compassion), was the perfect patron deity for a Mongol Khan. He had a black face with an angry expression, long canine teeth, and a headdress of skulls. He brandished weapons and danced upon a corpse. He was the protector of the faith, one might say the dark side of the Buddha of Infinite Compassion. Tibetan Buddhism has a subtle understanding of human psychology.

Khubilai and 24 of his courtiers were initiated three times into the Mahakala teachings. Chabi gave the Phagpa Lama a valuable pearl that she had received as a gift from her grandfather. He sold it and sent the money to Tibet, where it was used for the gold roof of the main temple.

Khubilai had outgrown his estate and needed a new administrative center, so he built a new capital building in Shangdu (Xanadu). Designed and built in the traditional architectural style by his Chinese chancellor, it was meant to impress upon his Chinese subjects that he intended to rule in the manner of a Chinese emperor. The building was both a practical necessity and also an example of Khubilai's rule by symbol.

The new building was bigger and more splendid than the imperial palace in Inner Mongolia, the Wan-an Kung or Palace of a Thousand Tranquilities. Built by Ogodei using craftsmen imported from Inner Asia, the palace was modeled on the palace of the Abbasid caliph of Baghdad, said to be the most beautiful building in the world. Khubilai's new Chinese administrative center roused suspicion among the senior officials in Mongke's court. They whispered that he intended to usurp the throne. The Mongol nobility were conservative, and gossip began to fly that Khubilai had "gone native," that is, become too Chinese. Jealous of imperial prerogatives, they resented the fact that his palace was more splendid than the Emperor's residence.

The courtiers convinced Mongke to send inspectors to look over Khubilai's tax receipts to determine if he was forwarding revenues to the central government in the appropriate manner. Khubilai was insulted and inclined to go to war, but his advisor and chancellor, Liu Pingqong, advised against such a rash course of action. He reasoned that the two brothers needed each other and had a mutual interest in uniting for the coming campaign to conquer southern China. Liu advised Khubilai to make peace.

Khubilai went to Khara Khorum to prove his loyalty to his brother and convinced him that he remained a true Mongol. He explained to Mongke that he observed all the Mongol rituals and ceremonies, he participated in the Grand Hunt, and he imported grass from the native pastures of Chinggis Khan so that his wives— all Mongol women—would give birth on Mongol soil. Mongke was convinced, and the brothers patched up their relationship.

With the brothers reconciled, they began the campaign in South China. While on campaign, Mongke died of disease in the battle-field, but Khubilai remained in the field and won a military victory. He then returned to China to stand for election. Though an aura of illegitimacy hung over the election because it was held in China, and not in the Mongol homeland, as was the tradition, Khubilai had sup-port from his brother Hulegu and others of the senior Mongol nobil-ity and the election stood. Khubilai succeeded Mongke as emperor and was enthroned in the year 1260. He set about reforming the central government, adding new bureaus, and undertook massive new civil engineering projects.

In the year 1272, Khubilai Khan founded the Yuan Dynasty and built a new capital Shangdu (Xanadu) in the Chinese style of architecture. His reunification of China began with the conquest of the south in 1274 and completed it by 1279. It must be regarded as one of the most important events in Chinese history, because he solidified the boundaries of China proper to roughly the same terri-tory that it occupies in to the present day.

❦

The Mongol aristocracy had always gathered in a Great Assembly and elected their leaders. Chinggis Khan did not believe in heredi-tary rule—many of the empires he conquered had men at the top who had come to power as the result of inheritance. In a complete break with Mongol tradition, Khubilai named an heir apparent, his son Jinggim. The appointment of a successor disqualified Khubilai's younger brother Arigh Boke from the imperial succession. This led to Arigh Boke's rebelling and attempting to break away from the empire. He was unsuccessful; Khubilai put down the rebellion and Mongolia remained within the empire.

Khaidu, the Khan of Inner Asia, Khubilai's first cousin and the son of Chinggis Khan's second son, Jagadai, was also disqualified from becoming emperor. Khaidu was a nomad traditionalist and resented giving the rich revenues from the Central Asian caravan trade to the Khara Khorum government. He moved his camp from the city to the countryside and reinstated the old nomad way of life. He rallied many of the nobility to his cause, and the Central Asian Khanate broke away from the central government. Khubilai considered his inability to keep the empire one of his greatest failures and it haunted him until his death.

❧

In 1274, Khubilai put the Mongol Imperial Army into the field against the Southern Song Dynasty. In a dazzling series of battles, General Bayan rode south and conquered the Southern Song. The Dowager Empress and loyal courtiers attempted to escape with the boy Emperor's brothers (who might someday have helped restore the Song Dynasty). The two brothers drowned at sea under suspicious circumstances. The Dowager Empress and the boy Emperor were captured and came under military escort of General Bayan to the Mongol capital, where the Dowager Empress delivered the Song Seal of State into Khubilai Khan's hands.

Before Khubilai ascended the Dragon Throne as Emperor of China and Son of Heaven, he arranged for the deposed boy Emperor to spend his days in a monastery in Tibet. Tibet was a good place for exile: organized as a special region of the Yuan Empire, ruled jointly by the Mongol emperor and the Sakya sect. As a place of retirement for a youth who could potentially be the object of a move to restore a Han Chinese to the throne, Tibet had the added virtue of being remote. There the boy Emperor would be out of sight and out of mind. It would have been simple for Khubilai to kill the heir to the Song throne, but instead, he packed him off to a monastery.

Traditional Chinese history considered the Mongol period to be a dark age, but generations of scholarship in the post-World War II era have shown it to be an era of change and innovation. A popular form of drama was born, the first novels were written, new genres of painting were created (horse painting, because the Mongols loved their horses). Even the famed blue and white porcelain associated with the Ming Dynasty has recently been discovered to have its roots in the Yuan period.

It was Khubilai's wish that the Song be welcomed back to the domains of the Chinese Emperor as a long-lost brother. He wished the Song to be treated with compassion and not be punished. By his decree, the flourishing Song economy was integrated into the economy of North China. Despite these brilliant accomplishments, the fact remains that traditional Chinese historians considered the Yuan a conquest dynasty and judged Mongol inhabitants of the Dragon Throne harshly because they were not Han Chinese.

The Great Buddhist-Daoist Debate

In the three great philosophic traditions of China—Confucianism, Daoism, and Buddhism—the Confucians were the normally the most influential, the Buddhists second, and the Daoists third. But a period of Daoist ascendancy began during Chinggis Khan's campaign in the Muslim lands. It was during this campaign that Chinggis heard of the Daoist sage Chang Chun and his famous Elixir of Immortality. The Supreme Khan was in his late 60s and must wished to extend his life, for he still had much to accomplish. He sent an imperial summons to "the Abode of Clouds and Mists," a Daoist monastery in North China. He requested that Master Chang make a "comfortable journey" (at the Emperor's expense) to meet the Supreme Khan in his camp in the West to discuss philosophy.

The old priest had previously turned down requests from the Song and Chin Emperors, but he accepted Chinggis Khan's invitation and set out with a disciple named Li.[1] Chang traveled the very great distance to Samarkand, where he met with Chinggis Khan. To his dismay, the supreme Khan discovered that the "elixir" was a system of meditation and yogic exercises, a spiritual discipline rather than a magic potion that he could imbibe. Despite his disappointment, Chinggis Khan received instructions for three days. The Conqueror had thousands of concubines and liked the company of beautiful women, but because the priest was ascetic, he wished to meet in a tent without female attendants.

The sage advised the Emperor to refrain from hunting at his advanced age. The Great Khan abstained for two weeks, but then resumed his habit. Hunting was his favorite pastime. He was also asked to refrain from intercourse with women, but it seems that he ignored this advice, too. Chinggis Khan was pleased with Master Chang's teaching and ordered that the philosopher's words be carved on a stone stele and that handwritten copies also be made so that his men might receive his instruction.

The Conqueror issued a decree, signed by him and sealed with his seal, granting the Daoist monasteries exempted from taxes and corvée in China. The Daoists had evidence of imperial favor and abused the privilege. Chinese Buddhists were without imperial support and were victimized by the Daoists.

The capital of Qungdu soon saw street battles between the Daoists and the Buddhists. The Daoists handed out printed texts in the streets of the capital, claiming that Lao Zi invented Buddhism. Other pamphlets claimed that Buddha was a Daoist saint. Mongol troops were often called out to put an end to the outbreaks of violence, but the abuses did not stop there. Claiming the patronage of Chinggis Khan, the Daoists seized Chinese Buddhist monasteries and ousted the Buddhists. They used axes to chop up big statues of the Buddha to use as kindling wood.

Emperor Mongke wanted peace between the religious factions in China, since civil unrest could spread and lead to a general rebellion against the Mongols. He called upon Khubilai to help restore order. Khubilai had an ingenious solution to the problem: in 1258, he organized a Buddhist-Daoist debate. Representatives of each of the opposing factions would present evidence before a group of judges. At the end of the contest, a verdict would be rendered as to the authenticity of the texts and the correct ownership of disputed monasteries. The Phagpa Lama helped to organize the proceedings.

The Tibetan Buddhist tradition placed an emphasis on learning, and their scholarly expertise exposed the Daoist's texts as forgeries having nothing to do with the Buddhist canon.[2] With the help of the learned Tibetan monks, the Buddhists outwitted the Daoists. The Tibetans also outdid the Daoists in their display of feats of magic. This was humiliating for the Daoists, who traditionally excelled in magic.

The judges decided in favor of the Buddhists and ordered that the Daoists have their heads shaved. As further punishment, they were ordered to cease printing the fraudulent pamphlets and were forced to burn all copies of the blasphemous texts that they had already printed. The Daoists also had to give back the monasteries they had taken. Some of the offenders were even ordered to join Buddhist monasteries. Khubilai's ingenious solution ended the unfair and corrupt influence of the Daoists and peace was restored in the streets of the capital.

Problems of Empire

Khubilai Khan was a modern ruler in the sense in that he saw kingship as a stage. His empire was vast and comprised many different nationalities and religions. He used Chinese forms of government to appeal to his millions of Chinese subjects. He built a Chinese capital, he used Chinese titles for his relatives, and he acceded to Chinese custom such as celebrating the Confucian ancestor rites and naming an heir apparent. He even used Chinese forms of taxation, since the populace understood them and did not object to them.

To appeal to his Buddhist subjects in Tibet and Inner Asia, Khubilai Khan presented himself as a Chakravartin, a Buddhist sage-king, and used Buddhist forms of phraseology and images of Buddhist origin in his decrees that were printed in China and posted in Central Asia and Tibet. The Yuan was the first dynasty in which Chinese emperors presented themselves as Chakravartins, The Ming and Qing would follow this example later on.

He used the religion to counterbalance the influence of Confucians and Chinese Buddhists. In fact, Tibetan Buddhists gained so much influence in the capital that the Chinese Buddhists complained about Tibetan monks easily gaining imperial audiences while Chinese Buddhists were seldom granted access to the Emperor.

Khubilai Khan's strategy of domination and control of the government was to play the factions at court against one another. The highest government positions went to Mongols. He employed Muslims in the Bureau of Revenue and also as tax collectors. This was a deliberate strategy to deflect Chinese resentment away from the Mongols and toward the Muslims. Uighurs from the western realms of the Silk Road and Inner Asia, of both the Christian and Muslim faiths, served as translators, clerks, and military administrators.[3] These were people of Turkic origin who were literate and possessed administrative skills.

Khubilai admired Chinese civilization but feared the power of the Confucians. Khubilai's distrust of the Confucians stemmed from his recognition that they could govern China without a military. He understood that they were a bureaucratic class that had been governing China for more than a millennium. Dynasties came and went, but the Confucians formed the backbone of the state. The Mongol population was much smaller than that of the Chinese, so Khubilai was careful not to place too much power in Chinese hands. He refused to reinstate the examination system for government office because it was founded upon mastery of the Confucian classics. In private conversation he ventured the opinion that the Confucians might have conspired to bring down the Chin Dynasty.

Although there were sound reasons why Khubilai Khan employed his multi-ethnic approach, some of the Mongol imperial family resented his approach. They were part of the old party of Nomad Traditionalists, conservatives who lived and worked at court and in the other khanates and believed in retaining the ways of their ancestors rather than succumbing to the habits of the sedentary world. Before long, civil war erupted among princes at the top of the Mongol government. The war disrupted travel and commerce throughout Inner Asia. Marco Polo, traversing Asia with his father and uncle, had to wait for three years in Bukhara because no traffic could get through to Qungdu, the Chinese capital. They could only proceed when they received an escort from an official sent by Hulegu, the Khan of Persia.

Marco Polo was an enterprising young man and put his delay to good use. During his stay in a lively caravanserai, he managed to learn the Mongolian language. He had already mastered Turkish and Persian, two of the other languages of Khubilai's court, and was soon to learn Chinese. This facility later led Khubilai to appoint Marco Polo as a special envoy. He was a European and outsider to court intrigues, but he could undertake special missions and report back to the Khan. In short, he was an extra pair of eyes and ears for the Emperor, a spy. Khubilai had a tendency to paranoia after a Chinese member of his court conspired in a rebellion against him, but he felt that he could trust young Marco. After the conquest of the south, Marco served as the Salt Commissioner of Yangzhou and excelled in a government post. Khubilai rewarded Marco and made him a nobleman, an honor that had not been granted to Marco in his native Venice.

The Priest–Patron Relationship

The arrival of Phagpa in the Chinese capital marked the beginning of the priest–patron (in Tibetan, *chö-yon*) relationship between Tibet and the emperors of China. This relationship is described as that between pupil and teacher, protégé and protector; according to legal scholar Michael Van Walt Van Praag, it is unique in the history of diplomacy. The Phagpa Lama was not subordinate to his mighty patron, but rather stood in the relation of priest to lay Buddhist. Begun by Khubilai Khan, some form of this relationship existed down to the fall of the dynastic system.[4]

In 1260, the Phagpa Lama presided over Khubilai's enthronement as the first Emperor of the Yuan Dynasty. The Lama also performed a Mahakala ceremony to dedicate Xanadu (in Chinese, *Shangdu*), Khubilai's new capital. The Confucians were horrified by the display of tangkha paintings of Tibetan Buddhist deities and the use of Tibetan ceremonies to dedicate the new imperial seat. Chinese Buddhists were envious. The spectacle was grand, but it was so un-Chinese.

Some Tibetan monks grew accustomed to their power and abused their privileges. They traveled about with weapons and used the imperial post roads not for official business, but to transport private goods that they traded for profit.

In 1264, Khubilai Khan issued a decree stating that the Buddhist church was independent of the worldly power of the Emperor and was exempted from taxes. Furthermore, the Emperor and empress gave generous presents. Riches found their way to Tibet, and this continued under the Emperor's successors. Khubilai's patronage of the Sakya sect assured their ascendancy over the other sects of Tibetan Buddhism for 75 years, laying the foundation for Sakya wealth and influence.

The Yuan government had several offices for dealing with Tibet and the Tibetan borderlands on China's western border. The Bureau for Buddhist and Tibetan affairs had a mostly military character. Postal stations were organized in Tibetan borderlands and in central Tibet to provide a courier service for transportation and traffic, a service that was used mostly by Tibetan clerics traveling between their homeland and China.

Phagpa became the Mongol viceroy of Tibet, exercising indirect rule while maintaining ties to the Mongol Court. He was also the Imperial Tutor as well as head of an entire branch of the central government of China (Bureau of Tibetan and Buddhist Affairs). Khubilai Khan could not do without the Lama at court—this is the origin of the office of the Panchen Lama, the second highest clerical office in Tibet. When the senior lama of the Sakya lineage was residing in China, the Panchen Lama ruled Tibet.

After the Phagpa Lama was appointed Imperial Preceptor in 1260, the position and influence of Chinese Buddhists in the capital gradually declined. Tibetan Buddhism became the state religion of China. The colorful ceremonies and superior magic in Tibetan religion appealed to the Mongol mind more than did the subtle philosophy and unconventional conduct of the Chan Buddhists. From a cultural viewpoint, the Mongols felt a close affinity with the Tibetans. The Buddhist cleric Abbot Hai Yun remained an advisor to Khubilai Khan, and Liu Pingqong (Khubilai's chancellor) was a master of all three schools of Chinese philosophy.

In 1265, the Phagpa Lama returned to Tibet because he missed his homeland, but Khubilai missed the Phagpa Lama at court and asked him to come back. In 1268, the Lama returned to the Yuan Court and had a reunion with Khubilai Khan. Phagpa left the Chinese capital for the last time in 1275, accompanied by the heir apparent, Crown Prince Jinggim. At Jinggim's request, the Phagpa Lama composed a "Textbook of Tibetan Buddhism."

At the time of his departure, the Lama presented Khubilai Khan the gift of a new alphabet, the so-called Phagpa script, which was capable of expressing the four official languages of Khubilai's court: Mongolian, Chinese, Turkish, and Persian. It was a magnificent gesture, one that had taken many years to complete. Khubilai had been looking for a way to write the difficult Chinese characters in alphabet form, thus eliminating the need to master Chinese characters. On his return to Tibet, Phagpa presided over a religious ceremony attended by one hundred thousand of the faithful.

The *chö-yon* relationship lasted from Yuan (1279–1368), through the Ming (1368–1644) and Qing (1644–1911). Tibetans view the relationship as having ended with the fall of Qing. The Yuan Dynasty conducted their relationship with Tibet through the Sakya lamas. After the Gelugpa sect rose to power in Tibet, Chinese emperors conducted their relations with the lamaist government headed by the Dalai Lama. The Ming granted titles and honors to senior Tibetan lamas, but used their relationship with the Dalai Lama to manage the military threat from the Mongols to the north.

The Chinese use the Qing period to justify their present occupation of Tibet. The Qing offered Tibet military protection on an emergency basis and posted an imperial representative (*amban*) in Lhasa. The priest–patron relationship ended with the fall of the dynastic system in 1911. At that time, the Thirteenth Dalai Lama evicted the *amban* from Lhasa and proclaimed Tibetan independence.

Tibet during the Yuan

From the Yuan Dynasty's point of view, Tibet was an autonomous province of the Mongol Empire with special institutions in the capital (the Bureau of Tibetan and Buddhist Affairs was part of the

Central Secretariat, the most powerful body in the central government). The status of Tibet was different from that of subordinate
states such as Korea. For example, there were no bureaus of Japanese
Affairs, Korean Affairs, Central Asian Affairs, Russian Affairs, or
Muslim Affairs

The office of the Panchen Lama was invented sometime around
1260. The Panchen Lama resided in Tibet and served as head of
the Sakya government there, but he was under the direction of the
Imperial Preceptor who resided in the Chinese capital. He was not
only the director of civil administration but also commanded the
militias of central Tibet. He held the title of Civil and Military
Myriarch for the Three Circuits of Tibet.

Tibet was never fully integrated into the Yuan. A census was
taken, taxes were levied, and a regular postal service was established.
The Mongols had the right to recruit troops in Tibet, but they
did not station a Mongol military governor there, as was the case
throughout the rest of the empire. Also, licensed border markets
continued to operate at the China-Tibet border, a trading concession
that did not exist anywhere else in the empire.[5]

The Yuan Dynasty lasted for nearly a hundred years after the
reunification of China in 1279. Khubilai Khan's descendants were
less talented rulers than he. Many ascended the throne at an early
age. Some were murdered, and most had short reigns. Toward the
end of the dynasty, the military garrisons were badly managed.
What was once the greatest army in the world failed to put down
local rebellions and could not control bandits who were bleeding the
populace.

The Yuan ended for a number of reasons: the flooding of the
Yellow River, crop failures, inflation, and internal strife. The Yuan
broke down over a fifty-year period. Various military elements struggled to put together a force strong enough to found a dynasty. Local
bandit forces became local militias, which eventually became local
rebellions. In the mid-fourteenth century, the Red Turbans emerged
as the strongest of the competitors. Composed mostly of a rag-tag
militia of adherents to a folk religion that attracted social outcasts,
the Red Turbans gained in numbers and strength and became a
rallying point for anti-Mongol sentiment. By the mid-fourteenth

century they became a formidable threat to the Yuan. Eventually the rebels rode to the capital and burned it to the ground. In 1368, the Yuan fell and the last of the Yuan emperors got on his horse and rode back to the steppes. A Han Chinese emperor would once again sit on the Dragon Throne.

PART 3

Ming and Qing Dynasties

Tibetan Religious Influence in the Chinese Imperial System

The Mongols Quit China

Zhu Yuanzhang, a rebel leader, founded the Ming Dynasty and ruled as the Emperor Hongwu. The dynasty that he founded lasted from 1368 to 1644, a period of more than two and a half centuries. His capital was at Nanjing in southern China, where his rebellion had its roots. The dynasty was the beginning of the modern era in China.

From the fall of Tang in the tenth century until the fall of the Qing in 1911, the Ming was the only Han Chinese dynasty to occupy the Dragon Throne. Considering the history of conquest dynasties, one begins to understand the obsession with Chinese unity that gripped the minds of many in the modern Chinese leadership.

An impoverished Buddhist monk, Zhu was born into a poor peasant family in modern Anhui province. He joined the Red Turbans, an offshoot of the White Lotus Society. (This was a sect of Buddhism that arose in the late Yuan Dynasty, attracting followers by proclaiming itself to be anti-Mongol.) Zhu rose to leadership

by marrying the adopted daughter of one of the rebel commanders. In a series of military campaigns, Zhu defeated his rivals and
assumed the top position. He led his rebel army to the capture of
Nanjing.

His army eventually grew strong enough to ride to the Mongol
capital and burn it to the ground. Zhu claimed the Mandate of
Heaven and proclaimed a new dynasty, the Ming. His reign lasted
thirty years, from 1368 to 1398. An era of prosperity, the Ming saw
the growth of urban centers and commercial expansion. Also during the Ming, China developed a manufacturing base built on the
traditional exports of silk, tea, and porcelain.

The return of a Han Chinese dynasty marked the return of the
old system of dominance of the Confucian scholar-gentry class.
They again rose to prominence through the examination system.
The traditional bureaucracy controlled China's military, its provin-
cial governments, and China's vast resources. With the rise of the
Chinese literati came a brilliant flowering of art and culture.

❧

The Yongle Emperor, fourth son of the Hongwu Emperor, was
the third emperor of the Ming and reigned from 1403 to 1424.
One of the greatest rulers in Chinese history, he moved the capital
from Nanjing in southern China to Beijing in 1421. He built the
Forbidden City, the imperial complex at the heart of Beijing. This
was a Chinese-style capital, with plum-colored walls, vast court-
yards, gardens, and ceremonial spaces. The complex of governmental and residential buildings featured gold-tiled roofs and marble
ramps carved with the imperial symbol: the imperial dragon playing
in the sky, chasing clouds.

The throne in the imperial capital aligned perfectly with the
points of the compass, as in a mandala. The forces of the universe
flowed to the emperor and from the emperor out through the gates
of the palace complex and the city gates to the Chinese populace.
The Son of Heaven, who ruled through the Mandate of Heaven, sat
at the center of cosmic forces. He was viewed as the conduit between
heaven and earth, between the celestial forces and his subjects. This

grandeur was not lost on visitors, delegates from the old tribute nations who came to the capital once a year: these were Koreans, Mongols, Muslims from the khanates of the Silk Road and Inner Asia, Tibetans, Vietnamese, and Japanese. The foreign envoys were required to perform the *ke-tou* (the knocking of the head) or flat prostrations in front of the throne.

Ming territory was considerably smaller than that of either the Yuan Dynasty (which preceded it) or the Qing Dynasty (which followed).[1] The old Mongol Empire had been vast, stretching from the Pacific to the Mediterranean. Under Khubilai Khan, the empire broke up. At the time of the founding of Ming, descendants of Chinggis Khan still ruled Russia and Persia, but these former imperial possessions were not incorporated into the Chinese state.

Yongle's rule saw many accomplishments. Among the most important was the restoration of the Grand Canal, the inland waterway that had fallen into disuse and disrepair by the end of the Yuan Dynasty. He used the waterway to transport foodstuffs, goods, and supplies to the new capital in the north. The Yongle Emperor was also the first Ming ruler to establish a formal relationship between China and Tibet.

Yongle was a serious practitioner of Tibetan Buddhism, and the religion's influence found its way into arts of the period. According to Watt and Leidy "The Yongle reign was a period of active trade and diplomatic exchanges between China and Central Asia and the Middle East, the influence of which can be seen in the decorative arts of this era: porcelain articles, for example, copied the shapes of Islamic glass and metalware vessels."[2]

Yongle inherited the workshops of the artisans who had provided decorative arts to the Dragon Throne during the Yuan Dynasty. Through these workshops, foreign influence became part of the artistic vocabulary of Chinese arts and crafts. The imperial workshops specializing in sculpture, lacquer, metalwork, ceramics, textiles, and ivory showed Islamic influence on metal, glass, and porcelain. Because Yongle was a serious practitioner of Tibetan Buddhism, the religion's influence found its way into arts of the period. From the Mongol Empire through the Ming, this

Tibetan-influenced art had "a seminal role in the development of later Chinese decorative arts."[3]

The early Ming saw the spread of capitalism, a result of burgeoning commerce in the cities. The famed Ming Voyages were a rare event in Chinese history: outward expansion and imperialism on the seas. Admiral Cheng Ho, a Muslim eunuch, made seven voyages from 1405 to 1433 under imperial sponsorship. Ambassadors of the states surrounding China traveled to the capital on a regular basis to present the Yongle Emperor with tribute. The emperor gave gifts as much as double the tributes' value, not only to demonstrate his generosity but also to show that he had no need for revenue.

One cannot overstate the point that Chinese history was written by Confucian intellectuals who held a Sinocentric point of view. For them, China was the center of the world—all other states belonged to the periphery. The flow of civilization proceeded from the Han center to the "barbarian" periphery. Civilization *was* Sinicization. For most of Chinese history, Confucian intellectuals harbored a prejudice against Buddhism as a foreign religion with other-worldly concerns. By contrast, the Confucians prided themselves on the fact that their worldview was concerned with practical matters in the here and now. Tibetan religious influence flowed to the Chinese center during the Yuan Dynasty, but regardless of the expanded presence of Tibetan Buddhist ideas and practice, the Confucian prejudice held true.

Foreign Relations during the Ming

Anxious to keep good relations, Emperor Hongwu sent envoys to Tibet in the winter of 1372–1373. He requested that all those who held office under the Yuan now renew their titles with the Ming. This appears to have been a formality. The Ming did not have administrative authority over Tibet, as the Yuan had through its Bureau of Tibetan and Buddhist Affairs. The dispensation of titles seems to have been a recognition of political realities rather than a formal submission of Tibet as a tribute state of the Ming.

In the south, Annam (modern-day Vietnam) had become a vassal state of China during the Yuan Dynasty. The Yongle Emperor of the Ming attempted to reassert China's relationship, but the Annamese would have none of it. In 1418, Le Loi—later to become emperor of Vietnam and the founder of a dynasty—led a revolt that lasted ten years. The Ming sent troops to counter the revolt, but they failed to suppress it. In the end, the Dragon Throne acknowledged Le Loi as King of Annam. His dynasty lasted until the eighteenth century.

During the Ming, the relationship between Japan and China was of tribute state to the Celestial Kingdom. The infamous Japanese pirates (*wak*) marauded the southern Chinese coasts for forty years, from 1550 to 1590, and presented a constant problem for the Ming. The Japanese also attempted an invasion of Korea, taking Seoul and Pyong-yang. The Ming came to the aid of Korea as a matter of self-interest, since China had every intention of protecting its network of vassal relationships in the region. The Japanese withdrew, and the Ming declared peace in 1607.

Far to the west, in Inner Asia, Tamerlane had reunited the old Central Asia Khanate created by the Mongol khans. Fortunately for China, Tamerlane died in 1405, before he had the chance to invade and wrest control of the empire.

The greatest military threat to China came from the Mongol tribes of the north. The early Ming emperors rebuilt the Great Wall, the eastern section in the fifteenth century and the western section in the sixteenth century. Employing the traditional foreign policy of using barbarians to check barbarians, the Chinese played the warring Mongol tribes—Tatars and Oirats—against one another. But the two sets of Mongol invaders broke through the wall. In 1449, Esen (leader of the Oirat army) kidnapped the Ming Emperor and held him for ransom. In 1550, the Tatar army, led by Altan Khan, raided Beijing. Peace with the Mongols came when they converted to Tibetan Buddhism. This brought into play the Ming's "triangular" strategy of using the high Tibetan lamas to control their warlike neighbors and to protect China's borders in the north and northwest. This was ingenious diplomacy, and as a result, Tibetan religious influence served a political purpose for China.

In the fifteenth and sixteenth centuries, monasticism grew in Tibet while the authority of the feudal lords decreased. During the fifteenth century, Tsong Khapa, a Tibetan religious reformer, founded the Gelugpa sect. The Gelugpa became the most important sect of Tibetan Buddhism and extended its influence over central Tibet. It also came to control the largest and most powerful monasteries. The Gelugpa was the sect of the Dalai Lama, and with the Gelugpa's ascendance, the clerical office of the Dalai Lama also began to serve as the secular head of the Tibetan traditional government.

As the various factions contended for political control of the country, Tibet became embroiled in civil war. Although some historians have attributed the conflict to a religious rivalry among different sects of Tibetan Buddhism, Professor Robert Thurman interprets the war as a secular conflict:

> During the mid-sixteenth century, there [was] intermittent conflict between the secular rulers of southern Tibet and those of central Tibet, which some historians...attributed to sectarian conflict between the Karmapa Lamas and their followers and the Gelugpa Lamas and their followers. More accurately the unrest was the result of a conflict between the secular warlord rulers of feudal Tibet and the increasing monastic institutions and their spiritual leaders.[4]

Rather than characterizing the nature of the Tibetan government as a state–church relationship, Thurman describes it as a unity of state and university. Instead of comparing the monastic establishment to the Western institution of churches, Thurman describes it as deriving from the great monastic tradition of India.

In the midst of the civil war between followers of the Gelugpa and the Kagyu, the Dalai Lama institution—which had taken the role of expanding the monastic universities of Tibet—asked its Mongol devotees to intervene and protect it from a secular ruler, the warlord King of Tsang (a region of central Tibet). This king was a devotee of the Karmapa, the aforementioned head of the Kagyu sect. The Mongols, converts to the Gelugpa (or Yellow Hat Sect), rode to the rescue of the Dalai Lama.

By the fifteenth century, the Gelugpa sect was firmly in command of Tibet. In 1642, the Fifth Dalai Lama took political responsibility for Tibet. The Dalai Lama became the head of the government. As Thurman puts it: "Tibetans preferred a monk-king to a warlord king." Meanwhile, in China, the Ming rulers—who understood neither the complexity of Tibet's politics nor the dynamics of its civil war—remained aloof.

The Great Fifth was the first of the Dalai Lamas to assume the temporal rule of Tibet. He undertook the building of the greatest work of native Tibetan architecture: the Potala Palace, seat of government and residence of the Dalai Lamas. He also created the new government structure as a center for all the monastic orders. The Great Fifth included in the bureaucratic ranks the former warlord families—after they gave up their rights to old landholdings and dissolved their private armies.

The late Ming was a time of shifting political fortunes and the rise and fall of ruling houses. The Ming fell in 1644, and a new foreign invader took the Dragon Throne. This latest conquest dynasty was the Qing, founded by Manchu invaders from northeastern China.

The Fifth Dalai Lama made a treaty with the new Qing Dynasty, pledging to keep peace in the region and to help reduce the threat of military aggression from the Mongols. This was a boon to the new dynasty, since the marauding Mongols were a problem for them.[5] Under the Dalai Lamas, the Tibetan role as interlocutor between the Chinese and the Mongols became an important feature of Asian diplomacy.

Tibet acknowledged Chinese suzerainty (overlordship) by accepting the renewal of titles that had originally been issued under the Mongol Dynasty. Scholars in today's People's Republic of China argue that this acknowledgment indicated that Tibet had submitted politically to the Chinese emperor. Perhaps this is self-serving. Most scholars outside of the PRC argue that the relationship was mainly ceremonial. The titles served a commercial purpose, as Tibetan envoys continued to make journeys to the Chinese court, pay tribute, and trade in the capital.

Tibetan Politics during the Ming:
The Dalai Lama Emerges

Buddhism retained its influence at the center of the Ming state, but in a diminished fashion compared with the dominant role it had played with the Mongol ruling elite during the Yuan Dynasty. The Ming Court did not understand the complexity of events in the Tibetan political world. The Emperor Hongwu sought relations with the Karmapa, head of the Kagyu lineage of Tibetan Buddhism who lived in the eastern Kham region of Tibet. The Karmapa had lost the Tibetan civil war. What motive could the Ming Emperor have for aligning himself with a prelate who was out of power? One suspects that a simple practical consideration underlay the political overtures: the desire to purchase horses from the Tibetan nomads living in Kham.

The horse markets of Mongolia were closed to the Ming court because of incessant tribal warfare in the northern regions. The Ming needed horses for the imperial cavalry, and the Tibetans of Kham, even though followers of the Karmapa, could supply them. The Karmapa declined an invitation to appear at the Ming court in Nanjing. Instead, Hongwu received several of the Fourth Karmapa's disciples as envoys. In a reciprocal gesture, Emperor Hongwu sent his private religious tutor to Tibet to obtain Buddhist scriptures. This was a formal demonstration of Buddhist devotion. This ritual had occurred before in Chinese history, certainly among the Mongol emperors.

A devotee of Buddhism, Yongle invited the Fifth Karmapa to his court in 1403. The emperor wished the Karmapa, Deshin Shelpa, to perform Buddhist ceremonies in honor of Yongle's parents, the deceased emperor and empress. The Chinese emperor sent gifts including a large ingot of silver, 150 silver coins, 20 rolls of silk, a block of sandalwood, 150 bricks of tea, and 10 pounds of incense. The Karmapa accepted the gifts and the invitation, after which he made the journey to the capital and performed the requested ceremonies. The imperial parents were designated posthumously as incarnations of Manjusri (the Buddha of Infinite Wisdom) and of the goddess Tara, respectively.

Following the example of Khubilai Khan in his reverence toward the Phagpa Lama, the Yongle Emperor sat on a chair that was lower than the Karmapa's when he was receiving religious teachings from him. Yongle bestowed upon the Karmapa the title of "Great Treasure Prince of the Dharma." Perhaps this bit of imperial diplomacy toward a Tibetan religious figure had an ulterior political motive. Yongle had usurped the throne from the Jianwen Emperor. The various rites performed by the Karmapa had the effect of legitimizing Yongle's rule. It is reasonable to suppose that the Ming court's patronage of high Tibetan lamas was meant to stabilize the border regions and protect trade routes, rather than to impose military or political control over Tibet. Mongol warriors continued to pose a military threat to China, a recurrent theme in Chinese history. The Mongol presence at the western Ming border diminished Ming contact with Tibet. In the fifteenth century, the Tumed Mongols moved into the Kokonor region of modern Qinghai and began raiding the Ming frontier.

Altan Khan ruled these Mongols from 1543 to 1583, but he did not make peace with the Ming until 1571. During the intervening years he conducted raids on China, even gathering enough strength for a raid on Beijing. Yet the Dalai Lama went to the court of Altan Khan and converted him to Tibetan Buddhism. This was the beginning of a renewed alliance between the Mongols and the Tibetans. Clearly, the real reason the Ming emperors needed a friendly relationship with Tibet was that Tibet had religious ties—and thus friendly relations—with the ruling families of the Mongols.

Despite the Ming's diplomatic relationship with Tibet, the formal relationship between the Ming court and Tibetan Buddhism ended in the sixteenth century. Confucian influence was paramount at the Ming court, and the Confucians despised Tibetan Buddhism. One of China's indigenous philosophies, Daoism, gained imperial sponsorship. Despite all the political fluctuations in China and Tibet, one thing remains certain: Tibet retained its independence during the Ming Dynasty.

Foreign Invaders Take the Dragon Throne

In 1644, the Manchus invaded China, defeated the Ming army, and founded the Qing Dynasty. Their dynasty was to preside over China until the fall of the dynastic system in 1911.[6]

The Manchus were related to the Jurchen who ruled China as the Chin, or Golden Dynasty, at the time of the Mongol conquest. They came prepared to rule. China had been defeated by yet another of the "northern barbarian" conquerors. As the barbarians took his capital, the last of the Ming emperors committed suicide by hanging himself.

By the time the Manchus invaded, the Ming Dynasty had already suffered a number of internal problems. The economy faltered despite a robust export trade in porcelain and silk. Even though there was prosperity in urban areas, famine and disease spread in rural areas. Gangs of the underprivileged turned into private armies of rebel peasants. Tax revenues were falling and so the army was not paid. Troop desertions led to border incursions by hostile populations.

Some elements of the Ming had managed to flee the capital and began plotting to overthrow the Manchu invaders. The Qing's first task was to bring all of China under Manchu control, and they immediately defeated the Ming rebels.

China had borders with fourteen states. Most of its ethnic minorities lived on the frontiers: Mongols to the north, Manchus to the northeast, Uighur Muslims in the far west, and Tibetans in the southwest. The Qing rulers reunited the country, strengthening its borders on all fronts. Preventing the border peoples from forming alliances with Russia, China's neighbor and competitor, was a major focus of Chinese foreign relations during the Qing. Governing the multi-ethnic frontiers was a problem for the Qing, and has endured as an ongoing problem to the present day.

An isolationist attitude toward foreign states was present from the beginning of the dynasty. Qing diplomacy with European nations was conducted through the Ministry of Rituals,[7] not through a foreign ministry. The Ministry of Rituals was responsible for the ceremony surrounding court visitation and tribute relations. This was assumed to be between the emperor and his vassal, a relation of superior to inferior. An exception to this manner of doing business was Chinese contact with Russia, which was handled through the bureau that dealt with the border peoples.

During the Ming, China's borders contracted. The Qing was a period of expansion: the Qing conquered Xinjiang—the new territories consisting of the old Muslim khanates on the oasis towns of the Silk Road. The Emperor Kangxi, who reigned from 1661 to 1722, was a talented and capable ruler—he combined in his person the habits of a Manchu autocrat with those of a Confucian sage-king. His reign was a time of stability. He established a functioning central administration and consolidated and expanded his borders.

Shi Lang, a Chinese admiral in command of a fleet of some 300 war vessels, captured the island of Taiwan in 1683.[8] The Russian czars were expanding into the east, increasing their Far East holdings. A furious Kangxi attacked the Russians in 1686 over a fortress town in northeast China. In 1689, Kangxi signed the Treaty of Nerchinsk, unusual for the Chinese in that it was a document drawn up between two equal parties.

Developments in the north were most threatening to the Qing. The Zunghar Mongols had been migrating over what is now Outer Mongolia and the province of Qinghai, and had control of the caravan routes of the Silk Road, the beginning of the overland trade route with Europe. They seized some important cities (all inhabited by Muslims) in the modern-day province of Xinjiang. Once Galdan, chief of the Zunghars, had acquired the revenues from the rich caravan trade, he had the means to finance further military campaigns. The Qing feared the rise of Galdan. They also feared that the Russians might forge an alliance with them, an ominous prospect. Russian territories in Central Asia bordered on Chinese Turkestan. The Qing did not want to lose a Chinese sphere of influence to the Russians.

Galdan defeated a number of Mongol tribes that had been unified under the Buddhist faith and united in their devotion to the Dalai Lama. Many of Galdan's warriors emigrated to Gansu, in the far west, where they might make further trouble. All of this was deeply unsettling to the Qing Dynasty. Qing forces set out to eliminate the Mongol threat. Kangxi himself took to the battlefield.

He led 80,000 troops across the Gobi Desert and attacked, forcing Galdan to retreat to the Kerulen River in the Altai region—the old native pastures of Chinggis Khan. Qing forces defeated Galdan in battle in 1696—the Mongol leader died the following year. Kangxi exulted over his victory, and wrote back to the capital that he could hardly express himself in brush writing. The victory marked the greatest extent of Qing territorial expansion and was the crowning achievement of Kangxi's career.

A fresh problem arose: new Zunghar leaders came forward and a power struggle ensued. The Dalai Lama was murdered in Tibet, and his successor was chosen in an illegitimate manner. Kangxi's Tibetan ally and interlocutor was now gone from the scene. When Kangxi found himself embroiled in conflict with the Zunghars again, he dispatched two Chinese armies to Tibet, one through the Kokonor region in Qinghai and the other through Sichuan.

The Chinese imperial troops reached Lhasa in 1720, occupied the capital, and supervised the selection and installation of a new Dalai Lama—one who was beholden to the Qing. A precedent had been set. This event marked the beginning of the Qing's armed intervention in Tibetan politics and in the selection of high lamas. By the time of Kangxi's death in 1722, Chinese power was at its peak, extending from Tibet in the southwest to Taiwan in the east.

In late Qing, a series of crises weakened the dynasty. The Chinese population expanded at too rapid a rate for the land to sustain it. Other problems were corruption of the bureaucracy and favoritism at the center of government. Ossification in the imperial system— and failed attempts at reform—eventually led to the downfall of the imperial system.

Finally, the Qing bungled a number of military expeditions at their borders. Campaigns in Burma and Vietnam failed, and these campaigns proved to be expensive. The Qing treasury was in no condition to continue supporting them.

Rebellions among the laborers who worked on the Grand Canal—barge pullers and coolies—joined with an underground folk Buddhist cult, the White Lotus Sect. They became a focus for the discontent caused by the rising population. Two Muslim uprisings in Gansu were suppressed, but there were White Lotus uprisings in

Sichuan, Hubei, Shaanxi, and Henan. In the midst of these failures, the Qing reorganized its military, one of the few successes of the dynasty's later days.

This military reorganization had important repercussions for Tibet. In 1910 and 1911, shortly before the fall of the dynasty, the Qing initiated a series of campaigns in Tibet. They conquered the regions of eastern Tibet and founded a new province, called Xikang. The ethnic Tibetan areas were incorporated into four Chinese provinces, the origin of the territorial dispute still being negotiated by representatives of the Dalai Lama today (see map, page viii–ix).

The Qing imperial troops defeated the defending Tibetan princes and established control over Lhasa. Objecting to the presence of a Qing garrison, the Thirteenth Dalai Lama fled to India. Qing forces, besting the difficult terrain, advanced to the borders of the British Himalayan possessions of Nepal, Bhutan, and Sikkim. The British were warned not to press their case regionally. These events marked the beginning of the rivalry of colonial powers for influence in the Himalayan region, a rivalry that would end only with the breakup of these empires in the aftermath of World War II.

❧

The Qing government was so committed to isolationism that it had no Ministry of Foreign Affairs. "Relations with non-Chinese People's were...conducted by a variety of bureaus and agencies that, in different ways, implied or stated the cultural inferiority and geographical marginality of foreigners while also defending the state against them."[9]

While Japan under the Meiji was opening and modernizing by learning from the West, the Qing shut out the West. The Japanese sent teams of experts to study Western science and technology. The Qing looked back to Chinese tradition, feeling that the answer for China lay there rather than in technology and science imported from the West. Western innovation was viewed almost as a pollutant. This was a fatal error.

The Industrial Revolution had created wealth in Britain, and with this wealth came a fashionable taste for tea, porcelain, and silk. The Qing were willing to sell items of Chinese manufacture to the

Europeans, but they had no desire to purchase anything from the foreigners. In their court documents, the Qing described Europeans as people with long hair and long noses, like demons. On the maritime coast, the Qing limited foreign trade to the port of Canton (present-day Guangdong), and traders were required to deal with specially designated Chinese commercial officials. Canton had a lively export porcelain industry, with small manufacturers creating goods for the foreign market. The imperial government granted licenses to *hong*, trading companies that engaged in commerce with foreigners.

The British were unhappy with the restrictive arrangement. In 1793, the British Crown dispatched Lord Macartney to negotiate directly with Emperor Qianlong. Macartney was a man of the world, well-connected in the spheres of British government and trade. He was a veteran diplomat who had served in previous postings to the Caribbean, India, and Russia. His mission was to secure access to more Chinese ports and a permanent British trade mission in Beijing.[10]

Although British requests for imperial audiences had previously been rejected, Macartney managed to secure an audience with Qianlong at the Jehol Summer Imperial Villa. The Qing sense of superiority was such that at the height of the British Empire—with British fleets the masters of the seas and the Union Jack snapping in the wind all over the world—Macartney was asked to perform the *ke-tou*. Macartney refused; he was not about to prostrate himself in front of an Asian monarch, even if that monarch was the key to British profits in Asia. The audience produced no good result. Macartney was unable to persuade the emperor to modify Qing trading restrictions. British frustration with the Qing attitude led to the two Opium Wars in the mid-nineteenth century. China was opened by force.

In early Qing, the Chinese economy was expanding. China was a continental economy rather than an international one— the market system of local, regional, and national markets was growing. Chinese merchants were extending their activities across provincial lines and into the South China Sea. The British were paying in silver, the demand was on the British side, but the Qing were aware of the exploitative activities of the British East India Company in India and feared British encroachment. Silver was the only commodity method of payment acceptable to China, but paying in silver was draining the British—they wanted to pay in opium, traded cheaply in India by the British East India Company. The Opium Wars were a drain on the economy. By late Qing, the economy was in decline.

The British Empire in South Asia extended from Afghanistan through the Himalayan kingdoms and through India to Burma. Since the late eighteenth century, it had sought trade relations with Tibet but without success. Britain thought influence in Tibet was necessary to safeguard its empire in India, the jewel in the imperial crown.

China and Tibet during the Qing

Tibet was situated on the Asian landmass at China's back door. The Mongols in the north remained a problem, and so the Qing created an Office of Border Affairs that employed as staff mostly ethnic Mongols and Manchus. Its main responsibility was to protect the strategic northwest from the incursions of would-be conquerors. The Office of Border Affairs regulated the caravan trade—viewed as incursions of foreigners onto Chinese soil—and placed Qing garrisons in the dangerous border areas to protect against Mongols, Zunghars, and Russians. The Qing also employed the time-honored device of marital alliance, betrothing imperial princesses to important Mongol princes. Muslims from Inner Asia and those of Chinese origin had freedom of worship, but the Qing office and the garrisons kept a watchful eye for the rumblings of sedition.

Tibet served as a buffer with the warlike Mongols and has had strategic value to China even as far back as the Qing Dynasty. The marauding Mongols were among the most devoted followers of Tibetan Buddhism, so the lamas were invaluable as interlocutors.

The British, through their colonial empire in India, sought influence in the Himalayan region. By expanding into Nepal, Sikkim, and Bhutan, in the early 1800s they had upset the traditional balance of power on the Asian landmass. The Qing sought to counteract British influence in the region, which led them to assert the Chinese imperial presence in Tibet.

Late in the dynasty, the Qing under Emperor Yongzheng placed troops in Lhasa, ostensibly to protect Tibet from the British. This pacified the Mongols, and thus the Qing neutralized one military threat. The Manchu-Tibetan relationship of the Qing period was the high-water mark of China's influence in Tibet.

During the late Qing, the Fifth Dalai Lama consolidated his rule over Tibet and summoned the Mongols to intervene in Tibetan affairs by supporting his struggle to assert authority over all of Tibet. The priest–patron relationship involved an understanding that the patron was obliged to protect the priest. Tibet had a weak military and had to summon surrogates for protection. Sometimes these surrogates were Qing and sometimes they were Mongols. The Tibetan-Mongol alliance was seen by the Qing government as dangerous, so the Qing began a 75-year long history of intervention in Tibet.

Michael Van Walt Van Praag, an authority on the special status of Tibet, states: "The dominant theme of the time...was the conflict between the Manchu emperors and the Mongol tribes striving to recreate an empire of their own."[11] During this period, the Fifth Dalai Lama and the Emperor Shunzhi reestablished their *chö-yon* relationship on the basis that they were equal sovereigns.

The Great Fifth, in keeping with the tradition of legitimizing Chinese imperial rule by bestowing sacred titles upon the emperor, recognized the Manchu emperors as the incarnation of Manjusri, the bodhisattva of infinite wisdom. This designation may have lent the emperor political clout when he was dealing with Tibet, since the sacred title gave the emperor the Dalai Lama's seal of approval. The Dalai Lama also contributed to the relationship by using his influence with the Zunghar Mongols to preserve the peace and contain Mongol expansionism. "From the Chinese records, it is clear that beyond the religious significance of the meeting between the Dalai Lama and the Shunzhi Emperor, the meeting was especially important given the Emperor's concern for the Mongol menace on the Empire's northern and western borders."[12]

By 1720, the situation had changed. During the reign of the Kangxi Emperor, the Zunghar Mongols invaded Tibet. Manchu troops came onto Tibetan territory to expel the Zunghars and to escort the Seventh Dalai Lama to Lhasa. By the early eighteenth century, Tibet had been in political upheaval for some time. Manchu officials arrived in the Tibetan capital to help reorganize Tibet's political administration and to discourage the Zunghars from attempting to exert control again. In 1721, a reorganized Tibetan government took power under the guidance of Manchu military.

Tibet then entered into treaty alliances with various neighboring states, including Sikkim. With the rise of another regional power, the Nepalese Kingdom of Ghurka, Tibet was invaded in 1786. At issue was the establishment of direct trade relations. The Qianlong Emperor, a devout follower of Tibetan Buddhism, sent troops, and a joint Tibetan-Manchu-Chinese army pushed the Gurkha forces out of Tibet. This was the fourth time in less than a century that the Qing had intervened in Tibet.

These interventions were expensive for the Qing. Tibet was far from the imperial center, and troops had to be fed, paid, and transported. The Qianlong Emperor demanded political reform in Tibet as well as the placement of a Qing official, an *amban,* to bring the conduct of Tibet's foreign relations directly under Qing supervision. By the end of the eighteenth century, the Qing exerted enough influence to close Tibet to outsiders. After this initial period of stabilization, the power of the Qing steadily diminished in Tibet, and the influence of the *ambans* declined. According to Van Praag:

> By the mid-nineteenth century, Manchu influence had ebbed to so low a point that the Tibetans could have expelled the amban and other Manchus from Tibet.... The total abandonment of the Qing Emperor's role as Protector of the Dalai Lama, his teaching, and his country—and therefore of the very essence of the relationship that had existed between the Manchu Court and Tibet—was indisputable by the middle of the nineteenth century.

In the nineteenth century, the Himalayas were a hotbed of shifting political alliances. The Ghurka invaded Tibet for a second time in 1842—this war was fought exclusively by Nepalese and Tibetan troops with no foreign assistance on either side. Eventually Tibet and Nepal signed a treaty, with Nepal demanding Tibet's complete separation from China and the payment of tribute to Nepal. Still, the *amban* managed to include in the treaty a declaration of respect for the Chinese emperor.

> The Manchu intervention in Tibetan affairs, which had started in 1720, came to a virtual end. Since the passing away of the Great Fifth Dalai Lama, the Tibetans had experienced Mongolian, Manchu, Gurkha and even Dogra interventions in their country in addition to frequent internal dissension....All of these interventions were essentially short-lived, although the Manchus maintained a formal *cho-yon* link with Tibet for over two centuries. By the time the Thirteenth Dalai Lama took over the reins of government in 1895, no Asian state could escape the attention of the Great Powers of Europe competing for influence and power. With the erosion of Manchu influence in Tibet, the interest of other empires increased, for a power vacuum could not exist in the very heart of Asia.[13]

The Political Value of Tibetan Buddhism: Managing the Marauding Mongols

Throughout Chinese history, Buddhism has been in and out of fashion among the Chinese elite. Sometimes the emperors and nobility were sincere practitioners of Buddhism; yet at other times it was branded a foreign influence and fell out of fashion.

The first Manchu emperors were opposed to Buddhism in both its Chinese and Tibetan forms. The reason for this was simple: The Buddhist worldview conflicted with their military needs. Monks devoted their energies to accumulation of merit for auspicious reincarnation, and this otherworldly focus inclined even lay Buddhists to nonviolence and rendered them ill-suited to military service.

Confucianism, by contrast, was a useful political philosophy because it was focused on this world and on practical affairs. The early Qing emperors adopted a new philosophy, the state's new orthodoxy. This was Neo-Confucianism, a revitalization and reinterpretation of the Confucian tradition that incorporated influences and ideas from Buddhist and Daoist sources.

Later emperors employed Tibetan Buddhism in the time-honored fashion to facilitate Mongol submission to Manchu imperial authority. Tibetan Buddhism was important to these emperors not as religion but as politics. Its principal use was in winning over the

Mongols—Qing emperors needed the steppe warriors as part of their system of defense. They used religious symbols to communicate across ethnic lines. This is the benefit that the Manchu emperors derived from portraying themselves as "perfect Buddhist monarchs, grand patrons of the True Law, and bodhisattvas."

The Qing emperors built temples for monks and gave generous gifts to monasteries. They undertook imperial sponsorship of the publication of Buddhist books on a grand scale. They printed them in the many languages of the people over whom the Chinese influence prevailed, including Tibetan, Mongolian, Chinese, and Manchu. The Qianlong Emperor was a serious student and studied Tibetan Buddhism and Sanskrit with lamas.[14] He gave his mother 9,000 statues of Buddhist deities on her 70th birthday. Both Kangxi and Qianlong made several pilgrimages to Mount Wu-tai, as did many of the Qing dowager empresses. As further evidence of the sincerity of his devotion, "Qianlong ordered a Manchu language Buddhist canon prepared for the benefit of his fellow Manchus (and perhaps to convince the Mongolian clergy of his sincerity about spreading the Law), a work that took nearly twenty years, involved more than five hundred translators, and for which a special agency of government was created."[15]

Qianlong was the first of the Manchu rulers to fully inhabit both his Manchu and Chinese identities. His approach harkened back to the universal appeal that Khubilai Khan sought. Qianlong attempted to appeal to the Chinese as a highly cultured patron of the arts and as a scholar of Chinese tradition; to the Tibetan Buddhists, he portrayed himself as a reincarnation of Manjusri, an important bodhisattva in the Tibetan tradition. To the troublesome Mongols, Qianlong was a true son of the steppes who respected the heritage of the nomad aristocracy.

Some of the fervor for a Chinese republic in the early twentieth century took the form of anti-Manchu activity. As a result of the Qing expansion, the multi-ethnic border states presently comprise half of Chinese territory and a very great proportion of its natural resources. To embrace greater China was to define China as a multi-ethnic empire, including all the nationalities that had been incorporated under Qing. This was the legacy left by Qing to both the Nationalists and the Communists. Both of them had to resolve China's identity in a new way.

Qing's relationship with Tibet was never a direct administration, nor did it involve the establishment of a Chinese governmental bureaucracy. There was no significant military presence in Tibet, and there was no management or planning of the Tibetan economy. The Qing were content with a watchful ceremonial and symbolic relationship, a presence to safeguard their commercial interests and their sphere of influence, backed up by force, when necessary.

Western Colonial Encroachment on the Maritime Coast

At the end of the eighteenth century, at the height of the British Empire, Western ships arrived in southern port of Canton (modern Guangdong). China viewed foreigners as a curse, and wanted a purely commercial relationship with them. The Qing discouraged the permanent settlement of foreigners and forbade Chinese to teach them the Chinese language. To correct the unfavorable balance of trade, the British began paying for goods with their ready supplies of opium instead of the silver China preferred.

The demand for opium grew, and the British East India Company and American clipper ships (America soon sought a piece of the lucrative trade) counted opium as their principal cargo. The Qing government finally decided to put an end to the opium trade, which Britain and America resisted. As a result, two Opium Wars were fought in the mid-nineteenth century (1839–1842 and 1856–1860). The Manchu had only antique cannons on the coast, and they had been left to rust. The cannons were of no use against British warships.

The first Opium War established the Treaty Ports (five towns along the seaboard from Canton to Shanghai) and gave the British the lease on Hong Kong. The British gained extraterritorial rights of governance in the Treaty Ports, including residential rights, consulates, and courts—where criminals were tried under the British Code. They secured a fixed tariff rate of 5 percent, a most advantageous rate that assured the profitability of their trade. The second Opium War gave foreign nationals access to ten more Treaty Ports and the right to navigate the Yangzi. It also granted freedom of travel in China. This brought the Western missionaries, whose influence began to spread.

✿

The Taiping Rebellion was the Chinese response to the Manchu government and to the outrage, humiliation, and weakness caused by the Qing Dynasty's failure to modernize and its inadequate response to the challenges posed by the West.[16] This uprising occurred at roughly the same time as the U.S. Civil War, but lasted fourteen years.

The leader of the rebellion was Hong Xiuquan, a candidate who had failed the imperial exams. His conversion to Christianity marked the beginning of personal epiphany that he was to lead China and become emperor. Hong proclaimed himself a son of God and claimed to be the younger brother of Jesus Christ and to converse with the Holy Ghost.

The insurrection began in Guangxi Province and spread among the working class of the south. At first Hong primarily drew followers from the remote regions of the south. The movement attracted outlaws and members of the triads (Chinese criminal gangs). Gradually the movement grew organized enough to build an army, and the rebellion developed into a military force to be reckoned with. At one time, the area of southern China controlled by the rebels had a population of 30 million. In these rebel-controlled territories, they instituted social reforms, including a prohibition against smoking opium and a ban on footbinding. Later reforms provided for land distribution and military organization and training.

In 1850, the Qing government sent out troops to put down the bandits. The imperial forces were defeated, and Hong Xiuquan proclaimed himself the Heavenly King of the Heavenly Kingdom of Great Peace (*Taiping*). Hong established a capital at Nanjing and prevailed in a series of successful military campaigns, eventually controlling much of the valley of the Yangzi River.

In what was to be a bloody war, the Qing army eventually defeated the rebels with the help of British and French forces. The war is estimated to have caused 20 million deaths. The Taiping Rebellion was a national tragedy.

❧

China has been attempting to modernize since the mid-nineteenth century. For almost two centuries, China's coming to modernity has been traumatic. The eminent historian Jonathan Spence attributes the failure of the Taiping Rebellion to Hong's inability to organize collective leadership and his failure to use anti-Manchu sentiment as a base of popular support.[17] Mao Zedong hailed Hong Xiuquan as an early revolutionary.

The 1880s were the high tide of Western imperialism in China. The Chinese ruling elite received a psychological blow when they realized that Japan, to whom China traditionally referred in racially demeaning epithets, had modernized and surpassed China, the mother culture. The Meiji Restoration brought a successful reform of the Japanese system and a positive attitude toward modernization— meaning Western science and technology. Their open, experimental approach had completely eluded the backward and xenophobic Manchus.

Japan was now a sea power vying with Russia for control of Manchuria on the Chinese mainland and the seaward approach to China, while China endured humiliation at the hands of foreigners. Japan would eventually have imperialist designs on China; World War II would see Japan invading China and setting up a puppet state on Chinese territory.

Young Chinese such as Sun Yatsen, political theorist and father of the Chinese republic, and Lu Xun, greatest of modern Chinese writers, studied in Japan and then returned to the mainland determined to change China. Eventually they did so. The first half of the twentieth century was one of the most turbulent in Chinese history. Considering its weakness and its failures, it is miraculous that the decrepit dynastic system had managed to last into the twentieth century.

For a brief period, the Qing attempted to modernize under Cixi, the Empress Dowager who ruled China between in late nineteenth-century. Spurred on by a desire to match Japan's achievements, a group of reformers made the effort to transform the government and inundated the Emperor with suggestions. The effort was doomed to failure because conservative factions within the court opposed the new ideas. Some of the reformers seem to have participated in a coup or a counter-coup. Cixi had been away from court, and when she returned she issued an edict against one of the principal reformers. The main reformer was executed, and others left China. The modernization effort ended in failure.[18]

Western imperial powers stepped up their aggression against China in the late 1890s and early twentieth-century. Germany seized the Shandong port of Qingdao in pursuit of mining and railway rights. The British demanded a lease on Kowloon, Hong Kong, and seized a Shandong harbor. The French demanded rights in the border areas next to their Indochinese colony. The United States demanded the right to trade, and Japan expanded its trade into central China. The exploitation of China was at its peak.

The Boxer Rebellion of 1898–1900 began in Shandong as a protest against foreigners, mainly Western missionaries and their Chinese converts. Fighters were recruited from the local peasantry, from the working class, from soldiers dismissed from duty, and even from petty criminals such as smugglers.[19] Women's groups also joined in the fight. The anti-foreign uprising spread across the northeast and culminated in an attack upon the foreign legations in Peking.

When Cixi heard that Westerners had seized a Qing fort, the first response of the Empress Dowager was to put down the Boxer Rebellion, but she changed her mind and supported it. The Empress Dowager was no fool—she began to see the rebellion as an expression of popular support for the dynasty. The attacks spread across North China.

The foreign diplomatic corps and their families retreated to a compound within Peking. A foreign force of soldiers from Britain, the United States, France, Japan, Germany, and Russia entered the capital and crushed the rebellion. The Dowager Empress and key members of the court fled to a temporary capital outside the city. Two hundred Westerners were dead—the Empress Dowager agreed to pay an indemnity.

The Empress Dowager returned to Peking in 1902. The foreign expeditionary force had occupied the Forbidden City, but Cixi moved back into the imperial residence upon her return. Sun Yatsen and Kang Yuwei, the two most important Chinese reformers, continued in their quest for change. Sun wanted to end the imperial system and found a republic. Kang wanted the Emperor to become a constitutional monarch.

China's quest for modernity was long and tumultuous. Sometimes the ideas for new systems came from an attempt to reform the traditional system, and sometimes the educated reformers attempted to use foreign ideas—particularly those imported from the West. In the end, when the dynastic system fell, there was nothing to replace it. The center could not hold. The country fractured into regions controlled by local warlords. Eventually a civil war erupted between the only two factions capable of establishing a central government and taking control of the country.

PART 4

Tibet and the Great Game

The Manchu, the Raj, and the Czars

Tibet Shuffled in the Great Game

In the nineteenth century, the sun never set on the British Empire. Britain was a maritime power, the empire circled the globe, and India was the jewel in the crown. This was the era of Rudyard Kipling, the time of the good officer as servant of the crown—shooting and playing polo and carrying the "white man's burden" of civilizing people of color. To describe this as a period of ethnic insensitivity would be a vast understatement. In the British Parliament, at the height of the Victorian era, Lord Macaulay famously stated that he would not trade the whole of Sanskrit literature for one shelf of a good English library.

Nineteenth-century British involvement in Tibetan politics—meddling in South Asian politics—helps to explain China's claim to Tibet. The Brits played a major role, first forcing themselves upon Tibet, then butting out with India's gaining independence, but the history has been poorly understood.

The United States has been engaged in a war in Afghanistan for the past decade. American scholar-generals have understood that a familiarity with the history of British imperialism—the legacy of the Great Game—is crucial for understanding the conflict. Afghan tribal fighters were familiar with the most difficult terrain in the world, and they were not intimidated by Westerners and their modernity. They had already beaten the Brits on more than one occasion, and in the past they had battled Alexander the Great and Chinggis Khan.

South Asia had always been a crossroads and now it was a crucible, the intersection of vital interests in a clash between ancient and modern cultures. Russia and some of the Central Asian republics were to the north, India was to the south, China was to the east, Pakistan was to the southeast, and Iran was to the west. Oil, heroin, and religious extremism—coupled with border disputes—produced a volatile brew of politics, insurgency, and hot wars. Also involved were three nuclear powers, two of which had gone to the brink twice in the past decade. Modern communications incorporated a formerly remote part of the world into global chatter, for good and for ill. Modern weapons emboldened the formerly disadvantaged. Smuggling, an ancient and honorable occupation in the region, continued, with drugs and weapons as valued commodities.

This most definitely was not your grandfather's "Roof of the World." Even the mountaineering assaults on Everest had gone high-tech. Vacationing travelers ventured across the Taklimakan Desert in Toyota Land Cruisers, their GPS units loaded with special maps. The new Karakorum Highway connected Pakistan to Xinjiang. The Qinghai–Lhasa railroad brought tourists by the thousands to the once remote Buddhist capital in the Himalayas. Kathmandu was no longer a stop on the hippie trail for hashish and spirituality, and even the Maoist guerrillas of Nepal had put down their arms and gone back to "video nights in Kathmandu" (the title of a Pico Iyer travel book about the changes that technology and globalization have brought to South Asia). Bangladesh ceased to be East Pakistan in the 1970s, but it was still poor, still ravaged by nature and a breeding ground for extremism. The civil war in former Ceylon (now Sri Lanka) had finally come to an end, with the Tamil Tigers losing their bid for secession.

❧

Peter the Great founded the Russian Empire in 1682. After the Mongol Empire, the Russian Empire was the largest land-based empire in world history, extending from the Arctic Ocean to the Black Sea and from the Pacific to Caspian and the Baltic Seas.[1] Intent upon connecting Russia with the Pacific Ocean port of Vladivostok, the czars Alexander II and Alexander III began building the Trans-Siberian Railway. It was completed at immense cost in 1891, during the reign of Czar Nicholas II.

World War I brought the Bolshevik Revolution in Russia and the end of the czarist regime. The USSR was born. The new communist government planned to bring science, modernization, and social justice to Russia. Its revolutionary leader, Vladimir Ilyich Lenin, believed in exporting his revolution to Asia in order to liberate the working classes of India from Britain. In Lenin's dream of the future, the East would be red. The imperialists and their Union Jack would be gone from the scene.

In the latter half of the nineteenth century, the British were deeply involved in South Asian politics—in India, Bhutan, Sikkim, and Nepal. All of these Himalayan states had relations with Tibet—reciprocal trade relations and regional political affairs—within the context of Buddhism. Religion *was* politics for the southern Himalayas. Already sitting on top of their Indian cash cow, the British sought to open trade relations with Tibet, a quest that began in the late eighteenth century. Russia, China, and Britain all sought influence with Tibet, and all feared that the others would gain the advantage of occupying the high ground of Asia. The Tibetan government rebuffed all such overtures. Tibet became a chess piece in an imperial board game. The only problem was that a real state and real people were involved.

The British misinterpreted Tibet's status as a "forbidden state," the idea that it was closed to foreigners. Because so little information was available about the actual state of affairs inside Tibet, the British assumed that the Manchu government was ruling Tibet directly. After they had defeated the Manchus in the Opium Wars, the British sought Manchu help in gaining access to Tibet. As early as the 1860s, Britain realized that its treaties with the Qing government, signed after the Opium Wars, did not give it the right to travel through Tibet. The British government acknowledged that the Qing government had the right to make treaties for Tibet.

The Tibetans feared the British might employ tactics of armed force, annexation, and unfavorable treaty agreements—methods that the Brits had used to good effect against other Himalayan states. For their part, the British thought that the Tibetan perception of them as greedy imperialists was backward, ignorant, and medieval. According to Tibet scholar Michael Van Praag, the Manchus ruling China feared "yet another base from which the British, Russians or French might approach their disintegrating empire. . . . Nevertheless, given the weak position in which the Qing Court found itself after the disastrous Opium war and the subsequent pressure caused by Western imperialist encroachment in China, concessions were made."[2]

In 1876, Britain and China signed the Chefoo Convention, which granted Britain the right to send an exploratory mission to Tibet led by explorer Colman Macauley. It also formalized the Chinese right to negotiate for Tibet, thus establishing Chinese suzerainty. The Convention was signed by the British viceroy in India and by the Chinese *amban* in Lhasa, but Tibet did not sign. The Tibetan government repudiated not only the treaty but also the assumption that the Chinese government could negotiate on Tibet's behalf, an early assertion of Tibetan independence.

The Tibetan Kashag called an emergency session and sent emissaries to all border posts. Its border officials were notified *not* to accept passports issued by the Manchu government for travel inside Tibet. "The Manchus dreaded the prospect of open Tibetan opposition to a mission traveling on passports issued by their Imperial government because it would expose the Emperor's total lack of authority over the Tibetan government. Moreover, an armed clash would undoubtedly be won by the British, who would bring Tibet under their influence."[3]

The Qing government settled with the British over an outstanding matter relating to Burma in return for Britain's abandoning the Macauley mission to Tibet.

In 1914 Tibet participated in the Tripartite Convention in Simla as a co-equal signatory with Britain. The main subject of discussion was the border between India and Tibet. The British representative, Sir Henry McMahon, met with Lochen Shatra, the Tibetan representative, and fixed the frontier at a point that was mutually acceptable to Tibet and Britain: the so-called McMahon line. The British and Tibetan governments approved the terms of the agreement. Documents were signed, and maps were redrawn to reflect the McMahon line.

Tibetan representatives were also engaged in discussions with Chinese representatives regarding matters that pertained to their countries, including trade. China refused to sign the documents because it did not agree with their resolution of the border issues. It is ironic to note that in the 1960s, China and India went to war twice over border issues, and these involved the McMahon line and other border issues that were a legacy of the British Empire in Asia. The present government of China refuses to accept the validity of the border created at Simla, because it would amount to acknowledging Tibet was functioning as an independent country that could negotiate borders without reference to China's sovereignty.[4]

The Great Game presented another challenge to China. As Britain extended its influence in South Asia, czarist Russia extended its influence into Central Asia—the resource-rich lands that were eventually incorporated into the USSR as the Central Asian Republics, the vast Muslim underbelly of the Soviet Union: "The Russian government realized—as the Manchus had for centuries—that in Tibet lay the key to influence over most people in Central Asia. Russian friendship and perhaps influence over the Dalai Lama could mean a certain degree of influence and even control over the Mongol Kalmucks, Buriats and other Buddhist peoples now within the Russian Empire's borders or sphere of interest."[5]

The late Qing period was one of internal corruption and decay. The dynasty was critically weakened by the Taiping Rebellion (1850–1864), and was fast losing its grip on the empire. Rebellions in China's far west created an even greater drain on the state's resources. The Sino-Japanese war of 1895 followed. With foreign wars and internal rebellions, the Qing seemed to have lost the Mandate of Heaven, the assent of the cosmos in the legitimacy of the dynasty. Throughout Chinese history, dynasties had fallen because they lost the mandate.

A Russian mission visited Lhasa in 1898; this was followed by an emissary from the Dalai Lama traveling to the Czar's palace in St. Petersburg. The czarist government was encouraged by the prospect of expanding to the east. The Russians also moved south, intending to fill the power vacuum in the heart of Asia.

Vying for influence in South Asia became an issue of national pride for the Chinese. The Qing government did not want to lose Tibet to the Russian sphere of influence. Britain also feared greater Russian influence in what the British considered their zone of influence in Asia. The British diplomatic corps were motivated once again to eliminate the Chinese intermediary and create direct contact with Tibet.

Tibet, on the other hand, considered the British a greater threat than the Russians. "There was a visible fear of British imperialism inside Tibet....Even when this 'fear of foreigners' was recognized, it was seen as irrational, backward, medieval, and hence wrong. The hegemonic imperial ethos prevented most commentators from accepting this fear as borne out of a legitimate understanding of the nature of modern Western imperialism."[6]

A young powerful Dalai Lama, the Thirteenth, took over the reins of the Tibetan government in 1895. He pronounced that the age-old relationship between the Dalai Lama and the Chinese Emperor was that of priest and patron, the old *chö-yon* arrangement, conceived of as existing between equals. Tibet's borders remained closed. The country was materially poor and backward: It had no roads, telegraph, electricity, plumbing, railway, or modern factories. Tibet had only a subsistence agricultural economy, which included some animal husbandry and crafts. It had inherited the high scholastic tradition of India in the form of Tibetan Buddhism—a tradition that was Tibet's principal treasure. It had a distinct culture as well as unique art and architecture, and its cultural life revolved around the events of the Buddhist calendar, with its seasonal festivals and celebrations.

The Great Thirteenth began to implement some forms of modernization. He ran into opposition from the conservative clergy, who saw reform as a threat to the status quo, he began to build a Tibetan military. To him, it was evident that the forces of the decaying

Qing dynasty could not defend the country. In 1911, when the Manchu government fell, the Great Thirteenth proclaimed Tibet's independence.

❧

Mapping was an obsession of the Victorian imperial adventurers. The Raj, the British colonial government in India, had successfully mapped the Himalayas. Tibet, however, remained a large blank on the map. The British had a strong desire to map Tibet. Call it a form of insurance, a way to anticipate a potential adversary's advance. Where a map exists, an army can travel.

White men, even if they were disguised in native dress, could not gain admission to Tibet at the border. The first team of cartographers sent by the viceroy of India was a group of Indian colonials (sepoys) who received special training from the British for their mission. The maps they made remain accurate more than a century later. The tasks of the Indian colonials also included spying in Lhasa. They provided an early firsthand description of the Chinese *ambans* stationed in the Tibetan capital. The head of the Indian team recorded that the *ambans* were dissipated and licentious and were hated by the Tibetans.

Lord Curzon, the viceroy of India and chief officer of the British Raj in Asia, did not like the implications of close Russian-Tibetan relations. Observation and intelligence gathered in the field convinced him that czarist Russia intended to dominate Asia. The viceroy wanted proof that Tibet had not allied itself with Russia, so he made up his mind to initiate direct relations with the government of Tibet—that is, without going through the Qing government. He began to send letters to the Dalai Lama in 1901, but the Great Thirteenth returned Curzon's letters unopened. This was a mistake.

Penetrating Tibet had become something of an obsession with Lord Curzon, and the Tibetan rebuff inflamed the viceroy. Curzon decided to send a mission to Lhasa—he intended to enter Tibet by force and demand that the Tibetan government enter into trade relations. He believed that imperial action (a blending of negotiation and force) might be required to convince Tibetans of their place in the larger scheme of things—namely, their recognition of British imperial interests.[7] Lord Curzon dispatched the Younghusband mission to Lhasa in 1904. Curzon hoped to station a British representative in the Tibetan capital. As with so many incidents in history, matters got out of hand.

Curzon placed Colonel Younghusband, a graduate of the Royal Military Academy Sandhurst, at the head of the expedition and gave him a post on the Tibet Frontier Commission. Younghusband was an avid imperialist. He shared the official British point of view that any Tibetan attempt to form a relationship with Russia should be countered—if necessary, by force. British opinion on Tibet was divided into the romantics and the realists. The romantics saw Tibet as a place of ineffable mystery that would be destroyed by the arrival of the modern world. The realists thought that the place was a filthy medieval backwater, controlled by superstition and ignorance that could only be improved by opening to the outside world.

Younghusband was a mystic by nature, which was unusual in a military man. He had been born and bred in India and had traveled widely in the Himalayas in his youth. He had written of the effect of the mountains and the people on his consciousness in his journal. He resembled many British colonials who felt that India and Tibet possessed the spirituality that the scientific, material West had lost. They felt that they had regained Paradise Lost when they entered Tibet. Younghusband's experience in Tibet was to have a profound effect on him for the rest of his life.

Francis Younghusband's career did not begin in Tibet. His first assignment as a servant of the British Crown was to travel across China to map Xinjiang. China's far west was of interest to the British because of the Russian presence in Turkestan. The Russian bear was nibbling away at the Chinese sphere of influence.

Upon successfully completing this epic journey across China, Younghusband received the Tibet assignment from Curzon to open negotiations at the Tibetan frontier with officials in a trading town on the border. The expedition was no small affair. Younghusband commanded 1,500 British troops, and the expedition contained a number of Ghurka companies of Nepalese. The mission had had four artillery guns and four machine guns; they also brought an animal train of 4,000 yaks, 7,000 mules, 200 ponies, 6 camels, and a human train of 10,000 porters. The train extended over four miles of Himalayan trails. It included four members of the British press, who relayed their stories back to London and New Delhi via telegraph. (Because there was no telegraph in the Himalayas, Younghusband strung a telegraph wire behind the expedition for this purpose.)

The Tibetan border officials were adamant. They wanted nothing to do with Great Britain. They wanted to be left alone. Ceremonial displays of British regiments in uniform did nothing to convince the Tibetans, since their own ceremonial outfits were more splendid. Tibetan officials asked Younghusband to turn back at the border. He ignored the request and advanced into Tibet with troops. Younghusband fought several battles, killed a great many Tibetans, and prevailed in the battle.

Although Lord Kitchener replaced Lord Curzon as viceroy in 1905, the opening of Tibet remained a goal. It was an imperial mission, not the obsession of one imperialist. Younghusband pressed on. The Tibetans had built a stone wall to block the mountain pass, but they were armed only with old rifles and swords and "protection amulets" from the Dalai Lama. The British responded with modern firepower, and Tibetan bodies were strewn all over the pass. Younghusband pressed forward, and again he killed and wounded hundreds of Tibetans.

When Younghusband finally reached the holy city of Lhasa, he became the first Englishman to gain entry to the fabled capital in more than a century. Lhasa wove a spell, with the gleaming white walls of the Potala Palace set against the deep blue sky.

The British discovered that their fears were unfounded: There were no Russian officials in residence nor any sort of Russian trading post or embassy. Younghusband met with Tibetan officials and concluded a treaty, the Anglo-Tibetan Convention. Under its provisions, the Tibetans promised not to have relations with any country other than China. The British levied a huge indemnity against Tibet, which was later revoked by London because Younghusband had exceeded his authority in pressing to Lhasa.

Tibet could no longer use the Qing government as a protector to shield it from the British. Once remote, it was no longer beyond reach—the Himalayas no longer served as a natural barrier against attacks. The Dalai Lama asked for assistance from China, Russia, and Nepal. The Nepalese refused to enter into the conflict, and no other country offered to come to the aid of Tibet. The Dalai Lama left Lhasa and fled to India in 1907, leaving the *amban* to assert Chinese authority over Tibet.

In 1906, an Adhesion Agreement with Britain was signed in Peking (as the Chinese capital was called at the time), after a series of treaty talks. The agreement formally recognized the Chinese emperor's special position in Tibet. Britain acknowledged the Qing Emperor's right to guarantee Tibet's territorial integrity. Tibet was not asked to agree to modifications in the treaty and the document was signed without the consent of Tibet. The Tibetan government stated that the Manchus had not fulfilled their traditional role of protecting Tibet and declared the treaty invalid. All this was to no avail. The pattern was set. Tibet was a small state whose future was decided by bigger, more powerful states.

The Russians believed that the Anglo-Chinese agreement was a threat to their regional interests, since they thought that the British had created Tibet as a British protectorate. In 1903 and again in 1904, the British assured the Russian government that Britain had no imperial intentions. The two powers signed a treaty to resolve territorial issues concerning Persia, Afghanistan, and Tibet. The two powers did not make any agreements concerning sovereign rights in Tibet and Persia, reassuring each other that neither had a right to do so.

Tibet was in the Qing Empire's sphere of influence, to the exclusion of all other powers except for the British. A British official, Charles Bell, neatly summarized matters as follows: the British knocked the Tibetans down and left them in a reduced state, making it easier for the Qing to return and reassert themselves. Confusion regarding the definitions of "suzerainty" and "protectorate" resounded loudly in the international community at the time of the Chinese invasion in 1950. These concepts and categories of state relations are the legacy of the colonial era.

The Qing government paid the indemnity owed to the British as a result of the Younghusband expedition. Although the payment came from China, the indemnity was rendered by an official of the Tibetan government at British insistence as a matter of form.

The British removed their troops from Tibet. A Qing special commissioner arrived and chased out the British officers who had concluded the treaties, an action that the British government protested. The Tibetans were not pleased with the actions of the special commissioner, but in the Dalai Lama's absence they were powerless to prevent the hostile behavior.

Qing armies took over a portion of the eastern Tibetan province of Kham and incorporated it into the Chinese province of Sichuan. This is the basis of the Chinese claim that eastern Tibet is part of China. Given the circumstances surrounding the annexation, this territorial issue could be argued either way.

The Dowager Empress Cixi was the de facto ruler of China. The boy emperor Pu Yi was too young to take the throne, and it was the Chinese custom that a regent exerted power until the heir to the throne came of age. The Empress Dowager and the Qing Court concluded that the relations with the Tibetan people would improve upon the return of the Dalai Lama, so they set about urging him to come back. The Dalai Lama returned to Tibet in 1909, but he was not happy with the situation there. The Qing general Zhang had occupied even more eastern Tibetan territory and was urging the Emperor to create a new Chinese province, Xikang.

Zhang's troops advanced upon Lhasa soon after the Dalai Lama's return. In 1910, the Qing imperial government issued an edict deposing the Dalai Lama and ordering a search for his successor. The Dalai Lama again left Tibet and took up residence in Darjeeling, India. He also reiterated his renunciation of Qing claims to Tibet.

The Tibetan populace resisted Chinese authority. Again the Qing government decided that it needed the Dalai Lama to rule Tibet. They invited him to return. He declined. At the same time, the British wanted a stable government in Tibet and considered the Qing government to be in violation of treaty agreements. The

British ambassador to Peking delivered several protests. This was a futile effort.

☙

After the fall of Qing in 1911, Tibetans attacked Chinese imperial garrisons in Lhasa and forced them to surrender. The Thirteenth Dalai Lama returned to Tibet and proclaimed Tibet's independence from China. With the fall of the imperial system in China, Tibet considered the priest–patron relationship officially over. The system that had been in place for centuries was no more.

The early twentieth century was an era of massive tectonic shifts in world politics. Momentous change followed upon cataclysmic change. In the wake of World War I, empires fell. The Ottoman and the Austro-Hungarian empires were no more. The Manchus fell in China. The Russian imperial system came to an end with the Bolshevik Revolution in 1917.

The new master of Russia, Vladimir Ilyich Lenin, did not change Russian expansionist policies in Central Asia. In *Setting the East Ablaze: Lenin's Dream of an Empire in Asia,* author/journalist Peter Hopkirk writes that by the year 1919, "the missionaries of Bolshevism had sworn to set the East ablaze using the heady new gospel of Marxism as their torch. If India could be torn by insurrection from Britain's grasp, then no longer would she be able to buy off her workers—unwitting shareholders in imperialism—with the sweated labor and cheap raw materials of the East."

From the end of the nineteenth century to the mid-twentieth century, when Tibet attempted to gain a hearing at the United Nations after the Chinese invasion, its position on its own sovereignty has never changed. What changed were British imperial interests in South Asia. When the British quit India in the wake of World War II, Britain no longer had an interest in maintaining a position in Tibet. The British now viewed Tibet as the responsibility of the newly independent India, an India struggling to govern itself, a vast, poor country, in the wake of a foreign power's departure. With domestic concerns presenting daunting problems—the partitioning of India and Pakistan was a human rights disaster of immense proportions—Tibet was not high on the priority list of India's Prime Minister Jawaharlal Nehru.

Tibet's geopolitical identity was carved out in the language of British imperialism: sovereignty, suzerainty, autonomy, and independence. The principle that China seized upon was sovereignty.

> The most significant aspect of the British imperialist policy practiced in the first half of the twentieth century was the formula of 'Chinese suzerainty/Tibetan autonomy.' This strategic hypocrisy, while nurturing an ambiguity in Tibet's status, culminated in the victory of a Western idea of sovereignty. It was China, not Tibet that found the sovereignty talk most useful.[8]

The governments of the world accepted the Chinese interpretation of its relationship with Tibet. The People's Republic cites history to legitimize its claim, but the legal concept of sovereignty derives from international relations of the imperial era. As applied by China in international dialogue, "sovereignty" serves as background music to the Chinese invasion—familiar and accepted, but rarely analyzed in sixty years.

On the other side of the argument, Tibetans and their supporters in the international arena reject the concept of sovereignty. Their argument is that China has no sovereignty and thus is illegally occupying Tibet. Tibet's position has always been that it is an independent nation. Advocates for an independent or autonomous Tibet point to a supporting body of evidence consisting of the claims of Tibetan civilization (history and religion), traditions of international law, and bodies of knowledge (morality, decolonization, nationalism, human rights, the claim of democracy and self-determination). The haze of categories of colonial relationships muddied the waters where the status of Tibet is concerned

It is true that some senior members of the secular government and the monastic establishment (the disgraced regent Reting and the self-exiled Tenth Panchen Lama) did side with the Chinese. For the most part, however, Tibet's position has been that it is entitled to self-determination. As proof, supporters cite Tibet's campaign to gain international recognition as a state in the 1948–1950 period by seeking redress from the UN and from various postwar powers.

Britain first ignored and then undermined the attempt. Britain was no longer protecting its financial interests in India.

India also did not support Tibet. The new postcolonial state of India wanted friendly relations with China and viewed its international stature as being more important than entering into a dispute with China over a minor state. In 1954, India officially recognized Tibet as an integral part of China.

The newly independent India honored British agreements from the Raj period that concerned Tibet. One example was the Simla Agreement of 1914, which set the McMahon line as the boundary between India and Tibet. The Tibetans argue that because the Chinese never signed the agreement, its formula of Chinese sovereignty/Tibetan autonomy has no binding effect.

Throughout the early part of the twentieth century, the Thirteenth Dalai Lama insisted upon Tibet's independence, its wish to be free of Chinese dominance, and its desire to practice Tibetan religion without interference. This was a nationalist aspiration. Tibet's early efforts at modernization were slow and ineffectual, but there is no doubt that it was an independent state from 1913 to 1951. The Qing representative had been expelled, and Tibet conducted its own affairs. The problem was that Tibet had not been recognized by any other country as an independent state.

❧

In their negotiating behavior, the Chinese show a predilection for having major points agreed upon in advance of formal negotiations. Down to the present day, the Tibetan Government in Exile's insistence on the return of ethnically Tibetan territory incorporated into Chinese provinces has been a deal-breaker. The Chinese will not consider returning what amounts to a quarter of their landmass. The ethnically Tibetan areas in Gansu, Yunnan, Sichuan, and Qinghai are protected under national minority provisions in the Chinese constitution.

Tibet lost the critical moment for recognition. Because of the murky situation in international law, Tibet could not advance its case for decolonialization before the United Nations. No country came forward to support Tibet's claim to statehood, because no power wanted to be accused of attempting to break up China. Thus, no nation supported Tibet's secession from China. Tibet had failed to meet the challenge of modernity. Melvyn C. Goldstein, a historian of modern Tibet, put it this way: "History is not nice."[9]

Why Now?

Recent pressures of population transfer are changing the ethnic composition of Tibet. The exile government refers to Chinese immigration policies as cultural genocide: the deliberate destruction of Tibet's faith and culture as a consequence of China's "Go West" policy. At issue is government-supported immigration aimed at the rapid economic development of Tibet.

The policy is nothing new in China. The PRC employed the same immigration policy in other minority regions, especially Xinjiang. History shows that the influx of Han Chinese changed the ethnic composition of Xinjiang and caused ethnic unrest there. Better jobs and higher pay are offered to Han Chinese willing to work in the provinces, often under difficult conditions. In Tibet, this means the physical hardship of the high-altitude environment.

In some ways, it has been a successful policy for China. Han majorities in formerly ethnic territories such as Xinjiang have made loyalty to Beijing a foregone conclusion, but as the 2009 riots in Urumqi demonstrate, the Chinese have to contend with underlying ethnic tensions.

In his 1988 speech before the European Parliament at Strasbourg, the Fourteenth Dalai Lama sought to preserve the ethnic character of Tibet. Giving up on the idea of Tibetan independence, he accepted the lesser goal of Tibetan autonomy. Given China's modern armaments, devolution of control would surely pose no threat to Chinese security.

The Dalai Lama's stance has met with a backlash among the younger generation of Tibetans, the Rangzen movement, who support the goal of independence and who are willing to advocate the use of violence. They openly oppose the Dalai Lama's insistence upon nonviolence. Aside from the philosophical objections that the exiled Tibetan leader has to the use of violence, the Dalai Lama has publicly rejected the idea of a Tibetan intifada as impractical, because such an approach stands no chance of success against superior Chinese forces. Lives would be lost and the desired result stands no chance of success.

The result is a stalemate on all sides. Yet with new thinking and new models, the situation could resolve into a win-win outcome. No one wants to interfere in Chinese affairs, but in 2008 intermittent crackdowns in Lhasa caused a firestorm of criticism in the international community. China recognizes that ongoing tensions in Tibet create a public relations nightmare for China in the global community. Foreign policy professionals have weighed in on all sides of the Tibet Question.

Former South Korean Foreign Minister Dr. Han Sung-Joo has identified the locus of the conceptual problem as far as diplomacy is concerned. "The Chinese have a concept of sovereignty in an age of interflow of influence." Dr. Han proposes that the region work with China in multilateral regional bodies such as ASEAN and retain some fluidity in dealing with all issues as problems to be solved in the normal course of business rather than as roadblocks standing in the way of progress. Issues within this framework would be Tibet's potential to de-stabilize China's relations with Western states and the eventual re-unification of the Koreas, which has the ability to de-stabilize the region.

The Chinese cannot do away with their worldview in an instant. The current generation of Chinese leaders may view these suggestions as concessions rather than as advantages, given China's fantastic economic success. Even Chinese officials who see things from a multilateral perspective are hard-pressed to explain their views to colleagues in the current atmosphere of nationalism. There is some evidence to suggest that the top leadership, including the hard-liners, are uncertain as to what to do about Tibet and are searching for a solution. The author suggests moving to the front of the agenda a regional economic body of the sort that has proved so successful for China in Southeast Asia, a body where China already has observer status. The problem of militant Islam and the upsurge in the narcotics trade in the South Asian region are the twin stimuli dictating a new solution in Tibet.

A new regional common market in South Asia and a newly diversified Tibet economy would achieve China's long-standing goal of economic prosperity for Tibet. From Beijing, Tibet looks like a poor stepchild out on the periphery. Seen from the point of view of Lhasa, if Tibet's role in the old regional political and trading patterns, which pre-date the Great Game and the Cold War, are restored, Tibet has the potential to be a regional leader and an exporter, not to China proper, but to the region.

The Chinese could project not hard power (military) or soft power (ethnic sensitivity) but smart power (political and economic solutions) into the South Asian region, a strategy that has not yet been tried. The Chinese have ignored the root causes of ethnic tensions in Tibet and instead have blamed the problems on outside influences. This has failed to convince the Tibetan masses. If Tibetans could exert more control over their political situation, it would diffuse ethnic tensions because it would address the root causes. South Asia is a region in the midst of crisis and change. The United States has announced its intention to begin to draw down its troops in Afghanistan in 2011. A new roadmap for Tibet, as outlined in the conclusion of this book, might benefit the whole region and have the added benefit to China of enhancing its expanding role as the major power there. Is it worth the experiment? China holds the cards.

Lord Curzon, British Conservative statesman and viceroy of India from 1898 to 1905. Suspicious of the Russian Empire's expansion across Central Asia, Curzon sent a British expedition to Tibet in 1904. (*Library of Congress*)

The Thirteenth Dalai Lama ousted the Chinese imperial bureaucrat from Lhasa at the fall of the Qing Dynasty and proclaimed Tibet's independence. A modernizing force, he earned the nickname The Great Thirteenth. (*Library of Congress*)

Colonel Francis Younghusband, center, was the first British Resident in Kashgar (in present day Xinjiang). The focus of British colonial activity shifted from South Asia to Central Asia in the late nineteenth century, as Russia expanded into Asia. The British government sent a number of missions to the area to make contact with the local government, and to collect intelligence on the Russians. (*1891. [Mss Eur F197/674(1)] © The British Library Board*)

Dowager Empress, Cixi, ruled China at the fall of the Qing Dynasty. In her later years, she was fearsome—the imperial court nicknamed her "the Old Buddha" indicating a masculine role, that of wielding absolute power. This photograph taken in her youth shows a feminine aspect indicating a potential route to power: It reveals how she might have charmed an emperor and gained power at the top of the Chinese imperial system. (*Time Life Pictures/Getty Images*)

Chiang Kaishek, generalissimo of Nationalist forces and later president of the Republic of China (Taiwan), lost the Chinese civil war to the communists. Here he reads the "creeds for party members" of the Guomindang and army notices to Central Training Corps, Chongqing, somewhere between 1937 and 1945. (*Library of Congress*)

Mao Zedong, first chairman of the People's Republic of China, and the Soviet leader Joseph Stalin in the early 1950s in Moscow. Soviet politician Nikolai Bulganin is in the background. (*Rolls/Popperfoto/Getty Images*)

The Dalai Lama on an elephant ride with Jawaharlal Nehru, prime minister of India and an elephant trainer, New Delhi, 1957. (*Office of the Dalai Lama*)

The Tibetan Uprising of 1959 in Lhasa led to the demise of the traditional Tibetan government. In this photo from the protests, the Potala Palace is in background. (*STR/AFP/Getty Images*)

The Dalai Lama (near left) on a visit Beijing in 1955, with the first premier of the People's Republic of China, Zhou Enlai (far right) and the Panchen Lama (near right). The six-month visit to Beijing occurred during the so-called Honeymoon Period (during the fifties) when the Dalai Lama believed that Buddhism was compatible with Marxism. (*Keystone/Hulton Archive/Getty Images*)

The Dalai Lama escaped to India in 1959. In this photo he is seated in dark robes and his usual glasses, center, surrounded by Khampa bodyguards. (*Popperfoto/Getty Images*)

An editorial cartoon from 1959 depicting the international response to the Chinese invasion of Tibet. The United Nations peers at the feet of a man labeled "Tibet" hanging from a tree while Soviet deputy premier Vasiliĭ Kuznetsov stands behind the United Nations representative, his hands clenched into fists, telling him that he is "being provocative, malicious, slanderous and nosy." (*Library of Congress*)

Communist leader and first president of the People's Republic of China, Mao Zedong, and Soviet premier Nikita Khrushchev in Beijing, 1958. (*AFP/Getty Images*)

Mao Zedong (right) with Deng Xiaoping (left) in Beijing. Mao died in 1976, with Deng Xiaoping succeeding him and undertaking Chinese economic reforms. (*Keystone/Getty Images*)

Reformist Communist Party leader Hu Yaobang (right) with then leader Deng Xiaoping (left) in Beijing in 1981. On April 15, 2004, Hu Yaobang died of a sudden heart attack in Beijing, sparking a spontaneous outpouring of grief. This led to six weeks of unprecedented, nationwide democracy protests that centered in Tienanmen. On July 4, the People's Liberation Army troops moved in to quell the protests, resulting in a bloody massacre. (*AFP/Getty Images*)

PART 5

Early Twentieth-Century China

The Nationalists Adopt Imperial Policy in Tibet

Failure at the Chinese Center

Flood, famine, popular uprisings, and rebellion in the army afflicted the late Qing dynasty. The treasury was bankrupt. The government borrowed vast sums of money to build a railroad network throughout the country then defaulted on the loans. Most significantly, the population doubled to almost 450 million by the mid-nineteenth century. China was not producing enough food to feed the burgeoning population, and in the late nineteenth century there was a famine. Corrupt officials and a land shortage combined to create an impoverished population. In traditional times, these would have been signs that portended the loss of the Mandate of Heaven and the right of a dynasty to rule, a traditional Chinese interpretation that the fall of a dynasty would not be in error.

This state of affairs led to popular unrest, which shook the foundations of the dynasty. The Taiping Rebellion (1850–1864), centered in southern China, was one of the most cataclysmic events in world history, taking some twenty million lives. The domestic situation was exacerbated by external challenges. For example, seven areas of China were designated as property of foreign powers, the best of examples being Hong Kong belonging to the British Empire. These concessions were outside the reach of Chinese courts, subject only to their own legal systems, and discriminated against the Chinese in their own country. The terms of foreign trade were often unfavorable to the Chinese.

Confucianism as a unifying ideology had lost its authority and appeal. A variety of imported Western philosophies drew adherents among the educated elite and spread among the masses: anarchism, republicanism, socialism, communism. The revolutionaries had been educated abroad and influenced by the West, but no new system emerged that was strong enough to replace the old one. The old China broke under the strain.

In the final years of the dynasty, the Qing tried to reform itself, and a National Assembly was formed to set about the job of creating a constitution and a parliament. But the effort was too little too late.

Much of the critique of China's old system came from students who had the wealth and backing to study overseas. Sun Yatsen, the father of the Republican Revolution, studied in Japan and was a nationalist. Nationalism was the wine that the reformers imbibed and it was anti-foreign. Many European socialist texts had been translated into Chinese, and socialism had its adherents in China, some of whom supported Sun. He also had the backing of women, who had not been a constituency in any manner in traditional China. Sun even had support among the criminal triad factions in southern China. His principal base was the amalgamation of anti-Qing groups called the Revolutionary Alliance, which advocated republican revolution.

Sun advocated revolution against the Qing and supported seven armed insurrections against the dynasty—three of them in Guangzhou, his strongest base. In 1911, the Republican Revolution overthrew the dynastic system that had been ruling China for two millennia. The last Qing emperor stepped down from the Dragon

Throne in 1912. "Although in 1912 many Chinese still favored a strong central authority, the institution of the emperorship along with the compromise of a constitutional monarchy had been rejected by most Chinese."[1]

A period of chaos followed the fall of Qing. Political power disappeared at the center and power spun out to the regional warlords, who provided military and political authority. Militarists, varied in their backgrounds and talents, ran the show in the provinces.

Two groups emerged from this period, republicans and communists. Chiang Kaishek was a republican nationalist who came from a privileged background and had a military education. He was Sun Yatsen's political heir, and he inherited the leadership of the Revolutionary Alliance, which later became the Guomindang, or National People's Party. The Guomindang (GMT) was formed in 1912 and subscribed to a theory of immediate rather than gradual change. At this time, the trend among modernizing nations was to become a republic. There had been a Chinese empire, but there had never been a modern Chinese nation-state. The GMT's idea was that the boundaries of the new Chinese state would incorporate all territory conquered by Qing. This required redefining the concept of Han Chinese: Minorities were now defined as having their origins in the Chinese race. Sun developed the idea of the five minorities of China being subgroups of Han Chinese. It was a popular theory but without basis in biology, anthropology, or genetics.

Mao Zedong came from a peasant family in Hunan. In his youth, he threw off the peasant life and the arranged marriage his family made for him and served in the anti-Qing army. Chinese intellectual ferment was centered in Peking University. Mao moved to Peking, took a job in the library, and attended classes. He began a course of study that was to expose him to the major intellectual trends of the time. In Peking, Mao, the young peasant from the provinces, absorbed ideas and developed the foundation of his theory: he defined the peasantry as the backbone of the Chinese revolution. The proletariat might be at the heart of the Russian revolution, but Mao knew China and China had a peasantry.

There was not enough proletariat in China to serve as the basis of a revolution.

❧

After the revolution, Sun Yatsen served as provisional president for a year and then resigned in 1912. His letter of resignation set forth the idea that China's elected head of state must obey the new constitution and be subject to its provisions. Gone would be imperial whim. China was to have rule of law, which would apply even to the head of state. The new constitution defined the rules for national elections for a two-chamber parliament, with representation in the lower chamber on the basis of one representative for every 800,000 persons. China's new government was to be installed in 1913.

In October of 1913, Britain gave diplomatic recognition to the Chinese republic. Japan recognized the new republic after China agreed to favorable railway deals. In North Asia, Outer Mongolia broke away from inclusion in the Chinese state and declared its autonomy, an action that was supported by Russia. Mongolia once again played an important part in events on the Asian continent, but that is a story for a later chapter.

On November 8, 1913, the National Assembly elected Yuan Shikai as China's first president. The United States sent its diplomatic representative in Peking to grant full recognition to the new government. Initially Yuan claimed that Tibet was a Chinese dependency, affirming the status of Tibet under the late Qing. This was a reaction to the perceived injustice of Western imperialism. It was nationalism, a reassertion of Han Chinese identity. This would not be the last time that Chinese nationalism would affect relations with Tibet.

At the fall of Qing, the Thirteenth Dalai Lama proclaimed Tibet's independence by ousting the Qing *amban* from Lhasa. Thubten Gyatso, the Great Thirteenth, as this powerful Dalai Lama was known, believed in modernization and tried to strengthen Tibet. He attempted to build and modernize an army to protect Tibet's eastern borders, a project that drained the central government's finances.

From these momentous events until 1950, Tibet functioned as an independent state.

Throughout China's Nationalist period, roughly the late 1920s through the late 1940s, Thubten Gyatso refused to accept the Chinese definition held over from Qing that the five nationalities—Han, Manchus, Mongols, Tibetans and Muslims—were part of China. He represented Tibetan interests in eastern Tibet (annexed by Qing) when the Nationalists dispatched two separate missions to Lhasa to discuss the status of Tibet under their government. The Nationalists could not exert control over all of China and had problems projecting their power into Tibet. The Great Thirteenth also attempted to renegotiate the old border dispute formerly settled with Britain at the Simla Convention.[2]

President Yuan Shikai was confronted with major challenges in creating a modern political system in China. The new parliament was supposed to equalize the relationship between the central government and the provincial governments. Yuan did not have a firm enough control over the military to maintain order or prevent mass protests and open rebellion in the provinces. After the election of 1912, the leader of the main political party was assassinated.

By 1914, Yuan assumed the powers of a dictator. He imposed censorship on newspapers and other publications. Yuan initially believed in constitutional monarchy, but after he took office he attempted to restore the imperial system *with himself as emperor.* He was thoroughly discredited and his reputation was ruined. In 1916, Yuan ended his attempted restoration of the imperial system. He died shortly thereafter.

The presidency and republicanism had taken a blow. A military coup attempted to restore the emperorship, but this too failed. The central government, the president, and the legislature came under the control of military men.

🙰

The Russian Revolution had a tremendous impact in China. Some Chinese political writers saw a comparison between the old authoritarian systems in both Russia and China, both of which needed to be reformed. The Soviet Union sent agents into the hotbed of political ferment that China had become. By 1920, the Chinese Communist Party (CCP) had been born.

In the 1920s, Nationalists and Communists formed an alliance for the building of a new China. Yet by 1927, the two groups were at odds. The Guomindang emerged as the strongest of the contending factions in the nascent civil war. The Nationalists drove the Communists out of the cities and tried to consolidate their control of the foreign enclaves and warlord territories.

The Nationalists and the Minorities

The changes that took place in early twentieth-century China shook the established order much as an earthquake shifts the ground. The old was gone and the new was struggling to assume a coherent form.

Chinese nationalism, the patriotic support for China as a modern "state," was something new in Chinese history. The main reason for this is that there had never been a Chinese nation-state, to use the modern political term. There had been a Chinese empire—an empire that ruled by the magnificence of its civilization and by reference to a classical set of texts—but not a Chinese state. The surging of nationalism represented a new and powerful political force and it emerged from the bottom up, much like the earlier Taiping Rebellion and the Boxer Rebellion. The up and coming leaders of the new China sought to harness the new political force. Their task was to find a central authority to replace the dynastic system and they sought modern political means to do it.

When Sun Yatsen died in 1925, Chiang Kaishek succeeded him as leader of the Nationalists. The Guomintang announced the formation of a government in 1928. The GMT tried, under successive leaders, to restore order and to found a central government. They established a capital at Nanjing, but they could not establish control over all of China.

The border regions—Tibet, Xinjiang, Outer Mongolia, and Manchuria—were controlled by warlords who continued imperial forms of rule: top-down imposition of authority backed up by military force. For all practical purposes, Manchuria, Mongolia, and Tibet were independent. "Recognizing the continued importance to China's security of the frontier 'buffer territories,' China's new leaders preserved the 'colonialist-imperialist posture' toward Tibet, Eastern Turkestan (Xinjiang) and Mongolia."[3] In fact, the Nationalist government wanted to preserve the Manchu idea of a multi-ethnic empire comprising the Han Chinese and "the four minority nationalities: the Tibetans, the Manchus, the Mongolians and the Moslems of Sinkiang."[4]

Sun Yatsen developed a theory of national origins. In his view, the "five nationalities" were one people who had shared a common origin since the Chin and Han Dynasties. He reasoned that the minorities numbered only about 10 million out of 400 million Chinese and concluded that, "for the most part, the Chinese people are of the Han or Chinese race with common blood, common language, common religion, and common customs—a single, pure race."[5] (Chiang Kaishek later endorsed Sun's theory of the unity of nationalities.)

When he came to power, Sun Yatsen called for self-determination for the minority regions, an idea adopted from the American president Woodrow Wilson. In contrast, Chiang Kaishek—whose goal was to reunify China—did not endorse the concept of autonomy for the minorities. Chiang had decided to assert power over the border regions, which he regarded as an indivisible part of the Chinese motherland. If minorities were branches of Han Chinese, then self-determination for minorities was unnecessary. China was one and indivisible.

The Chinese minorities did not agree that their histories and cultures did nothing more than entitle them to be minor branches of the Han Chinese. The minorities understood their identities to include their own ethnicity, religion, customs, foods, and culture. The Muslims of Xinjiang, the Buddhists of Tibet, the Mongols of Mongolia, and the Manchus in Manchuria did not see themselves as branches of the Han. This was of no concern to Sun Yatsen or Chiang Kaishek, whose racial and national views became institutionalized as part of China's school curriculum under the Nationalists. The ideas eventually permeated the population and influenced popular thinking; as such, they formed part of China's modern consciousness.

In the 1980s, while on a trip to China, the author interviewed an influential Chinese-American art historian who grew up in Shanghai. He was born into a prominent banking family, but after the communist takeover in 1949, the family emigrated to America. This erudite and well-traveled man, who took his degrees at American Ivy League institutions, subscribed to the antique nationalist racial theory. He vividly remembered the "five races" of China that he learned in school and they remained part of his consciousness into his middle age. This one example illustrates how the theory of the "five races" served as a kind of Chinese background lighting illuminating the communist theory of nationalities.

Between the Dalai Lamas

At the fall of Qing in 1912, the Thirteenth Dalai Lama ended the official Chinese presence in Lhasa. This event seemed to hold the promise that Tibet might modernize along distinctly Tibetan lines, but the promise never came to fruition. Tibet could not escape history. It was a small, weak state and it had a long way to go to enter modernity. History overwhelmed Tibet, even the Tibetan government undermined the trajectory of Tibetan modernism. To paraphrase from James Joyce's *Portrait of the Artist as a Young Man,* history was a nightmare from which Tibet was unable to awaken.

The Thirteenth Dalai Lama was strongly opposed to any Chinese presence in Lhasa. The Great Thirteenth believed that a well-trained army would serve as a deterrent, so he attempted to strengthen the Tibetan army. They had antiquated weapons and no training. His efforts fell short, and Tibet's military deteriorated after his death. His view, as stated in his last will and testament, was that Tibet should develop good diplomatic relationships with its two powerful neighbors, China and India, and that it should station troops at the frontiers that bordered hostile forces. As circumstance would have it, he was too late and too slow in modernizing Tibetan armed forces.

The Thirteenth Dalai Lama warned the Tibetan leadership about the threats to the Buddhist faith, particularly from what he termed "the red ideology." He witnessed what the communist system had done in Mongolia. He feared the imposition of such a system on Tibet. In centuries past, Mongolia had been a Chinese tribute state, but had proclaimed its independence after the fall of Qing. The communists came to power and created the state's modern identity as the Mongolian People's Republic. Mongolia drew close to the new Soviet Union and avoided the fate of becoming a province of China, much to the annoyance of the Chinese. The communists persecuted the Buddhist religion: they blocked the search for the reincarnation of a Grand Lama, they confiscated monasteries, and they forced lamas and monks into the army.

The Nationalist Chinese government was anxious to reestablish a Chinese presence in Lhasa, but their effort failed. Attempting to control Tibet by interfering in its politics of succession, the Nationalists did manage to influence the selection of a new regent and the Panchen Lama, the Buddhist cleric second in importance to the Dalai Lama. This was the extent of their influence.

The system of government by Dalai Lamas has one main inherent weakness: succession. During the period between the death of a Dalai Lama and the investiture of a new one, a regent exercises political power. Once the Dalai Lama is discovered, if he is too young to assume power then the Panchen Lama becomes the leader of Tibet. This way the Chinese could control the selection of the future Dalai Lama.

Throughout the history of the Dalai Lamas, the regency was a time of weakness in the traditional Tibetan government. The Thirteenth Dalai Lama died in 1933, after which a dispute erupted over the regency. The Fourteenth (and present) Dalai Lama, Tenzin Gyatso, was not born until 1935. He was discovered by the traditional methods and brought to Lhasa with his family to begin training for his eventual accession to the rulership of Tibet.

Unable to gain political control of Tibet, the Panchen Lama went into exile in Mongolia, a country that revered him as a spiritual leader. He then moved to China, where he remained for a decade. While the titular ruler of Tibet was sojourning in China in self-inflicted exile, the Nationalists began using him to influence affairs in Tibet. Upon the death of the Thirteenth Dalai Lama, the

Panchen Lama announced to the Kashag that he wished to return to Tibet and to bring with him Chinese diplomatic personnel and a military escort. He announced his intention to build roads, to establish a telegraph system and a modern postal system, and to construct a system of grammar schools that would teach Tibetan and Chinese languages as well as science. The Panchen Lama claimed that the Nationalist government would provide the funding—nearly a million Chinese dollars, a massive expenditure by Tibetan standards. The Tibetan government was wary of establishing a precedent by inviting Nationalist troops onto Tibetan soil. They insisted that the Panchen Lama return to Tibet by sea, not by the overland route through China. In the end, the Panchen returned to Tibet through India without Chinese troops.

The Tibetan government had been encouraging British influence because they hoped that the British would give them military aid to keep the Chinese out. Yet at the same time, the Panchen Lama was scheming with the Chinese in order to counter British influence in Tibet. The Panchen Lama was not alone in politicking for a Chinese protectorate in Tibet. However, a crisis was averted when the Panchen Lama died on December 1, 1937—the same year in which the Sino-Japanese War broke out.

The Japanese invasion of China in 1937 had put an end to the maneuvering over Tibet. On the Chinese mainland, the two contenders in the civil war—the Nationalists and the Communists— joined forces to oust the Japanese. Tibetan politics were no longer a principal concern of the Chinese.

The British established a permanent mission in Lhasa in 1937, which remained until the Communist invasion of 1950. The government of the People's Republic of China (PRC) assumed authority over selection of the Panchen Lama, a claim with roots in the politics of the Nationalist period. This was not the first time that the Panchen Lama was used by the Chinese for political reasons, and it would not be the last.

British interests in East Asia were aligned against the Japanese goal of pan-Asian unity under the hegemony of the Japanese Emperor Hirohito.[6] In 1937, Britain was on the verge of recognizing Tibetan independence, but backed off when Japan invaded China.

His Majesty's Government did not wish to seem anti-Chinese at a time when China was the victim of Japanese aggression.

At Whitehall, the seat of British government, those who were known as the Raj faction pushed for diplomatic recognition of Tibet; the Hong Kong faction of British diplomats advocated not recognizing Tibet. The Raj faction lost the bureaucratic skirmish, and the British government chose not to recognize Tibet's independence. Tibet thus had no standing in international law, which was the source of its problem at the time of the Chinese invasion. How different the course of Tibetan history would have been had British recognition clarified Tibet's status.

The Nationalists Lose

Between 1930 and 1932, the years leading up to the Japanese invasion of Manchuria, China and Tibet went to war over the Sino-Tibetan border in the Eastern Tibetan province of Kham.[7] The Nationalists sent General Huang Musung, vice-chief of the general staff, on a mission to Lhasa. General Huang arrived with a delegation and extended his condolences regarding the death of the Thirteenth Dalai Lama.[8] "The Huang condolence mission was aimed at inducing Tibet to admit it was one of the five races (ethnic groups) that made up the new Republic of China, by emphasizing the commonalities between China and Tibet as opposed to the alien British."[9] His diplomatic objective was to discover whether Tibetan desire for independence (and insistence on its eastern border) had diminished following the death of the Great Thirteenth.

Huang presented a three-point proposal on behalf of the GMT government: Tibet would be recognized as part of China, the Chinese would take responsibility for Tibetan defense, and an *amban* would return to Lhasa and take up residence there as the representative of the Nationalist government.[10] The Tibetans did not have a strong enough military to fight off the Nationalist army, but they did not want their entire eastern border to fall to the Chinese. Hence they adopted a policy of a rapprochement with China. Subsequent to Huang's mission, China incorporated the Tibetan border region of Kham into the Chinese province of Sikang. Although the Nationalists could not exert their control over all of China proper, they inherited a stronger situation in the border regions. They were fully capable of annexing eastern Tibet.

The root of the problem for Tibet was its weak military, and Britain would not agree to aid Tibet in the event of a Chinese invasion. Because Tibet no longer had the British to serve as a protector, its only viable alternative was yielding to the pro-Chinese groups in Tibet by seeking a bilateral agreement with China.[11] In the absence of any British military support, some Tibetans believed that an alliance with the Chinese was necessary. Their motive was a tactic of last resort: Tibet wanted in on the postwar peace conference so that it might gain Britain's political support in its quest for independence. This was a colonial gambit in which an emerging small state sought leverage in the post-colonial world, but it was not to bear fruit. Tibet was caught up in the surging storms of nationalist determination in the twentieth century, but, to use a nautical metaphor, the ship of state lacked a strong enough engine to get up a head of steam.

❧

The events recounted here are the basis of the Tibetan Government in Exile's claim to the ethnic regions known in Tibetan as Kham and Amdo, which were incorporated as autonomous entities into several Chinese provinces. During this period, the Nationalists were waging a propaganda campaign to convince the international community that Tibet was a protectorate of China, a campaign to which the Tibetan government did not respond. Sir Basil Gould, the British political officer in Sikkim, feared that Chinese propaganda might lead to international support for a Chinese takeover of Tibet after World War II. He recommended a number of countermoves to the British government in Delhi: having the British government in India accept a Tibetan representative, sending the United States an envoy with a gift for President Roosevelt— anything to create political theater for Tibet's independent status. Gould's reasoning was that Tibet would be an important postwar buffer for the British government, and he wanted to rouse the Tibetans to action.

India had achieved its independence from the British and was now self-governing. This was an inspiration to nations wishing to emerge from their former colonial masters, and India's opinion—that Tibet be recognized as independent—bore some weight with Britain. India's request that the British receive a Tibetan representative reached London at the worst possible time. The proposal arrived at Whitehall just after the Foreign Office had rejected India's proposal to recognize Tibet. The Foreign Office voiced objections to Tibet's establishing diplomatic relations with the British Raj and the United States. The Foreign Office knew that the Chinese were attempting to undermine Tibetan independence, but they wanted Tibet to settle their differences with China. The underlying reason for this position was simple: Britain did not want to go to war with China over Tibet.

Gould arrived in Lhasa in August 1944. The political climate was one in which British friendship and reliability were being increasingly questioned. Gould met with the Kashag on September 7 and informed the *shapes* (high Tibetan officials) that Britain would agree to Tibet's negotiating directly with China so long as Britain was kept informed. Gould then asked the *shapes* point-blank whether the Tibetan government still claimed to be autonomous. When he received an unequivocally affirmative replay, he told them: "I have treated this [whether Tibet desired autonomy] in a serious manner because the British Government have lately been rather disturbed by what they call the supine attitude of the Tibetan Government towards China."[12]

✿

Sun Yatsen had supported the principle of self-determination for minority peoples, but his successor Chiang Kaishek repudiated the policy. This was a setback for Tibet. Tibet had consistently argued that China should return lands that are ethnically Tibetan and belonged to Tibet in the past (a position that did not change upon initiation of talks with the PRC). Sun Yatsen wished to have talks with Tibet regarding the disputed territories; Chiang Kaishek did not. Under Chiang, the Chinese republican government declared its intention to maintain imperial China's policies in regard to the border areas. Chiang Kaishek ignored the wishes of his mentor Sun and reverted to the Qing policy of referring to Tibet as part of the motherland.

When civil war eventually broke out in China, the Nationalists and the Communists competed for the prize of controlling China's destiny. In 1937, Japan invaded China and set up a puppet government in Manchuria. Nationalists and Communists abandoned the civil war and joined forces to expel the Japanese. Japan was defeated in 1945 and the war for control of China resumed. Eventually, the Communists defeated the GMT.

PART 6

Mid-Twentieth-Century China

The Communists Retain Imperial Policy in Tibet

Closing China's Back Door

Much has been written about Mao Zedong as a utopian thinker, a giant of twentieth-century history who despised bourgeois thinking and bourgeois forms of government, and who believed that socialism and communism were superior forms of government. Josef Stalin, the leader of the USSR during World War II, held the honor of being the only man who intimidated Mao, probably because Mao was the junior partner in the early years of their relationship. Stalin believed that, after the war, the Soviet Union would emerge as the unrivaled military power on the Eurasian continent. The USSR had helped the West achieve victory over the Axis powers. Stalin believed that the Soviet Union's position as the dominant power on the Asian continent was to be his reward for helping to defeat Nazism in Europe. The USSR emerged from World War II as a victor, while the PRC inherited massive problems.

Mao and Stalin were cold-blooded practitioners of geopolitics.[1] Both Stalin and Mao had the imperial taste, a predilection that drew more on national tradition and history than on communist ideology. Both indulged in the colonial strategy of creating buffer zones at the perimeters of their territories. Military-political interests and national security were the ultimate standards by which their policies evolved. In public, both men enunciated the ideological line of communism, using its familiar anti-imperialist rhetoric. In private—as shown by newly opened Cold War archives of the USSR and the PRC—both were realists.

One year after the Communist victory in 1949, Mao Zedong sent the People's Liberation Army (PLA) into Tibet. Mao officially pronounced that China had "freed" Tibet from a feudal and parasitic landowning class, namely the aristocracy and the monasteries. This was his stated objective, but his motive was strategic, not ideological.

The Chinese civil war, the Japanese invasion of 1937, and the Century of Humiliation at the hands of Western colonial powers created in Mao a determination to secure Chinese borders. The imperial idea of creating a buffer zone at the edge of empire appealed to Mao, and he had decided that the Chinese border should be the southern Himalayas. He intended to prevail strategically against threats, real and potential, from a long list of countries: Britain, the USSR, India, Pakistan, Afghanistan, and the Asian republics of the Soviet Union.

Mao considered that the legitimacy of the government of the PRC rested in part upon its ability to restore Chinese unity. He was wise enough to know that Tibet was a special case. It was the only border state with which Mao signed any type of formal agreement.

By 1944, Stalin had fomented a Uyghur and Kazakh nationalist uprising against Chinese authority in Xinjiang. The insurgents, with the help of Soviet advisers and weapons, consolidated control of northern Xinjiang and proclaimed a short-lived Republic of East Turkestan. In 1945, at the end of World War II, the Nationalists were in power in Nanjing. Stalin pressured the Uighur insurgents to compromise with the Guomindang government. Nationalist leader Chiang Kaishek negotiated for China. This was part of Stalin's scheme to improve the Soviet relationship with Nanjing. The short life of the Turkish republic in Xinjiang came to an end, but it is a hallowed memory for Turkish separatists in Xinjiang even to the present day.

Another factor influenced Mao's thinking: the possible escape of Muslims, Kazakhs, Tajiks, and other minorities across the border to Russian territory in the Central Asian republics. Mao was sensitive to Soviet meddling and interference on the long Soviet border with Xinjiang because he feared a Soviet invasion.

After the defeat of Japan and Japan's departure from the Chinese mainland, the Nationalists and the Communists resumed the civil war. In 1948, before the communist victory, Mao attempted to arrange a meeting with Stalin in Moscow, but the civil war and the imminent defeat of the Nationalists kept Mao in China. Stalin kept postponing the meeting. In a telegram to Mao in early 1949, Stalin wrote: "We do not think that Outer Mongolia would renounce its independence in favor of autonomy within the Chinese state, even if all Mongolian regions were joined into one autonomous unit. Clearly, the decisive voice here belongs to Outer Mongolia itself."[2]

In 1949, the communists won. Mao stood at a microphone at the Gate of Heavenly Peace, Tiananmen, and announced the founding of the People's Republic of China. In the old news photographs, he does not appear triumphant, but wears a frown, as though the enormity of the task before him has just begun to impress itself upon his consciousness. He wanted China and he had it, and judging from the photograph, the reality of the situation seems to have stunned him.

After a series of failed attempts at meeting Mao in Moscow, Stalin sent envoy Anastas Mikoyan to Xibaipo in China for secret meetings in 1949. Mongolia had declared its independence in 1911, but considered itself aligned with the Soviets, rather than as a province of China. Therefore, in discussing the future of Mongolia, Mao did not negotiate with Mongolia but dealt with Moscow. On this occasion, Mao asked for the USSR to accept Mongolia's return to China. Mikoyan replied that Mongolia had grown used to independence and was unlikely to reunify with China by its own choice. Mao assured Mikoyan that he did not follow the Great Han chauvinistic line.[3] Mao meant that he would not assert that a Han Chinese decision about Mongolia's future.

Mikoyan agreed with Mao that one should not give independence to the national minorities. In his report to Stalin, Mikoyan confided that Mao was "glad to hear this advice but you could tell by his face that he had no intention of giving independence to anybody whatsoever."[4]

> Religious reforms were marked by the curtailment of Buddhism, demolition of temples, and mass execution of lamas. Expropriationist state policies undermined the livestock economy. Prosecution of mostly imagined "enemies of the state" and "Japanese spies" silenced all opposition. Mongolia followed closely in Soviet footsteps and political initiative was severely constrained.... [Politicians] who dared to oppose Stalin and criticized, implicitly, Soviet policies, discovered the limits of Mongolia's independence: they were arrested and executed in Moscow. By the 1940s, political power was in the hands of Soviet supported Marshall Khorloogiin Choibalsan, Mongolia's "Stalin."[5]

Because he feared that Mongolia would become a province of China, the new ruler of the Mongolian People's Republic aligned his country with Russia. "Choilbalsaan reasoned that a closer relationship with the Soviet Union was a better option for Mongolia than being a Chinese province, since the Soviets supposedly did not pose a threat to the existence of the Mongolian nation. China, on the other hand, posed a very real threat in the eyes of the Mongolian leadership."[6] The new rulers of Mongolia hoped that they would eventually take control of Inner Mongolia, weaning it away from Chinese influence.

The comparison between the Bolshevik takeover of Mongolia and the Chinese "liberation" of Tibet is obvious. Communist ideology saw religion as the enemy of the people, and ethnic chauvinism against the target country played a significant role. In both cases, the geostrategic concerns of the big state trumped the human rights concerns of the smaller state.

The point here is that because Mongolia had support from an outside power, it was able to remain outside the Chinese state. Tibet had no support and succumbed to invasion. India was not strong enough to support Tibet, and Tibet lost British support after Indian independence. The United States had no real interest in the region, other than its Cold War aim of harassing China by supporting Tibetan guerrillas inside Tibet. Buddhism was the real loser here, because even though Mongolia retained its independence, the religion did not fare well under the communists.

Who Is Chinese?

When the PRC decided to incorporate the territory occupied by the Qing, China had to confront the problem of national minorities. The border states were now included in a multi-ethnic Chinese state. The peoples who inhabited China's periphery—Tibet, Inner Mongolia, Manchuria, and Xinjiang—were citizens of the PRC, governed by bureaucracies of the Party. The red background of the flag of the People's Republic represented "red" China. The former tribute states were represented by four small yellow stars forming a semicircle around the big yellow star of China. This was a new definition of China.

In the early years of the PRC, Soviet minority policy influenced the Chinese revolutionaries of the Long March generation, especially those educated in Moscow. Mao experimented with Lenin's model, a federal structure with minority republics. Lenin had envisioned autonomy for the minorities, up to and including independence. Yet the experience of the Long March led Mao to modify his thinking. As the Communist forces retreated into the southwest, Mao saw firsthand the intensity of anti-Chinese sentiment among the minorities, especially in the Tibetan areas of China's western provinces.

When Stalin succeeded Lenin, he reduced the rights of the nationalities in the Asian Soviet republics. Mao chose Stalin's model.

Chinese minority areas under the first constitution were not republics but "autonomous regions" or other autonomous entities, such as provinces.

Ideology and extreme social engineering characterized the policies and the relationship between the big socialist states and the small, independent but strategic states at their borders. When the People's Liberation Army moved into eastern Tibet, it justified this action by announcing to the world that it was enforcing a treaty between the Qing Dynasty and the Tibetan government. Previously, Tibet had skirmished with Chinese Nationalists in eastern Tibet and had arrived at various border settlements, none of them permanent. The Great Thirteenth and two Chinese missions had disagreed over the border, with the Dalai Lama demanding the return of ethnic Tibetan regions that had been incorporated into China, both centuries ago and more recently.[7]

Four types of governments had ruled China between the end of the dynastic system and the establishment of the People's Republic—imperial, military, republican, and communist—but Mao went back to Qing to legitimize his claim to Tibet. Mao, the anti-imperialist, sought legitimacy for his invasion in the language and statecraft of colonialism. He employed the old colonial formula that the Simla Conference produced: Chinese suzerainty and Tibetan autonomy.

The PLA began its military campaign in the Kham region of eastern Tibet, a region populated by the Khampa nomads who had been under nominal Chinese rule during the Qing and the Nationalist periods. The PLA troops had been on military operations in China's west, and Mao was still fighting remnants of Nationalist forces in the southwest. In October 1950, three divisions of the China's Eighteenth Army attacked at the Kham frontier. This frontier was protected by 3,500 regular solders and 2,000 Khampa militiamen. Some Tibetan units put up a sturdy defense but were decimated; others retreated.[8]

Once its battle-seasoned troops had been deployed, China offered the Lhasa government a "peaceful liberation." Mao wanted Tibet, but he did not want to incite the international community's disapproval. He wanted to come into Tibet by agreement rather than by aggression. He urged Tibetans to "return to the Chinese motherland." If necessary, force would be used to induce Tibet's compliance, but it would be better if Tibet agreed voluntarily. Mao wanted to make the arrangement official, to get it in writing.

The offer of a shotgun wedding threw the Tibetan government into disarray. Tibet had a weak army, just a few thousand troops, which was no match for the battle-tested People's Liberation Army. In command of the Tibetan troops was the governor of Cham, Jigme Ngabo. Regarded by some as a traitor to the Tibetan cause, Ngabo decided to surrender rather than fight. He may have wished to save the lives of his troops, and no doubt he realized the futility of fighting against the PLA. The Chinese insisted on taking a group back to Beijing for negotiations.

At the time of the Chinese invasion of Tibet, The Fourteenth Dalai Lama was still a teenager; in 1950 he was 16 and had not yet attained his rulership. Interregna such as this were always a time of uncertainty in Tibetan politics. With the ruler not yet in control of the country, the government was divided into factions: the regent Reting was in disgrace, the Panchen Lama was in exile, and members of the Kashag who were acting on the Dalai Lama's behalf were divided.

Tibet's acting government chose a group of officials to meet with the Chinese and instructed them on what points they were allowed to negotiate. In 1951, these representatives were brought to Beijing, isolated from their superiors, and asked to sign the so-called Seventeen Point Agreement. According to the Lhasa government, the representatives signed the agreement without authorization. There is some controversy about this. The PRC claims that the Dalai Lama sent a telegram authorizing the execution of the agreement.

On the basis of this agreement, Tibet became part of the People's Republic of China. Tibet would cease to conduct its own foreign affairs; China would station troops in Tibet and be responsible for its defense. This document put into concrete expression the relationship of Chinese sovereignty over Tibet. The Seventeen Point Agreement remains the legal basis of China's claim to sovereignty, despite the controversy over its legitimacy. Because of it, no country in the world recognizes the Tibetan Government in Exile as the legitimate government of Tibet. Thus Tibet became the only former tribute state with which Mao's government concluded any sort of agreement. Mao promised good relations with the populace and respect for the religion.

The Dalai Lama was shocked when he heard the content of the agreement in a radio broadcast. However, neither the Dalai Lama nor the Tibetan Government repudiated the Agreement until 1959, when the Dalai Lama went into exile in India. The delay proved to be fatal. The lack of repudiation was the major sticking point in Tibet's subsequent attempts to win support for its independence.

There was no local communist party for Mao to use as a political base when he entered Tibet, so he offered a deal. He suggested a "Go Slow" policy, the most ethnically sensitive relationship that communist ideology would allow. The traditional government would remain in power, the authority of the Dalai Lama would continue, and the religion of Tibet would be respected. The language and culture of Tibet would remain intact. In fact, terms of the Seventeen Point Agreement include the stipulation that Tibet was to have autonomy.

⚭

Tibet's status in international law was clouded by terms and treaties that were the legal remnants of the fluctuating relationships among colonial powers in South Asia. Because of Tibet's military weakness, Britain was the muscle behind Tibet's ability to retain its independent status. India's achieving its independence in August of 1947 changed the traditional balance of power in the region.

During the nineteenth and early twentieth centuries, the British considered Tibet to be important for securing their dominion during the Raj. As Britain advanced in the subcontinent, the Chinese lost influence. In 1934, the Guomindang attempted to restore Chinese influence in Tibet by sending a diplomatic mission. This marked the first appearance of a Chinese official since the *amban* was expelled at the fall of the Qing Dynasty in 1911. It was also the first time that

Tibet had direct dealings with China since the British-sponsored Simla Convention of 1913–1914.

The Chinese delegation was led by General Huang Musang, vice-chief of the general staff of the Nationalist army. Huang proposed that Tibet be considered as part of China, making the Chinese responsible for Tibet's defense and for stationing an *amban* there.[9] The Tibetan government granted the Huang mission the right to allow China to conduct its foreign affairs with the proviso that Tibet not be considered a province of China. But as with so much else in dispute between China and Tibet, this story has two versions.

The Chinese claim the mission was a success; the Tibetans claim that they rejected the mission and asked for the return of territories east of the Yangzi River. The Tibetans also claim that they stipulated India (still a British colony) was to act as mediator at any negotiation. This would mean, to Tibet's benefit, that an international character would attach to the negotiations. The Chinese were opposed, as they were anxious to keep Tibet an internal matter. The Guomindang set up an office in Lhasa and viewed this as validating the Chinese claim to Tibet. The British also set up an office in Lhasa, dispatching Sir Basil Gould in 1936.

The Tibetans claimed that they had never accepted Chinese sovereignty, but even the establishment of the British mission did not gain them formal *de jure* acceptance of their independent status. It looked like independence, but it was fuzzy in terms of international law; Tibet's legal status was thus betwixt and between. In the summer of 1949, the Kashag expelled all Guomindang representatives from Lhasa. Had the British official from the Indian government, Hugh Richardson, instigated this expulsion? The Chinese thought so, but Richardson never admitted to it.[10]

In the aftermath of World War II, Britain no longer saw itself as having a national interest in South Asia and so pulled out of the region. As far as the British were concerned, its responsibility for Tibet had devolved to India. Both India and China had always exerted influence on Tibet. Tibet was a strategic fulcrum between these two great powers.

In India, Prime Minister Jawaharlal Nehru was not willing to antagonize Mao in order to support Tibet. Nonetheless, within little more than a decade, India and China went to war over a border dispute. It would be the first of two border wars—disputes over territory have only begun to be resolved in the twenty-first century.

❧

The Korean War began to dominate the headlines, forcing events in South Asia into the background. In October of 1950, the North Koreans crossed the 38th parallel into South Korea. General Douglas MacArthur then crossed the 39th parallel into North Korea. The Chinese announced that they would enter the war on the side of North Korea if the United States crossed into the North. Tensions were running high in North Asia when China invaded Tibet on the seventh of October.

The Chinese invasion employed 40,000 PLA troops that intended to surprise and overwhelm the Tibetan troops from three directions. The Tibetans' only advantage was their knowledge of the terrain. News of the Chinese advance reached Jigme Ngawang Ngabo, governor of the Tibetan province of Chamdo. He requested instructions from Lhasa but was unable to reach the government. Chamdo was abandoned by Governor Ngabo and officials of the Lhasa government. The Chinese surrounded the Tibetan troops, who surrendered. The Communists did not march immediately on Lhasa; they waited while envoys carried messages back and forth prior to the Communist's official pronouncement of their Tibetan liberation.

Tibet sought international support, especially from the United Nations. The delegation from El Salvador requested that the General Assembly place the invasion of Tibet by a foreign power on the agenda, but none of the major powers supported this request. In the end, the UN decided to postpone any inclusion of the Tibet Question on its agenda.

The Tibetans were left to negotiate with the Chinese on their own. The delegation, led by Ngabo, arrived in Beijing on April 2, 1951. It would be up to the delegation, their Chinese hosts declared, whether Tibet would be liberated peacefully or by force of arms. The Chinese wanted to make certain that the delegation had been invested with authority to sign the document. The agreement was signed on the May 23, with Ngabo affirming that he was authorized to sign. The Chinese assumed that the agreement went into effect immediately. It is not clear why the Tibetan side did not wait for authorization from Lhasa, but they did not.

From its anti-communist perspective, America saw a Cold War interest in aggravating the Chinese in Tibet. Hence, for a short time the CIA granted covert support to Tibetan insurgents. They trained exiled Khampa in Nepal and in Mustang, Colorado, and then dropped them into Tibet. However, the United States did not want to drag Tibet into the middle of a Cold War confrontation on the Asian subcontinent. Although the United States offered to grant asylum to the Dalai Lama, it did not step up and take Tibet's case to the United Nations.

Tibet did not conceive of itself as requiring liberation, but it was an isolated and pre-modern country. The next two decades would prove to be devastating for Tibet's religion, culture, environment, and economy.

At Stalin's Knee: The Evolution of China's Minority Policy

In 1917, the Romanov czars fell from power and Bolsheviks became the new masters of Russia. The Bolsheviks held onto the Asian territories conquered by the czars.

Josef Stalin served as Commissar of Nationalities before he succeeded Vladimir Lenin as head of state. As such, he was the ideological father of Soviet nationalities theory and policy. Stalin believed that minorities suffered both from class oppression and from Great Russian chauvinism: the belief of the dominant ethnic Russians that the minorities were inferior. From the inception of communist rule, the minority nationalities of the Soviet Asian republics suffered from the effects of this chauvinism—the preference for Russian nationals and the Russian language in politics, education, housing, and jobs.

This is not to say that Stalin was a fan of such minority customs as self-flagellation in certain Tatar tribes or the Turkmen nomad's exaggerated devotion to their horses. Stalin thought the magnificent Akhal-Teke horses were a symbol of the Turkmen's backwardness and ordered that the horses be sent to sausage factories. Stalin gave the Turkmen tractors and settled them in apartment buildings in his attempt to modernize them. The nomads hated the apartments. Rather than destroy the horses, the Turkmen released their beloved Akhal-Teke horses into the desert, their original habitat, so that they might later recover them and reestablish the breed. (The Akhal-Tekes are among the ancestors of the modern thoroughbred and were highly prized by Chinese emperors, so much so that they were called the Horses of Heaven.) Stalin died, the Soviet Union passed into the history books, the Central Asian republics won their independence, and the Turkmen reestablished the breed. The old nomad customs proved to be more durable than the USSR.

In expounding his version of communist theory, Stalin followed his predecessors in viewing national characteristics that existed in bourgeois society as bourgeois and those that existed in proletarian society as proletarian. Neither type of national characteristic was defined as ethnic. In retrospect, this seems to have been a rather significant misunderstanding. Class identity was paramount and this was a feature of the theory of economic determinism.

In his writing, Stalin seems to have been of two minds. On the one hand he believed that, ideally, assimilating nationalities would confirm the theory that proletarian culture (class) would nurture national culture and that national culture would enrich proletarian culture. On the other hand, Stalin's experience during the revolution in Baku (the capital of Azerbaijan, a former Muslim khanate) led him to a different conclusion:

> What would be the result of national cultural autonomy?...To organize (the Tatars) into a national cultural union would be to...deliver them to the mercies of the reactionary mullahs, to create a new stronghold of spiritual enslavement of the Tatar masses to their worst enemy....The national problem can be solved only by drawing the backward nations and peoples into the common stream of a higher culture. It is the only progressive solution.[11]

Shortly after the Bolshevik Revolution, a provisional government came to power in Russia. Among its first actions were the abolition of czarist restrictions on the minorities. Because of the delay of important land reforms critical to the peasantry, a peasant revolt broke out in minority territories, with populations claiming for themselves land belonging to Russian colonists. The provisional government ruled against the minority peasants.

As a general rule, however, the right of minorities to secede was an article of faith among Leninists. In fact, the Bolsheviks actually recognized the secession of twelve minority states who declared their independence after propagandizing the peasantry to revolt against the Russian chauvinists. Yet, by 1921 the Red Army had regained control of the minority areas. Stalin had changed course and now proclaimed that demands for independence were counterrevolutionary. So much for minority self-determination.

After the USSR was formed, Soviet minority policy fell into three distinct periods. The first was a period of ethnic sensitivity. From 1922 to 1928, Stalin made an attempt to integrate minority areas into the socialist state. Non-Russians shared power with Russians. The goal of this was friendship. The Constitution of 1924 was ethnically sensitive: It granted autonomy to the minority areas, including the right to secede and to be educated in local languages. The Latin alphabet was used to Romanize these languages, replacing Arabic as the script of the Muslim minorities.

These efforts of the Soviet government reflected both humanitarian and economic motives. They brought civilization to the less fortunate minorities while taking their natural resources (e.g., Azerbaijani oil and Turkestani cotton). However, the industrialization and collectivization caused dislocations that created problems, and soon many local leaders believed that one dictatorship had been replaced with another with little real progress for the minorities. Stalin became disillusioned with his attempt to grant local autonomy and integrate minorities into the mainstream gradually.

The second period of Soviet minority policy, 1929–1953, was assimilationist and at times exterminationist. Minority differences were no longer tolerated and were fated to disappear. Minority peoples were forced to learn Russian, and Cyrillic alphabets were employed for writing even non-Russian languages. During this period, several nationalities—the Kalmuks, Chechens, Balkans, and Crimean Tatars—were purged entirely via deportation to Central Asia and Siberia.

Stalin died in 1953, which for a short time resulted in the liberalization of minority policy (except with regard to the Jews). From 1953 to 1958, the third period of Soviet minority policy, Khrushchev took the USSR on the road of revisionism. He theorized that even a taste of freedom would create the desire for more freedom, so he changed course by backing away from a policy of national autonomy.

In evaluating half a century of Soviet policy toward minorities, social scientist June Dreyer concludes that—even where the standard of living improved and where Russian became the national language—minority consciousness did not wither away. In fact, it increased. Many scholars predicted that frustrated nationalist aspirations would lead to secession unless the communist state decentralized.[12] The laboratory of history has demonstrated the accuracy of this prediction. Ethnic tensions resolved themselves when the Soviet republics in Central Asia gained their independence at the breakup of the Soviet Union. Holding on meant fracture.

❧

The problem of ethnic minorities has proved to be a conundrum for China. As was the case with the USSR, the policy of the PRC has seesawed between ethnic sensitivity and assimilation over time. "The socialist scriptures could be used to support either nationality diversity or proletarian conformity, nationality autonomy or strict central control."[13] Thus, assimilationist and accommodationist approaches are both ideologically orthodox. In the Chinese Communist Party's following of the Stalinist model in Tibet, there have been accommodationist periods followed by assimilationist periods. Neither has worked and neither has produced the results that China hoped for.

In the early 1920s, the Chinese Communist Party considered Tibet, Mongolia, and Xinjiang to be autonomous states in a Chinese federal republic. The CCP intended to build the new Chinese nation on the Soviet model. The Party manifesto declared that the autonomous states had the right of self-determination, including the right to secede. Even though the principles were enshrined in the Chinese Constitution of 1924, the various bureaucracies within the government interpreted the ideology to fit the prevailing political winds at the highest levels of power. The work of the various national minorities commissions was subject to fiat from the top, not only from Mao but also those officials favored by the powerful Central Committee of the Politburo.

Although some minorities were offered seats in the first National People's Congress (NPC), this was just for show. The main reason is that the NPC functioned as a rubber stamp and not as a true legislative body. In no sense was the NPC a co-equal branch of government. Power came from the man at the top of the party and from those around him who deliberated behind the plum-colored walls of Beijing's leadership compound, Zhongnanhai.

During the Long March of 1934–1935, Chinese Communists passed through the eastern Tibetan regions of southwest China. Mao witnessed the Tibetan animosity toward the Han and came to recognize that many of these nationalities strongly resented Chinese. Given the choice, most would prefer secession to being included in a Chinese federal republic.

The lesson was not lost upon Mao. After the Long March, Mao never again promised minority peoples the right to secede. He believed nationalities were the product of economic systems, so national differences would disappear once socialism had transformed a society. Class would triumph over ethnicity. Lenin was out; Stalin was in. If ideology described reality, Mao would not have had a problem in Tibet. The delivery of science and technology would have erased the concept of Tibetan-ness from the minds of every living Tibetan. This has not been the case. Prosperity and the improvement of a living standard does not change ethnic identity. It is more deeply rooted in the human being than class identity. Ideology often dies a hard death when confronted with actual conditions and the issue of ethnicity is a perfect example. The war in the Balkans during the 1990s proved the point: systems of government changed but ethnicity endured.

Material from declassified Soviet archives reveals a closer link between Stalin and Mao than was previously supposed. Stalin looked down on Mao, provoking a sense of outraged dignity in Mao. Stalin also proved to be a double-dealer. He meddled in Manchuria, and he engineered the secession of Outer Mongolia. This rankled Mao. During the 1930s, Stalin's expansionist ambitions led him to covet Xinjiang—a huge province rich in natural resources that China needed for the development of heavy industry. Mao had no intention of letting it secede or allowing Stalin to annex the province into the Soviet sphere of influence (as had happened with Outer Mongolia).

After the Communists defeated the Nationalists, China embarked on an ethnically sensitive policy in minority areas. This accommodationist policy included cultural development, the use of local languages, and exemption from Chinese marriage and tax laws. Minorities attained new social rights; discrimination was banned. China brought medicine and education to backward minority areas. Chinese cadres were punished if they violated the rules laid down for the treatment of minorities.

Nonetheless, a separatist movement grew up among the Uighurs. These mostly Muslim residents of Xinjiang had seceded and set up the independent East Turkestan Republic during the 1944–1949 period. Xinjiang minorities demanded that Han Chinese emigrate out of the newly formed minority regions and leave them as an exclusively national area; this was a reaction to Han chauvinism. The Party took the blame, and military government personnel were given strict rules to respect local customs and practices. Offenders were punished. Despite these policies, the Han Chinese continued their migration into Xinjiang, where today they are the majority population.

In the 1950s, Mao adopted the assimilationist approach: PRC policy was now to minimize minority differences and integrate minority areas into the Chinese economic and political structure. Separatism was seen as an imperialist plot by outsiders against the integrity of the motherland. The concept of "splittism" was born.

Mao included minorities in the Hundred Flowers campaign of 1956–1957, during which artists and intellectuals were encouraged to criticize the Party. No one could have been more surprised than Mao when the campaign brought more criticism than Mao would have wished. He didn't like it, and in 1953 he launched the Anti-Rightist campaign to denounce those who had spoken out against the Party. When Chinese cadres paid attention to popular litera-ture in minority languages, they discovered the shocking fact that the nationalities did not consider Chinese culture superior to their own—the minorities preferred their own cultures. This seems like simple common sense, except when one considers the traditional Chinese attitude about the superiority of its civilization.

When political winds at the center changed, the border regions had to bend or break. The theoretical struggle in minority areas turned Han Chinese against local nationalities. In the border regions, "bad elements" (separatists) were vocal in their criticism of Han chauvinism. For their politically incorrect stances, their unso-cialist points of view, many minority nationals were punished and imprisoned. The period of ethnic sensitivity had come to an end. The period of assimilation had begun.

᭪

The Great Leap Forward (1958–1961) was Mao's plan to rapidly industrialize China by using its massive manpower. At the same time as the rapid industrialization, the Great Leap also called for agriculture to be collectivized on a huge scale. The goal was to catch up to the West's level of industrial output. It was China's idea that it could match Great Britain's steel output by collecting scrap metal and creating steel in backyard steel furnaces.

None of these initiatives proceeded on a sound scientific basis. It was theory run amuck. The backyard steel furnaces were a dismal failure, as were the vast People's Communes. Droughts and floods resulted in crop failure. Production statistics for grain had been greatly overstated, and the result was food shortages and mass star-vation. This was a disaster of epic proportions from which China's economy took decades to recover.

During the Great Leap Forward, minority studies went out of vogue. The Party line was that the process of assimilating nationalities into the dominant culture would speed economic development. Multiple languages were a roadblock to the unity of the motherland, so learning Chinese became mandatory. Not surprisingly, minority peoples viewed the Party line as a Han chauvinist attempt to obliterate their ethnic identities. Throughout this period, Tibet was exempt from most of the reforms enacted in other minority areas.

As government policy, the Great Leap Forward was one of the most massive failures in history: an example of ideology trumping pragmatism resulting in the deaths of millions from famine. The period was disastrous for minority areas. Following this colossal failure, the accommodationist policy was reinstated. Peasants and herders were allowed plots of private land and private animals. In 1965, the central government installed the administrative apparatus of the Tibetan Autonomous Region (TAR). Tibet now had a communist government.

Bad as the Great Leap Forward may have been, it was nothing compared to the long nightmare of the Cultural Revolution that followed. The period from the late sixties to the seventies took as its goal the destruction of the Four Olds: old ideas, old culture, old customs, and old habits.

Mao sought to tighten his control on the party and the bureaucracy. He sensed that an elite was forming among the party members, something that might be considered the emergence of a privileged class and he did not like it. He himself was accused of fomenting a cult of personality, similar to that of Stalin's. When his policies were criticized in the brief Let A Hundred Flowers Bloom campaign, Mao knew that many in the bureaucracy wanted political and economic reforms. In brief, for the subject is too complex to treat fully here, Mao saw these bureaucrats as deviating from the revolutionary path. He reached down into the younger generation of students to correct what he saw as an error, the formation of a privileged class among the bureaucracy. The Red Guards were ideologically correct, the vanguard of the proletariat, the most radical leftist faction defending the revolution. They brandished their little red books containing the sayings of Chairman Mao and had his backing to stamp out any deviation from the Maoist line. The Red Guards were given free rein, and the country was treated to the spectacle of the young chastising those in power. The Red Guards asked that the special status of minorities end and advocated that minorities be treated exactly the same as Han.

Radical elements labeled Politburo member Liu Shaoqi a "splittist." He was attacked for his 1937 statement that supported self-determination for all China's minorities and because he had encouraged the Party to help minorities form autonomous governments. The leadership now called into question the Constitution of 1954 on the grounds of its stance on regional autonomy. The draft of a new constitution began circulating in 1968; this document proclaimed the unity of all nationalities and held that nationality struggle was class struggle.

The attack on the Four Olds was especially pernicious in minority areas—particularly in Tibet, because the campaign opposed the institution (and popularity) of Buddhism. For the Han cadres in Tibet, the Buddhist religion was seen as the remnant of a feudal culture. The cadres viewed the old system as a parasitic oppressor, a roadblock to modernity.[14]

Collectivization arrived in Tibet. China's new Constitution of 1970 did not proscribe the use of minority languages, but it was silent on the subject of minority customs.[15] In the final analysis, the Cultural Revolution did advance the CCP's own goals for minority nationalities. The economies of minority areas were further integrated into the Chinese economy, and minority rights were cut back.

❧

Founded on century-old thinking about ethnicity, minority theory and policy at the center of the Chinese state has swung between polar opposites. Neither sensitive accommodation nor hard-line assimilation has been able to resolve ethnic tensions peacefully—nor will it, because the definition of ethnicity in the ideology is in error. One could say that the PRC has employed the wrong tools for the job.

The West has been far from perfect in regard to minority relations, but the communist system has no workable solution—the history of the past sixty years is ample demonstration. The fault is in its
system and in the thinking that underlies that system.

From the time of its incorporation into the People's Republic,
Tibet was always treated as a special case. Because of its unique culture and history, Tibet proved to be the most resistant of all the
minority territories to the Chinese attempt to deliver the benefits of
socialism to the minorities.

In the beginning, Mao was in no hurry to force socialism upon
Tibet because Tibet was just emerging from feudalism and was not
yet ready for socialism: his plan was to win over the masses while
leaving the traditional Tibetan government in place. Mao intended
to secure the good will of the elites, the lay aristocracy and monk
officials who staffed the Tibetan government. He ordered a "Go
Slow" policy. Mao intended to rule Tibet by proxy, through Tibet's
traditional government but superimposing over it a (Chinese) communist structure.

The 1950s: Go Slow and Court the Elites

At the heart of the relationship between the PRC and Tibet lay a fundamental misunderstanding. Tibetans believed that the Seventeen
Point Agreement guaranteed them autonomy. The Tibetan government interpreted this as guaranteeing Tibet a special status within
the People's Republic, much like Hong Kong after the handover from
the British.[16] Critical to the Tibetan masses was the continued pri-
macy of the Dalai Lama's role in Tibetan affairs and religious life.[17]
To satisfy China's security concerns, it was critical that China be
responsible for Tibet's foreign relations and that the PLA would garrison the region. The Chinese saw Tibet as being ruled from Beijing,
not from Lhasa. Zhongnanhai, the Chinese leadership compound—
not the Potala—was to have the final word in Tibetan affairs.

One goal of the traditional Tibetan government was that the
Tibetan Autonomous Region, under the control of the Dalai Lama,
not be subjected to the same reforms as the rest of Tibet. Ethnic
Tibetan areas in the four Chinese provinces (Gansu, Yunnan,

Sichuan, and Qinghai) had already experienced the same reforms as China proper and the reforms brought unrest. These regions—called Kham and Amdo in Tibetan—were the starting point of the rebellion that culminated in the Tibetan Uprising of 1959 against the invasion, when rebels and refugees fleeing the Chinese in eastern Tibet arrived in the TAR and ignited the popular uprising. The Chinese characterized this revolt as one instigated by the ruling class in an effort to bring back feudalism. By contrast, Tibetan historian Tsering Shakya describes it as a national revolt.[18]

The Fourteenth Dalai Lama, Tenzin Gyatso, had read the last testament of the Great Thirteenth, and he and the Tibetan government were well aware of the destruction of Buddhism in Mongolia under the Soviets. Still, the Fourteenth had hope: he had studied Marxism and thought that it could benefit Tibet in terms of helping the masses, redistributing wealth, and encouraging the principle of self-reliance. In a 1999 interview with *Time* magazine, the Fourteenth Dalai Lama stated:

> Tibet at that time was very, very backward. The ruling class did not seem to care, and there was much inequality. Marxism talked about an equal and just distribution of wealth. I was very much in favor of this. Then there was the concept of self creation. Marxism talked about self-reliance, without depending on a creator or a God. That was very attractive. I had tried to do some things for my people, but I did not have enough time. I still think that if a genuine communist movement had come to Tibet, there would have been much benefit to the people. Instead, the Chinese communists brought Tibet a so-called "liberation." These people were not implementing true Marxist policy. If they had been, national boundaries would not be important to them. They would have worried about helping humanity. Instead, the Chinese communists carried out aggression and suppression in Tibet. Whenever there was opposition, it was simply crushed.[19]

A "honeymoon" period came after the signing of the Seventeen Point Agreement. Mao ordered a "Go Slow" policy. He intended to court the elites first, leave the traditional government of Tibet in place, and prepare the way for the socialist transformation of Tibet. The first Chinese to enter Lhasa were General Zhang Guohua and several thousand PLA soldiers flying red banners. Party cadres accompanied the Chinese army into the Tibetan capital. There was no local communist organization in Tibet. The general did not install a regional communist government, nor did he attempt to build a communist party. This was the meaning of the "Go Slow" policy. Meanwhile, in Beijing, a Tibet Work Committee that reported directly to Mao was assigned to carry out the planning for the socialist transformation of Tibet.

Some progressive Tibetans—and there were many who saw the need for modernization—thought that socialism might bring modern infrastructure to Tibet: hospitals, schools, modern communications, and (small) hydroelectric plants. As one of its first tasks, the PLA built two new roads connecting Tibet to China. This was a success. The Chinese paid the Tibetans for their work, which brought a cash economy, a first for Tibet. Still, the PLA was living off the populace and this caused a strain on the subsistence economy. Tibet was still subject to the ebb and flow of politics at the center. For example, when China's economy nosedived in response to the Great Leap Forward, salaries for Tibetan workers were cut.

Chairman Mao's instructions to the army and the cadres stationed in Lhasa were "to adopt policies that would win over the 'patriotic upper strata' of Tibetan society." This "go slow" approach was a novel one because it worked from the top down—in contrast to classical communist method of organizing, the transformation of the masses. Mao hoped that this tactic would isolate those members of the elite who harbored ideas of Tibetan independence. Shakya recounts an anecdote about Mao's response to criticism that his "Go Slow" reform in Tibet would proceed at the pace of a tortoise. Mao supposedly retorted that reform would advance at an even slower pace than a tortoise.[20]

The traditional Tibetan economy consisted of subsistence agriculture in the central provinces of U-tsang along with nomadism and animal husbandry on the eastern plateau (Kham and Amdo). The PLA camped outside the TAR capital of Lhasa; the arrival of thousands of outsiders caused tremendous disruption in Tibet's traditional economy. Mao had instructed the PLA to pay for their supplies, but food shortages led to rising prices. The Chinese were beginning to discover that Tibet's high plateau economy operated on a delicate balance. The Chinese had moved in unaware that their numbers might cause an unintended effect and the economy could not sustain the influx.

From the beginning there was a clash of cultures. The Chinese lack of familiarity with Tibetan customs caused tension and misunderstanding. The socialist revolutionaries saw Tibetans as feudal and backward. The Tibetan peasants had their own opinions of the Chinese invaders: they could not believe that the PLA were so foolish as to burn discarded yak horns for fuel, since the fires sent huge clouds of smoke into the atmosphere over Lhasa and left the air with a foul stench.[21]

In a show of good will, the Chinese permitted the religious festival of Monlam to take place. It was traditional for the Dalai Lama and the aristocracy to give alms at this time of the year. The Chinese participated in the alms-giving, part of Mao's policy of courtship of the aristocracy. The top Party officials also hosted banquets for the elite in Lhasa, occasions that included the screening of a film that showed the PLA successfully fighting the Guomindang and the Japanese. This propaganda underscored—for the benefit of any Tibetans who might have been contemplating armed resistance—the futility of opposing a modern army. It was the first time that Tibetans had seen modern warfare, and the screenings were wildly popular.

General Zhang deployed propaganda teams to the villages to prepare the peasantry for socialism. Meanwhile, the Chinese opened a medical clinic in Lhasa and offered free treatment to the citizens. Despite these friendly overtures, the PLA remained a burden on the populace.

Anti-Chinese complaints circulated in the Lhasa gossip mill. At this stage of occupation, the Chinese thought that that any large religious gathering had the potential to turn into a demonstration. The Chinese military disbanded the Tibetan Army, leaving its now unemployed soldiers to return to their home villages. This dislocation further fueled anti-Chinese sentiment. The masses were unhappy with the rising prices, and (according to the Indian representative in Lhasa) there were epidemics of smallpox and flu.[22]

These disruptions in the Tibetan way of life were severe enough to cause the villagers to present a petition at PLA headquarters. The petition informed General Zhang that the presence of the Chinese Army was creating unfavorable living conditions. The Tibetans knew the limits of the economy and demanded Chinese troop reductions to the level military retinues of the Qing *ambans*: a total of some 300 troops. Such reductions were not feasible from the Chinese perspective, since such a small garrison would not enable them to hold the country. General Zhang did not see the warning signs of popular unrest, but assigned blame. He considered the petitioning villagers a reactionary element. He put Lhasa under curfew and sent a letter to the Dalai Lama and the Kashag. Zhang's intent was clear: If the Kashag could not maintain law and order, the Chinese would.

Zhang demanded the names of the former Tibetan soldiers who had participated in the protest. The Kashag may not have known the names, but in any case it refused to supply them to the general. In order to maintain security, the PLA brought troops to Lhasa that had stationed at the borders. Zhang wanted sufficient men on hand in case of trouble in Tibet. This incident marked the inauguration of mistrust between the Kashag and the Chinese.

Soon another incident added to rising tensions: Armed Tibetans fired on the PLA guards of Jigme Ngawang Ngabo, a Tibetan member of the delegation that signed the Seventeen Point Agreement. He had since been appointed as a deputy commissioner. Whether the attack was aimed at Ngabo or his PLA guards remains a matter of conjecture, but the Chinese pressured the Kashag to control anti-Chinese sentiment. The Chinese believed that two popular Tibetan prime ministers were responsible for the protests and demanded their removal. The Kashag eventually dismissed the ministers, but this caused still further resentment. There was no mistaking the situation. The Chinese were in complete control. Realizing this, some aristocrats in the Tibetan government resigned their posts and departed for India.

Meanwhile, the Chinese attempted to repair the damage done to the Tibetan economy. They courted the prosperous trading families and bought surplus items at a good price. They created a board to solve the problem of food shortages. With an improvement in the economy, public anger against the Chinese diminished. This strategy further reduced the Tibetan government's power and increased popular acceptance of the Chinese. Land reform was next on the Chinese agenda. The Chinese began surveying the manorial estates of the Tibetan aristocracy and the monastic estates that supported the huge religious communities. The idea for land reform was to break up the estates and redistribute the land. Land redistribution was the most successful and popular of the Chinese reforms.

By 1954, the Chinese had met their initial objectives in Tibet, and in 1955 they invited the Dalai Lama to visit Beijing. The National People's Congress was in session, and its principal task was to adopt the 1954 Constitution. The Chinese believed that it was important for Tibet to be represented. The earlier constitution, based on the Soviet model, described China as a federal state with Tibet, Mongolia, and Xinjiang as republics. The document contained a provision that the republics had the right to secede. The 1954 Constitution ruled out this secession option.

The Tibetan delegation to the National People's Congress celebrated Tibetan New Year in Beijing that year. They were present when Mao announced the formation of a Preparatory Committee for the Autonomous Region of Tibet (PCART). Its purpose was to "spread reforms and integrate Tibet into the administration of Greater China."[23] In fact, the PCART was simply a temporary administrative structure meant to facilitate transition from rule by the Dalai Lama to rule by the Communist Party.

The early work in Tibet (from 1951 onward) was carried out by the Tibet Military Commission. By the late 1950s, the Chinese had created an infrastructure and so could administer Tibet without any help from the Tibetan government. Tibetans perceived the Chinese military as an antagonistic foreign element. For this reason, the PLA would be useless as agents of reform. The Chinese created a civilian commission in preparation for including Tibet in the administrative structure of greater China. This civilian commission was meant to garner popular support for the task of planning and implementing the new administrative structure of the Tibet Autonomous Region (TAR).

The Tibetan government in 1955 was divided into three parts: the Dalai Lama in Lhasa, the Panchen Lama in his traditional seat in Shigatse, and the People's Liberation Commission. In 1956, an

800-man delegation of Chinese arrived in Lhasa, the core of the new Chinese government. The Panchen Lama had been dealing directly with the Chinese throughout the 1950s, and the Chinese had been taking advantage of the rift between the number-one lama and the number-two lama, the Dalai Lama and the Panchen Lama, respectively.

One result of this initial reorganization of the Chinese presence in Tibet was the reduction of the Dalai Lama's power and prestige. The Kashag was unable to respond effectively to the downgrading of its traditional role. "The decline in the Dalai Lama's authority was more complex than a mere loss of political power in the Western sense; it was equated with the degeneration of Buddhist Tibet. The Chinese...were seen not only as political foes, but [also] as 'enemies of the faith.' "[24] This set the stage for the uprising.

The 1959 Uprising began in Eastern Tibet among the Khampa, but eventually it spread to central Tibet and from there to the rest of the country.

Eastern Tibet (Kham and Amdo) had known Chinese rule as far back as the Qing dynasty. In recent times, the eastern plateau had come under the authority of the Chinese Nationalists. This was not as direct nor as pervasive nor as constant as communist rule.

Of all previous Chinese rulers, only the Communists asserted direct rule over traditional Tibetan communities. Persuaded by assurances of noninterference with religious institutions, some lamas in eastern Tibet accepted the communists.

By 1954, the communists had completed their land surveys and study of land ownership, both of which were a prerequisite to land redistribution. Much was made of the breakup of the old estates and the deeding of land to peasants. Also preliminary to socialist reform, for the first time the communist began to divide the populace by class identity. These measures were a change from the traditional Tibetan view of society and were unpopular.

The next reform was the most unpopular of all, the policy of settling the nomads. The Khampa nomads of the eastern plateau have a well-deserved reputation as fierce warriors. They were a caste of mounted soldiers with a heritage of independence. It was part of their heritage that they went about armed. The Chinese realized how unpopular their reforms were with the Khampa and attempted to confiscate their arms. The Khampa refused to give up their weapons. Chinese reforms caused uprisings in Qinghai, Sichuan, and Yunnan and ignited the Khampa revolt that would last for would soon spread to the entire country.

One might ask, what were the Chinese thinking? The only answer is: old ideas, old ideology. These decisions took place before the age of multiculturalism, the idea that all cultures have an intrinsic value and looked backward to their roots in the old Soviet model.

Many Khampa refugees fled to India, and some of them became the core of the brief CIA-backed insurgency that was a feature of the Cold War. Thousands of refugees from eastern Tibet flooded into Lhasa. For the first time, Lhasans heard of monasteries being destroyed on the eastern plateau and of monks being killed by Chinese troops. Tibetans again complained to the Chinese about the destruction of the religion. Even those who believed in the communist reforms demanded that religious institutions be left alone.

❧

In 1956, the Dalai Lama visited India. His contacts with the British proved fruitless in terms of international support, and the Americans declined to support Tibet's case for independence at the United Nations. The United States offered covert support (financial support to insurgents, training, and weapons) for armed resistance inside Tibet. At independence, India had inherited responsibility for Tibet from the British. India, too, refused to support the Tibetan case for independence at the United Nations. India's first Prime Minister, Jawaharlal Nehru, gave domestic politics top priority, not foreign relations. At the time of the Dalai Lama's first visit, Nehru he did not want to antagonize the Chinese.

Nehru counseled the young Tenzin Gyatso that the status and prestige of the Dalai Lama would be diminished if he remained in exile in India. Nehru urged him to return to China and work out his differences with Mao. Chinese Foreign Minister Zhou Enlai paid a state visit to India at this time and met with the Dalai Lama in the Chinese Embassy in New Delhi. Zhou conveyed Mao's promise that reform in Tibet would be postponed for five years. In March of 1957, the Dalai Lama returned to Lhasa. The Chinese removed some of their cadres from the PCART and increased the number of Tibetan members. They also simplified the committee's structure and eliminated some of its departments.

This was a crucial time because the Chinese economy was faltering. The government was strapped for cash and had to cut back expenditures in Tibet. They also took responsibility for the failure of reforms and cited Han chauvinism, the lack of sensitivity to minorities, and the absence of minority participation in reforms as the principal reason for their failure. At this time the Chinese were in a phase of ethnic sensitivity and admitted that they had failed to win over the populace.

In late 1958, the Chinese insisted that the Kashag suppress the Khampa revolt. The request must have seemed ironic: General Zhang—having weakened the Kashag—now demanded that it suppress a rebellion. The Chinese were unwilling to provide the Tibetan government with arms, which meant that Tibet was powerless to suppress the rebellion. 1958 ended in stalemate: neither side wanted to be scapegoated for suppressing the rebellion. Ultimately, the PLA put down the rebellion in Kham.

In 1959, the unrest spilled over into Lhasa and subsequently spread across the country. In the midst of this turmoil, an incident occurred that triggered the flight of the Dalai Lama into exile. The Chinese organized a dance performance in honor of the Dalai Lama to be held at the Chinese military camp, a location the Dalai Lama himself had chosen. Normally theatrical events were held at the Norbulingka Palace, but the theater at Norbulingka Palace was not big enough to hold the invited guests. Those close to the Dalai Lama feared his going to a military camp, in case he might be abducted and taken to China. His retainers tried to convince him not to attend. The Dalai Lama—along with an entourage consisting of family members and a few government officials—attended the show. The Chinese had no reason to think that anything was amiss. [25] The next morning, however, a crowd assembled at the Norbulingka. The peaceful demonstration turned into an angry protest.

Some aristocratic officials supported the protest, seeing it as a last chance for Tibet to evict the Chinese. The Dalai Lama knew that such a course was futile. The Chinese saw the Kashag as faithless, breaking previous agreements. The Chinese deduced that they had no firm and reliable partner in the elites. Communication between the sides broke down.

Up until this time, the Chinese had been working with the Tibetan elite. The elites—aristocratic and monastic—determined which reforms were acceptable to Tibet and which were not. The protest was a turning point: Either the Chinese would have to concede ruling power to the Tibetan government, or the Tibetan government would have to admit that the Chinese had full authority in Tibet.

The Dalai Lama stood between the two factions. He had made personal agreements with Mao and had a personal understanding with him; he was also leader of the Buddhist faith, loyal to Tibet and the Kashag. There was no winning position for him.

The protest worsened and turned into a popular uprising as masses joined in. The Kashag distributed arms to the populace. The Chinese leaders called in the PLA to suppress the revolt, but the resistance of armed citizenry was no match for China's seasoned troops. Loudspeakers in the public areas announced after a time that the PLA had taken command of both the Potala and the Norbulingka. With their status far from certain, many of the aristocracy went into exile. The Dalai Lama left Lhasa and made the dangerous trip to India into exile. The uprising was suppressed. Mao was upset with this turn of events. He still viewed the Dalai Lama as key to winning over the Tibetan populace. When the Dalai Lama left Tibet, Mao pressured the Indian government not to grant him asylum. Mao wanted the Dalai Lama in Tibet.

The 1950s was a period of gradualist reform, a minuet performed by a group of aristocrats taking place within the crystal palace of the old Tibetan system. It was a beautiful illusion, created by Mao as a transition to a socialist Tibet. Mao intended to destroy the old system, and after the uprising, he ended the period of "go slow and court the elites." The crystal palace, the illusion that the old system could function under the communists, was shattered. The minuet of government by aristocrats was over. The suppression of the uprising created the first extensive Tibetan diaspora.

Foreign Minister Zhou Enlai announced that China no longer felt bound by the provisions of the Seventeen Point Agreement. As a treaty between the PRC and Tibet, the agreement was thus rendered null and void. Zhou also announced that as far as China was concerned, the Uprising of 1959 sounded the death knell for Tibet's traditional government. The period of Chinese accommodation to the Tibetan minority had come to an end. As a consequence of the uprising, Tibetans witnessed the demise of the lamaist state.[26] Beijing dissolved the traditional Tibetan government and replaced it with a Chinese provincial government in which Chinese cadres took the highest positions.

The socialist transformation of Tibet began in earnest. Socialism would come from the bottom up, with reforms and education imposed by a Chinese vanguard. Revolutionary work among the masses began. In the Dalai Lama's absence, the Panchen Lama functioned as the head of the Tibetan government. He also worked on the committee for the inauguration of the Communist government of the Tibet Autonomous Region. Soon he would find himself demoted from favor and considered an obstruction by Beijing. He would be replaced by a secular Tibetan, ultimately.

Mao believed that religion was the product of an antiquated class system and would fade away when the revolution established the dictatorship of the proletariat. He had addressed the issue in his writings on revolution. The problem was that no proletarian class existed in the old Tibet, a nation of peasants and herders. Mao sought to replace Buddhism with communism. Mao believed that an improved standard of living—the elimination of poverty—would end the reliance of the masses on religion. In short, Mao had concluded that, in the new Tibet, class identity would trump ethnicity and religion. Chinese lenience, a concession to Tibet's special status in the PRC, had ended.

The Cultural Revolution: Fast Track to Socialism

The Chinese communists failed to grasp an essential fact about Tibet: It was not merely a state but a civilization. Its boundaries were not physical but metaphysical, encompassing the entire Tibetan-speaking world: that of U-tsang, central Tibet, and Kham and Amdo.

It is odd that the Chinese were so myopic, but ideology—the instrument of their mission to modernize China—blinded them. Tibet was, in the most basic way, a 1,000 year-old civilization with Buddhism at the heart of its culture.

The reality did not jive with ideology. In the Maoist perspective, religion was an outgrowth of the economic system. If feudalism was destroyed then Buddhism would eventually disappear—or so the theory went. History trumps ideology, even in China today, where there is a resurgence of religion, even after sixty years of communist rule.

Everywhere that Buddhism has traveled it has come wrapped in art and culture. The Chinese Communists could have recognized this from a close examination of Chinese history. Buddhism came to China from India, but blended with indigenous artistic traditions and left a magnificent legacy, the Buddhist-inspired art of the Tang and Southern Song dynasties. To label the performance of a religious ritual as an instance of separatism or "splittism" was as nonsensical as claiming that the performance of the tea ceremony in Japan was an act of treason against the Japanese state. The error stemmed from communist theory.

᪥

Mao Zedong had a bad year in 1959. His attempt to rapidly industrialize China—the Great Leap Forward—had been a complete failure. Even the Chinese leadership attacked him for the disaster he had visited upon China. The political culture swung to the left in a demand for revolutionary purity. The policy of persuasion in Tibet was repudiated and gave way to a new policy: assimilation via rapid integration into the Chinese state. Tibet was the tail and the dog was in Beijing, wagging ferociously.

Stalin died in 1953 and Nikita Khrushchev assumed the leadership of the USSR. Khrushchev shocked the world with his denunciation of Stalin and his cult of personality and his attempts to reform the Soviet economy. Mao was particularly sensitive to the issue of cult of personality, since he had inspired a cult of his own personality in China (see cartoon referred to in Online Resources, page 218). Mao branded Khrushchev a revisionist and a "capitalist roader." It was the beginning of the Sino-Soviet split. Some brotherly solidarity still existed between the USSR and the PRC. When the matter of the Tibetan Uprising came up before the United Nations Security Council, the representative of the USSR defended China. Representatives of communist countries in Eastern Europe were not on board. They criticized China for its failure to establish correct minority policy.

The Chinese leadership in Beijing interpreted the Tibetan Uprising as a civil disturbance that could have been predicted and prevented rather than as a revolt. Afterwards, the leadership neither blamed nor purged the Chinese cadres in Tibet.

Responsibility for Tibet had been divided into the Northwest and the Southwest Military Regions. The Panchen Lama had close ties with Fan Ming, ruler of the Northwest Military Region, and therefore no disturbances occurred at the traditional seat of the Panchen Lama's Tashilumpo monastery. Once the Tibetan Uprising had been suppressed, the Panchen Lama sent a telegraph to the Chinese leadership in Beijing congratulating them on putting down the revolt and reassuring them of his loyalty to the CCP.

In order to preserve the illusion of autonomy as provided by the Seventeen Point Agreement, the Dalai Lama previously had been appointed chairman of the Provisional Committee for the Tibet Autonomous Region (PCART). This made him the central figure in the new Tibetan politics. The PCART included eight hundred Chinese and was organized into fourteen departments with responsibility for converting the administration of Tibet into a Chinese regional structure.

Mao regretted the Dalai Lama's departure to India. He understood the Dalai Lama's stature and authority, and he believed that he needed the Dalai Lama for the CCP to successfully administer Tibet. With the Dalai Lama in exile, there was no central government in Tibet. The Chinese were operating in a vacuum. Their only choice was to replace the Dalai Lama with someone who might inspire the support of ordinary Tibetans. The Chinese appointed the appointed the Panchen Lama to be acting chairman of the PCART. He became the Tibetan face of the Chinese government in Tibet.

Many of the Tibetan aristocracy had fled into exile; those who remained behind were given positions on the committee. After the flight of the Dalai Lama, the first task of the PCART was to condemn the disturbance and to secure a pledge of Party loyalty from its members.

The Chinese intended to form a mass political culture. Traditionally, the lower strata of Tibetan society believed that politics was the business of the aristocracy. In order to reeducate the masses, the Party's theoretical journal published an article claiming that if the Tibetan aristocracy were allowed to continue in power, then the reactionary remnants of the old system would attempt to reestablish feudalism. This is how the CCP justified the initiation of its new policy, the political transformation of the masses. As with everything concerning Tibet, the word issued forth from the top of the Chinese leadership.

During the 1950s, Mao's policy in Tibet was aimed at eradicating poverty. That era had come to an end; the Dalai Lama was gone. It was no longer necessary to win over the elites, and there were no more obstacles to socialist transformation. The Chinese administrative structure had replaced the traditional Tibetan government. Chinese cadres had been surveying and categorizing the class background of the population. Each person was assigned a class identity. This labeling of each individual as an aristocrat or a member of the masses led to the arrest and imprisonment of many of those who had taken part in the uprising. The PLA established control over the areas of resistance still remaining in the country; the Chinese divided the Tibetan leadership who remained in Lhasa, preventing them from presenting a united front against the Chinese.

Beginning in 1966, Tibet was embroiled in the politics of the Cultural Revolution. The movement began in Beijing but came to Tibet. Its economic goal was the destruction of the class structure of feudalism; its political goal was the indoctrination and control of the masses. In Tibet, the era of mass rallies and "struggle sessions" began. In theory, the Cultural Revolution was supposed to eliminate "nationality" and its loyalties. The Red Guards initiated a frontal assault on Tibetan culture and religion. "The... Tibetan masses were the victims of a struggle waged in Beijing."[27] The Red Guards organized mass mobilization campaigns: meetings and rallies organized to condemn the 1959 Uprising. Those who failed to condemn the revolt were branded as reactionaries and categorized as coming from a bad class background. This damning label was critical because Chinese cadres were now focused on class struggle: Those with bad class backgrounds were subjected to struggle sessions intended to revolutionize their thinking and their relationship to society.

The first of the Chinese land reforms in Tibet broke up the estates belonging to the aristocrats and distributed land to the bottom tier of society. Thus the peasants benefited and realized a measure of prosperity after the completion of reform. Tibetan society traditionally respected trade, and many former serfs soon began engaging in capitalism. Revisionism reared its ugly head in Tibet in the form of capitalist roaders.

The second set of land reforms established communes. In many cases, serfs who had been given land were now forced to give it up. This resulted in a novel phenomenon: Newly prosperous former serfs who were supposed to be the main beneficiaries of socialism, now wanted to delay socialist reform. The commune system was an effective means of social control. In fact, "The highly organized life in a commune allowed the Chinese to reshape every aspect of the Tibetan way of life."[28]

At first, the Chinese did not attempt to break up the monastic estates. They did, however, limit the celebration of religious festivals for fear that massive gatherings of Tibetans from all over the country would lead to anti-Chinese demonstrations. Eventually the time came for the reform of monastic estates.

Mass monasticism was a unique feature of Tibetan Buddhism—about 10 percent of the adult male population became monks. The revenues from the land supported the monastic population, and the agricultural products contributed to the traditional economy. The reform policy interrupted this flow of revenues, leaving the monasteries unable to support their resident monk population. The Chinese were ambivalent about disbanding the monasteries, since thousands of monks would then join the ranks of the unemployed.

Party leaders invited the Panchen Lama to criticize the progress of reforms inside Tibet. At this time, the Panchen Lama spent half his year in Beijing, where it was his task to attend committee meetings as well as meetings of the National People's Congress. Believing that the Chinese leadership wanted a sincere analysis, the Lama delivered a 70,000-character critique. He criticized the punishment of many innocent people after the revolt. The Panchen Lama also claimed that local Chinese cadres were falsifying reports about conditions in Tibet to officials in the central government. His most damning claim was that Chinese reform was destroying Tibetan identity and the Buddhist faith. Zhou Enlai ordered corrections to local policies in Tibet, and this eased tensions for a time.

The Chinese victory in the Sino-Indian border war boosted the leadership's confidence. Mao was once again in firm control of the Party leadership. Policies in Beijing took a hard turn toward the left. From his ideological standpoint of permanent revolution, Mao criticized the USSR as revisionist and has having abandoned the true socialist road. He also castigated the emerging market economy among the peasants in China's vast rural areas.

The Chinese leadership's previous indulgence of the Panchen Lama's document turned to vivid denunciation of its author as a "capitalist roader."[29] For defending the monastic estates, he was accused of wanting to bring back feudalism. The Panchen Lama was purged from the Party and removed from office. He was neither an acceptable substitute for the Dalai Lama and a focus of inspiration for Tibetans, nor a suitable figurehead for indirect Chinese rule in Tibetan society.

The communization of agricultural in nomadic areas continued, although the process did not lead to any good results. Official Chinese propaganda touted the line that the masses were happy, but this was far from the truth. Agricultural production dropped and normal patterns of trade were severely disrupted. Foolish mistakes were made. Wheat was planted instead of barley, the traditional staple of the Tibetan diet. The Chinese failed to plan for enough grain storage to last through the Tibetan winter, resulting in critical grain shortages. The disruption to the fragile Tibetan ecosystem, and the loss of animals due to settling of the nomads, resulted in shortages of butter. The pasturelands at the Roof of the World could not support agriculture. Tibet now required subsidies from Beijing.

The Cultural Revolution's class struggle and assault upon tradition obscured the reality of the Tibetan situation. For the Chinese, the main threat to communist rule in Tibet was separatism. For the Tibetans, the main threat to their way of life was an attack on religion. The Chinese interpreted any expression of Tibetan ethnicity—especially any observance of Buddhism—as a sign of separatism.

In 1966, local Red Guards in Lhasa undertook the task of destroying the Four Olds in Tibet. What followed was nothing less than the deliberate destruction of Tibet's cultural heritage. By the count of the International Campaign for Tibet, some 6,000 monasteries were destroyed. "In every village, the people were...[compelled] to destroy religious and cultural artifacts."

The films *The Last Emperor* and *The Blue Kite* contain dramatic portrayals of a common practice of the Red Guards during the Cultural Revolution: the denunciation and humiliation of those identified and branded as class enemies. In *The Last Emperor,* the deposed Son of Heaven Pu Yi undergoes criticism designed to eradicate class consciousness from his mind. In *The Blue Kite,* the person subjected to criticism has a paper dunce cap on his head and is forced to sit on a stool surrounded by tormentors. He is insulted, sometimes spat upon, sometimes beaten. The same thing (and far worse) happened to lamas, monks, and nuns in Tibet. Red Guards destroyed monasteries and hacked religious sculpture to bits. They destroyed religious objects and in some cases shipped the more valuable ones—those made of gold and silver or other precious metals and gems—back to Beijing.

Buddhism was at the center of Tibetan culture. When the Chinese attacked Buddhism, they attacked Tibetan identity. The Red Guards saw their assault on Tibetan culture was the last step on the way to assimilation with China. Tibetan dress vanished, replaced by the blue Mao suit or a PLA uniform. Tibet had metamorphosed into a suburb of Beijing.[30] The dictatorship of the Red Guards triumphed over the concept of regional autonomy.

❧

After ten long years, the Cultural Revolution came to an end in 1976.

During the political purges in China in the 1980s, those who participated in the Cultural Revolution were removed from the CCP. Many Tibetan cadres had participated in the Cultural Revolution, but they were not removed from the party. By this time in Tibet, many of the Tibetan cadres held senior posts in the regional Communist Party. They remained in office.

Unlike the Chinese who were purged, Tibetan cadres were promoted. Hu Yaobang believed that they could be reformed. These were men loyal to the center, and the Chinese could not do without them.[31] Was this, as Shakya contends, a classic tactic of colonialism, getting the indigenous collaborators on the side of the master? Or was it a pragmatic recognition of necessity, a form of power politics, with the end justifying the means?

The winds of modernity had been blowing through the Himalayas for almost a century, but until the arrival of the Chinese, Tibet seemed immune to change. One factor, the accident of geography, changed the country's destiny: Tibet was strategically located between China and India. It was, in a sense, the fulcrum of Asia. In the postcolonial period following World War II, Tibet became caught up in the politics of the Cold War.

Mao, Zhou, and Tibetan Buddhism: The Propaganda War in Tibet

From the Chinese invasion in 1950 until the Tibetan Uprising in 1959, Buddhism and Marxism co-existed in Tibet, although in a decidedly uncomfortable manner. After the Uprising of 1959, Mao Zedong and Zhou Enlai decided upon the rapid integration of Tibet into the Chinese economy. In communist states, propaganda is used to gain support for new policy.

The Propaganda Department of the CCP's Central Committee was a bureau, not formally part of the PRC's government apparatus. It was the highest office enforcing media censorship in China, and it was in charge of propaganda. The Propaganda Department initiated a campaign that portrayed Tibetan Buddhism as an evil brew of superstition and black magic. In official Chinese publications, Tibet was described as a backward, primitive place, a land of darkness and otherness. There is some debate in China as to whether this was Mao's formulation or Zhou's interpretation of Mao, but in any case Tibet was described in a classical four-phrase Chinese formulation: "Tibet was the most backward, the most reactionary, the most barbarian, and the most dark."

The propaganda took various forms. In 1963, millions of Chinese saw a socialist realist film entitled *Jampa,* about a Tibetan serf who resided on the estate of a noble family. The film was intended as a story about class oppression of the poor by the rich landowning class. It showed this class dealing out brutal punishments, signifying that all of Tibet was victimized. In the story, the peasant Jampa—in response to repression by the serf-owning class—refuses to talk and became mute. His liberation comes when he joins the Red Guards. The film perpetuates negative stereotypes of Tibetans as dark and violent, primitive and savage, superstitious and uncultured. During this period, when Chinese parents wished to frighten their children, they told them to be quiet or else they would call Jampa, the Tibetan bogeymen.[32]

The idea of Buddhism as a dark alien force is nothing new in Chinese history. Confucianism was the state ideology, a this-worldly system of ethics and philosophy focused on practical matters of behavior, governance and rule. Dynastic histories in Chinese were written by Confucian intellectuals who prepared for civil service by taking exams based on the Confucian classics. In the Tang and Song dynasties, there was a vogue for Buddhism among the elite, the imperial clans and the literati who ran the government. Most Chinese intellectuals were not Buddhists, however, and through most periods in Chinese history there has been a negative bias against Buddhism in official Confucian sources as well as in private literati sources.

As state ideologies, Confucianism and Marxism have some common characteristics: a focus on this world and on materialism, a concept of benevolent rule, and a concept of improving the lot of the masses. They also share a preference for trusting an enlightened elite—a vanguard of the educated—to rule for the benefit of the masses.

The Chinese leadership was ignorant of Tibetan Buddhism and misinterpreted Tibetan Buddhist symbols and rituals. In a scholarly deconstruction of the meaning of Tibetan religious rituals, Jeffrey Hopkins (Professor Emeritus of Tibetan and Buddhist Studies at the University of Virginia) explains that the Chinese, in their analysis of the Tibetan religion and its effect upon the populace, misrepresented the sophisticated iconography of Tibetan Buddhism mostly through ignorance. For instance, the Chinese Communists were revolted by the skull cups used in tantric rituals. They cited the skull cups as an example of barbarism, claiming that Tibetans drank human blood from the skull.

In reality, the top half of the skull—removed after death—is used in ceremonies as a symbol of impermanence and a reminder of the impermanence of life. Its ceremonial function is to exhort devotees to the practice of meditation. The Tibetan Buddhist tradition is perhaps unique in its focus upon preparedness for death and in its view of death, so the skull serves both a symbolic and a pedagogic purpose. While many ritual objects are used in initiations and ceremonies, the emphasis in Tibetan Buddhism is on the *inner* realization of compassion and wisdom culminating in the attainment of enlightenment.

The iconography of Tibetan religious paintings (tanghkas) includes the portraits of wrathful deities. According to Tibetan Buddhism, these wrathful deities have an inner nature of compassion and are meant for the practitioner who wants to make use of the force behind such levels of consciousness. A practicing Buddhist would have to cultivate compassion and wisdom for a long time before undertaking this type of meditation. The Tibetan tradition deals with subtleties of Buddhist psychology, and in this sense the representations of wrathful deities are meant to illustrate psychological truth.[33]

Another example of Chinese misinterpretation involves the depiction of Buddhas and their female consorts in sexual congress. Although depicted using human forms, these are not pornographic images, but are meant to symbolize the union of wisdom and compassion. Admittedly, the image is easily misunderstood by those unfamiliar with Buddhist concepts, but over the centuries, some of those for whom these were instructional materials were not literate, and this is a very direct way of communicating a spiritual truth. Tibetans are not puritanical and do not attach a sense of sin to such images.

The misunderstanding and mischaracterization of Buddhism found its way into the propaganda used to justify Chinese intervention and rule. Propaganda was essential to the Chinese claim to Tibet and is part of a pattern of exaggerated territorial claims on China's part, a formulaic part of its statecraft. In *The White House Years,* former Secretary of State Henry Kissinger took note of this Chinese propensity in the context of the Sino-Soviet dispute. In regard to a report of a trade agreement between Moscow and Peking, Kissinger quipped:

> I did not believe that Sino-Soviet differences lent themselves to simple reconciliation. No commercial gesture could alter the fact that forty Soviet divisions were poised along a 4,000-mile border not recognized by China. Nor could commercial transactions still the uneasiness with which Soviet leaders were bound to view the 800 million irredentists to their south, eyeing covetously the vast and rich empty spaces of Siberia, so unattractive to Russians.[34]

The Soviets ignored all such territorial exaggerations, viewing as mere rhetoric the Chinese public posture of irredentist claims. Nonetheless, Brezhnev positioned troops on the Chinese border as "the gun upon the table."

The intended role of propaganda in a communist state is to sell state policy to the masses. But even in China, people pay only lip service to communism and its rhetoric. The real glue of the state is nationalism, a kind of gut-level patriotism meant to rectify the humiliations of the past.

The central government launched an anti-Confucian and anti-Lin Biao campaign in the early 1970s, when the radicals of the Cultural Revolution were in control. The campaign was exported from China and adapted to conditions in Tibet, where it took the form of anti-Dalai propaganda. The Dalai Lama was branded a "jackal" and a "wolf in monk's clothing." The propaganda campaign also had a social engineering component: Tibetan customs were branded a hindrance to modernization. Although the Panchen Lama had gone along with the Chinese, he wrote an extensive critique of Chinese rule. For this he was branded a Confucian.[35]

The Tibetan people submitted to meetings and struggle sessions and to more propagandizing about the evil of their own culture. After the later uprisings in 1987 and 2008, Chinese hard-liners returned to the old phraseology of the Cultural Revolution and promulgated another round of anti-Dalai propaganda.

❦

The advent of modern technology—the internet, cell phones and text messaging—represents something new for China: a nonmediated, people-to-people exchange. The government filters and censors Western companies, in particular social networking sites such as Facebook. According to the Open Net Initiative, a collaborative partnership of leading academic institutions (Harvard, Oxford, the University of Toronto, and Cambridge University), the government filters works by blocking specific websites and addresses as though they never existed.[36] It is plain from the evidence of their various cyber-penetrations of foreign governments and industries that the Chinese government has made cyber-warfare a priority.

Does propaganda work? In the age of information, the government is not the lone voice preaching to the masses. Tibetans inside Tibet have access to radio stations—including the Tibetan-language broadcast of Voice of America and the BBC world news—as well as to other alternative voices avail no longer monopolize media, which has become democratized. Tibetan musicians perform in America at such august organizations at the Asia Society and have even become pop stars inside China.

China is not immune to these trends. Technology brings change. The Chinese people are sophisticated enough to know they are being propagandized, since they have been exposed to communist rhetoric since the founding of the PRC. The official pronouncements amount to so much background noise, and the young know how to get around the Party's firewalls. The Chinese government has been liberalizing state media at the local level and allowing for more reportage that need not pass state censorship. This has afforded some of the Chinese populace an alternative to the official view put out by the state-owned media.

Western technology companies—Google, IBM, and Microsoft, to name the largest—have complied with Chinese censorship requirements by blocking sensitive subjects (e.g., Taiwan, democracy, Tibet, Tiananmen, pornography) in order to do business in China. This compliance with censorship requirements has met with some criticism at U.S. Congressional hearings. In early 2010, Google announced that it would no longer employ the government-mandated filters on its Chinese search engine. This decision was based, in part, on evidence that Chinese government hackers were breaking into the Gmail accounts of Chinese dissidents.

The free flow of information and the free use of modern technology presents a problem for the Chinese government, a problem that it well recognizes. As stated by the intellectual property lawyer Jerome Cohen: "A modern economy depends upon the free flow of information. How can the state block information for political purposes while freeing it for economic purposes?"[37] One or the other has to give.

Are the Tibetans fooled by the propaganda? The Tibetan people have retained their earthy sense of humor despite their experiences of the last sixty years. Their street songs, as reported by anthropologists and journalists, contain jokes about the communists. The Tibetans know when they have been handed a line.

Tsering Shakya summarizes the situation as follows:

> In Tibet, everything from newspapers and magazines to music distribution is kept firmly under control, whereas all over China, there are increasing numbers of independent publishing houses. The joke in Tibet is that the Dalai Lama wants "one country, two systems" but what people [in Tibet] want is "one country, one system"—they want the more liberal policies that prevail in China also to apply in Tibet.[38]

The Chinese are left with a conundrum: their massive investment indicates their intent to bring prosperity to Tibet. Yet they have had mixed success. Much of their economic effort has foundered upon the rocks of political ideology and upon its seesaw approach to the problem of minority populations—neither accommodation nor assimilation has worked.

If the Chinese were to reform the political system in Tibet, it would have to be accompanied by a positive propaganda campaign to counteract the forty years of negative propaganda. Perhaps it would be best left to Tibetans to form their own self-image rather than view themselves through an imported filter of either the traditional Han Chinese chauvinism or the communist worldview.

Despite the years of negative propaganda, Tibet has become a magnet for Chinese tourists seeking spiritual regeneration. In addition, there has been a resurgence of the Tibetan Buddhist faith in China. Times have changed to the point where Chinese yuppies and members of the newly affluent middle class are among the most prevalent tourists to Tibet, where they seek lessons in meditation from lamas. The malaise of the new Chinese materialism has created in many Chinese the longing for spiritual regeneration. In a recurrent theme of Chinese history, what might be considered a fringe cult represents a threat to the established order. Rumblings emanating from the bottom of the heap mean that the structure might fall. History is replete with the stories of peasant uprisings, many inspired by religious cults. The arcs of historical change are in motion in Tibet, in China and in the region. If nothing is done, future unrest is likely. The Chinese must answer the question, what is to be done in Tibet?

PART 7

Late Twentieth-Century China

Hu Yaobang and the Liberal Policies of the 1980s

The Deng Era: The Ups and Downs of Chinese Policy in Post-Mao Tibet

Mao Zedong died in September of 1976. Posters and statues honoring him occupied public spaces from the Forbidden City and Tiananmen Square to provincial airports and railway stations. Mao portraits decorated peasant homes and the walls of urban proletarian apartments. His moon-shaped face gazed out from the office walls of Party functionaries and decorated Party department stores. Work sessions and struggle sessions began with songs and poems to the Great Helmsman. Mao, to say the least, was the dominating figure of a personality cult. He had survived guerrilla warfare, the Long March, and the defeat of the Japanese, he had brought the PRC into being and he piloted the socialist ship of state in its formative years. The nation was shocked at his passing and grieved. Mao's body was embalmed, placed in a crystal coffin, and moved to the Mao Mausoleum in Tiananmen Square, where it remains a tourist attraction.

Zhou Enlai, first Foreign Minister and later first Premier of the PRC and second only to Mao in the Chinese leadership, and Zhu De, the greatest military expert of the revolutionary generation and instrumental in the founding and leadership of the People's Liberation Army, had both died earlier in the year. Mao's widow, Jiang Qing, and the Gang of Four, members of the hard-left faction and prime movers behind the Cultural Revolution, were arrested within a month of Mao's death.

Hua Guofeng succeeded Mao as Chairman of the Central Committee of the Chinese Communist Party, but Hua was outmaneuvered by Deng Xiaoping who then became the party's chairman. An era of change was at hand. China was about to open. Under Deng's leadership, China entered an era of pragmatism. Economic policy was liberated from ideology and grounded in performance. The era of the Four Modernizations—in agriculture, industry, technology, and defense—had arrived. Market Stalinism was born. Two slogans sum up the zeitgeist of the period: "It doesn't matter whether it's a black cat or a white cat, as long as it catches mice" and "to get rich is glorious." For Tibetans inside Tibet and for the exile community, the Deng era held promise, and his new policies were met with enthusiasm.

China's economy had been in the doldrums for two decades following the ill-fated Great Leap Forward. Deng introduced elements of capitalism as a means of jump-starting the process of revitalization.[1] Changes proceeded as ripples from the center to the periphery, ultimately reaching Tibet. Beijing relaxed some of the political controls that were staples of the Cultural Revolution: class struggle, education of the masses, and communization. The Party adhered to the idea that the creation of a true proletarian class consciousness would eradicate national differences. The operative theory for the new leadership was this: Tibet would not be rapidly assimilated but instead would absorb "Chinese-ness" gradually. The new leaders blamed the Gang of Four for errors in executing the nationality policy. In Deng's view, there was nothing wrong with China's policy. The problem was with its implementation.

This was an attempt at equality, but the fundamental flaw was China's skewed vision of ethnicity. It was not the "tossed salad" model, in which all ethnicities are components of the salad yet retain their separate identities, nor even the "melting pot" model in which all ethnicities blend together and, out of the many, one dish is concocted with a distinctive flavor. Rather, China employed the "absorption" model. It was an old idea in new communist clothing: Sinicization is civilization. The barbarians must come to the party to be civilized.

Tibet's fragile economy had suffered from fundamental errors in economic planning, a misunderstanding of the local economy and Tibet's place in the region. The command economy, with choices dictated from the top down, achieved the opposite of Mao's goal of bringing prosperity to Tibet. During this period, the disparity in standards of living between China and the minorities widened. Statistics showed Tibet to be the poorest of all the minority regions. The standard of living of the average Tibetan worsened.

Beijing decreed that economic development was to become a top priority for Tibet. One stumbling block remained: those sympathetic to the Cultural Revolution remained in place in the local Tibetan Communist Party. They were not purged until the mid-1980s.[2]

The Party Secretariat appointed a five-man work committee on Tibet. The members were cadres with long experience in Tibet. The committee saw the problem as economic backwardness and perhaps an inequality in education. It never saw the problem in terms of China's basic relationship with Tibet.

The Chinese leadership believed that reconciliation with the Dalai Lama was necessary for the improvement of China's relationship with India. After all, the Tibetan Government in Exile (TGIE) was headquartered on Indian territory, in Dharamsala. The leadership realized that success in Tibet hinged on winning the Tibetan masses over to their side. It even appeared as if China's leadership had concluded that the return of the Dalai Lama and his followers would be a positive step in resolving the Tibet Question.

In 1978, in a gesture of good will toward Tibet, China released a group of prisoners, granted Tibetans the right to travel abroad to visit relatives, and initiated a policy of issuing visas to Tibetans living abroad to visit Tibet. Informal talks between Chinese government officials and Tibetans represented by Gyalo Thondrup, the Dalai Lama's elder brother—took place in Hong Kong. In 1979, Deng Xiaoping invited Gyalo Thondrup to Beijing and told him that, "apart from the question of total independence, all other issues could be discussed and all problems could be resolved."

During the 1979–1980 period, the Dalai Lama sent a fact-finding delegation to Tibet to obtain firsthand observations of the changes in Tibet that had occurred during the twenty years of communist rule. The Chinese may have supposed that the Dalai Lama would be impressed by the material progress made under the PRC, but the opposite was true. The fact-finding committees found terrible economic conditions.

Hu Yaobang, now party secretary, recommended a system that would permit Tibetan autonomy under the leadership of the Chinese Communist Party. The deal included exemption from taxes, permission for some private trade in agricultural products and products of animal husbandry, and allowance for cultural revival in Tibet—as long as that revival did not interfere with cherished socialist values. Hu also argued for establishing more schools at all levels, requiring Han nationals working in Tibet to learn Tibetan, and ensuring that two thirds of the cadres working in the Tibet Autonomous Region (TAR) government were Tibetan. Many of these reforms were put into practice.

The ethnically sensitive policy that had been in place in the 1950s was swept away by the assimilationists during the Cultural Revolution. In the 1950s, Mao had allowed the traditional Tibetan government to remain in place; by the 1980s, Beijing no longer made provision for a separate Tibetan government in Lhasa. The government in the Tibetan capital was communist and came under the leadership of the central Chinese government. The reins were not to be as tight as during the Cultural Revolution, but they were still tight. The view of Tibet would be the view from the center, not from Tibet or the South Asian region.

China continued informal discussions with representatives of the exile government. In 1981, the Dalai Lama wrote a letter to Deng Xiaoping that referred to Tibet and China as separate countries. China began demanding that the Dalai Lama recognize that Tibet had been part of China from time immemorial. This, the Dalai Lama was unwilling to do.

In 1981, Hu Yaobang met secretly with Gyalo Thondup in Beijing and presented him with Chinese terms for rapprochement with the Dalai Lama. While the Dalai Lama approached the problem as one between the governments of two countries, China took the position that it was dealing with a provincial region of China. At issue were the terms and conditions of the repatriation of the Dalai Lama and the rules governing his status and conduct.

The Chinese leadership had devised a new policy. They created a new face for the Communist Party in Tibet, at all levels of the party structure. They would also promote better-educated Han Chinese who could implement reforms without exemplifying the Great Han Chauvinism, meaning the anti-Tibetan prejudice of those cadres who had risen during the Cultural Revolution. The Chinese central government was able to implement this change in personnel because of an improved security apparatus that included better surveillance equipment, more plainclothes police, and more police stations in trouble-prone areas.

Hu offered the Dalai Lama the ceremonial post of vice-chairman of the National People's Congress and committed the Chinese government to his financial support. Accepting this offer may have solved some of the Chinese problems in Tibet. On the other hand, the Dalai Lama's accepting the offer would mean that, after years of declaring Tibet's right to self-determination, he would be accepting China's sovereignty over Tibet. Acceptance would not have secured for Tibet what Hong Kong was later to secure: the "one country, two systems" solution. This came about as a result of the definition of Hong Kong as a Special Administrative Region, or SAR, that entitled it to various protections and exceptions under Chinese law. Hong Kong was an economic powerhouse for China. Tibet was not, so the Chinese could afford to refuse Tibet's negotiating for the return of Kham and Amdo and the terms of repatriation of the Dalai Lama, as well as specific items pertaining to the governance of Tibet, such as policies relating to the Chinese management of the economy and the environment.

❦

On the thirtieth anniversary of the signing of the Seventeen Point Agreement, in 1981, Hu Yaobang went to Tibet to announce a new beginning. The past thirty years had been a series of mistakes, and Hu was ready to admit that the CCP had failed in Tibet.[3] Tibetans (those inside Tibet and those in exile) saw the Four Modernizations policy as a hope for a better future.

Hu appointed the liberal Wu Jinghua as regional party secretary in Tibet. A member of the Yi minority from southwest China, Wu had sympathy for Tibetan culture and often went about in Tibetan dress. The years under his stewardship were the best for Tibet since the invasion. He had served as first deputy minister of the State Nationalities Affairs Commission under Deng, where he was responsible for the development of liberal policies concerning minorities.[4] For the first time, Tibetans openly expressed resentment that no Tibetan had been appointed to the top post in Lhasa. Beijing claimed that no Tibetans who had reached the appropriate age had the appropriate experience. A far more likely explanation is that even the liberal Hu did not trust a Tibetan to govern Tibet.[5] "Tibetan party leaders occupied a precarious position in the CCP. They were faced with the ever-present danger of accusations of showing 'local nationalism' and of putting ethnic interests over the wider concerns of the Party and the motherland."[6]

In the 1980s, the Chinese reintroduced the United Work Front, a group meant to smooth relations with Tibetans who were not Party members. The role of the group was mainly public relations combined with community development, the hallmark of the CCP's work in Tibet during the 1950s.

❧

In part because of the criticisms of the Tenth Panchen Lama, by 1986 Tibetan was adopted as the main language of the administration on a trial basis. Primary schools would also use Tibetan as the language of instruction. Ethnic sensitivity was in. The study of Tibetan language was in.[7] The study of Chinese language was out.

The new language policy called for Tibetanization of the party. The goal was that, within a few years, two-thirds of the cadres in Tibet would be Tibetans. Also, Chinese cadres would be required to study the Tibetan language. "[Hu's] strategy was to withdraw thousands of Chinese cadres from Tibet, and he intended to achieve this by retiring, dismissing or transferring them to China. Of all the recommendations, this would have the most impact on Tibetan society."[8]

The central government at long last realized how badly Tibet had been mishandled.[9] Determined that the mistakes of the past would be rectified, Hu dealt with another source of tension. He recognized that Tibetans saw the PLA as a foreign army and resented them as an army of occupation. To improve relations, Hu ordered the Party's propaganda arm to educate the military on Tibetan religion and minority policy.

Deng believed in opening up China, Hu followed Deng's line in Tibet. Hu believed that opening Tibet was the only way to improve the local economy. The Chinese leadership realized that tourism could be good business in Tibet. Tibetan Buddhism was a fast-growing religion in Europe and the United States.[10] The world wanted to see Buddhist Tibet. This necessitated building an infrastructure, and the Chinese government struck up a joint venture with the American firm that runs the Holiday Inn chain of hotels.

The central problem in Tibet was the suppression of freedom of religion. The leadership had always taken the party line that minorities would in time choose to acculturate, meaning, to choose the Chinese way of life.[11] So far this had not proved to be the case. Assimilation had not occurred. Tibetans remained Tibetans. Pragmatism held sway in China. The new economic reforms ushered in an era of more cultural expression and religious freedom. The Chinese leadership had come to see that pursuing a policy of ethnic sensitivity might be profitable.

Deng's new liberalization policies for China included agricultural reforms. The regional government announced that permission would be granted for household-based agricultural production. This meant the Party would allow private farming. The new policy marked a complete shift in direction, so it was to be implemented gradually. There would be no more "shock therapy" for Tibet. Party cadres in Tibet were charged with the task of implementing a new, commodity-based economy. The new game plan was to diversify the Tibetan economy from its tradition base of agriculture and animal husbandry.

Hu relaxed restrictions on the Chinese, permitting them to enter Tibet for business and commercial enterprise. Loosening up the economy meant opening up to investment—one cannot run a modern

economy without information and opening up to the global information superhighway meant loosening Party control. This was the era
of liberalization. The Open Tibet policy meant a relaxation of tight
restrictions on trade, so that state-owned enterprises and individual
entrepreneurs were free to open businesses in Tibet. That was the
theory. In practice, the new openness facilitated the immigration and
relocation to the Tibetan plateau of great numbers of Han Chinese.
Dorje Tseten, a deputy party secretary in Tibet, objected that Tibetans
would not be able to compete with Chinese and that the immigration
of many Han might create problems of disparity and dislocation.

Because of their superior skills, higher educational level, and
Chinese language skills, the new residents put Tibetans at a competi-
tive disadvantage in the job market. (The same held true for the influx
of Chinese-speaking Hui Muslim entrepreneurs—Chinese-speaking
Muslims from China proper, rather than Turkic-speaking Muslims
from Xinjiang.) This was the outcome predicted by Dorje Tseten at
the policy discussion meeting of the Second Tibet Work Forum in
Beijing, but Hu Yaobang dismissed his analysis as alarmist and voiced
the opinion that the problem could be handled by local laws.

Many Tibetans believed that Chinese immigration was necessary
for Tibetan economic development—unlike Tibetans, the Chinese
were a skilled labor pool. The Chinese also possessed technical skills.
Throughout the 1980s, the Chinese developed institutes in China that
trained Tibetans to meet the demand for skilled and technically sophisticated labor. A trained Tibetan labor force—training to be supplied by
the government—would eliminate the need for outside expertise.[12]

The new situation did not work to the advantage of Tibetans.
The influx of Chinese blunted opportunities for Tibetans. This led
to resentment of the Chinese and to accusations that the PRC was
turning Tibet into a multi-ethnic region where Tibetans were in
danger of becoming a minority in their homeland. Was this a good
model for development, as Beijing contended? Or was it cultural
genocide, as Dharamsala contended?

Was Tibet unique, or was it just another country? Was the
increase in population of Chinese and Hui Muslims simply the
result of workers seeking better jobs, part of the "floating population" phenomenon that exists in China proper? Were the Chinese

and the Hui thus obeying the law of supply and demand, or were the Tibetans' suspicions justified? Was Tibet's future to become a multi-ethnic state? Was the destruction of "traditional" Tibet legitimate without the consent of the Tibetans? At the root of these questions is the issue of who decides. The Chinese leadership clearly prefers top-down decisions; while Tibetans believe that sovereignty should emanate from the bottom up, from Tibetans.

❧

Lhasa was once a showcase of indigenous architecture, but with the construction of modern utilitarian structures, the character of this capital city has changed, most say for the worse. The new Chinese construction was aimed at economic development, but it was decidedly not a product of modern urban planning and lacked aesthetic quality by comparison with the old city. The Chinese planning for the development was not up to international standard, but more of a commercialization of Old Lhasa.

Regardless of the botched development, China's attempt to improve its relationship with Tibet was a public relations success. With the advent of the new policies came increased international acceptance. International agencies wanted entry to Tibet, including the World Food Program and the United Nations Development Program.

One snag in these developments involved the Dalai Lama's proposal that Tibet become a nuclear-free zone. The Chinese, however, had already moved their nuclear facilities from Lop Nor (a salt lake in the Taklimakan Desert of Xinjiang Uighur Autonomous Region) to the Tibetan plateau. The Dalai Lama objected to the storage of nuclear waste on the Tibetan plateau. His proposal was intended to preserve Tibet's fragile and endangered ecosystem and reflected the Buddhist point of view of nonviolence. The Dalai Lama's plan is a way of diffusing regional military tensions, but does it gel with China's security interests? Three nuclear powers inhabit the Himalayan region: China, India, and Pakistan. Does the concept of a Zone of Peace conflict with China's interest in force projection?

Another ecological consideration is that five of Asia's major rivers have their headwaters in the Himalayas. Millions of people all over Asia are affected by environmental policy at the Roof of the World. What happens in Lhasa does not stay in Lhasa.

The Dilemma of the Dalai Lama

The Chinese leadership actively sought reconciliation with the Dalai Lama as a means of improving the relationship between Tibet and China. In 1981, Hu Yaobang met secretly with Gyalo Thondup in Beijing and presented him with the Chinese terms for rapprochement with the Dalai Lama. At issue were the conditions for the Dalai Lama's repatriation and the ground rules governing his status and conduct. The Dalai Lama rejected Deng's offer.

The Dalai Lama also rejected Hu's offer of the ceremonial post of vice-chairman of the National People's Congress. Some historians have called this a missed opportunity. Perhaps it was, perhaps not. Had the Dalai Lama accepted the Chinese offer, he would have alienated a segment of the exile community that sought more than autonomy—the faction that wanted complete independence. The Chinese position ruled out discussion of ethnic Tibetan areas incorporated into Chinese provinces. Discussion of any problems relating to events before 1959 were off the table. This method of setting a fixed agenda in advance of negotiations is a standard Chinese negotiating tactic, as many a Western businessman can attest.[13]

Although Deng said that anything other than independence would be on the table in discussions with the Dalai Lama, would he have made a deal for real autonomy? Perhaps not. The lamaist government was no longer in existence. The exile government had changed from the old mixed secular and monastic system to a parliamentary system with democratic features. If the PRC were to reconcile with Tibet, what would the arrangement look like?

Officials of the exile government believe that the Dharamsala-based government is a continuation of the government that has ruled Tibet since the seventeenth century. The exile government derives its legitimacy from the Tibetan tradition that the seat of its government is wherever the Dalai Lama resides.

In 1959, at the time of the exile, the Dalai Lama continued in his function as head of state. He reorganized the central government and the various branches of the exile government, such as the Library of Tibetan Works and Archives. He also created various new relief agencies and educational agencies. The Gelugpa sect of Tibetan Buddhism, of which the Dalai Lama is the spiritual head, has a strong tradition of scholarship and prides itself on its system of theological debate.

The Dalai Lama determined that the parliament would eventually be elected by popular vote. He also decided that the new cabinet would not be appointed by him. The popularly elected parliament would choose the cabinet on the basis of merit and ability and not on the basis of noble birth—the traditional qualification for governmental officials in Tibet. The parliament was no longer answerable to the Dalai Lama, although the 46-member cabinet remained accountable to him.

He called together a large congress of several hundred important leaders—tribal chieftains, families, civilians, and priests—at Bodhgaya, the place where the Buddha attained his enlightenment. These leaders came from all three parts of Tibet: U-tsang, Kham, and Amdo. (U-tsang is now called the Tibet Autonomous Region, and the other two regions are those incorporated into parts of China's Gansu, Qinghai, Yunnan, and Sichuan provinces.)

During the creation of the exile government in the early sixties, the Dalai Lama announced that it was time for the Tibetan government to modernize. The Dalai Lama undertook research on constitutions and on parliamentary systems, beginning with the works of Thomas Jefferson. This fact-finding period was similar to the research into Western systems undertaken by the Meiji government of Japan in the late nineteenth century. It sounds peculiar for a head of state to appoint a parliament, but the Dalai Lama, out of necessity, appointed both cabinet and parliament. The tenure of those first appointments ranged from fifteen to twenty years.

In the early 1960s, the exile government drafted its first constitution. The Dalai Lama offered to resign as head of state, but this was unpopular in the community. The new constitution is an important document. Its first article reads: Tibet shall be a democratic country. It also states that Tibet should occupy the territory that it occupied at the time of the (1950) Chinese invasion. This territorial dispute over the ethnically Tibetan areas of Kham and Amdo has been ongoing for most of the twentieth century, and it remains the main obstacle to substantive talks between China and the Dalai Lama.

The Dalai Lama has come to believe that Tibet should have a popularly elected president. De-emphasizing his traditional role as the head of a theocratic state and moving closer to Western parliamentary systems, the Dalai Lama does not want to be the head of a nation. In fact, he sees the dual secular-sacral function of the Tibetan head of state as a weakness in the system and believes that the office of Dalai Lama belonged to a different time. For the modern era, what Tibet needs is a civilian head of government and a cleric as head of the Tibetan religion—in other words, a division of church and state. Finally, Tenzin Gyatso also believes that the constitution should not speak of him as a person but instead should address the structure of government. In the interim he has agreed to continue as executive head of the government, although he insisted (over popular objection) on an impeachment clause in the constitution.

In 1990, the exile government adopted the new constitution. The Dalai Lama no longer appoints even cabinet ministers, who are now appointed by the popularly elected representatives of the parliament. The Exile Parliament of Tibet consists of 46 representatives from all three regions of traditional Tibet but also includes one representative from North America and one from each of the Tibetan exile communities (such as those in Switzerland and Great Britain). In what must be the world's most unusual election process, at the time designated for parliamentary elections the Tibetan Association of Washington (or Geneva or London) organizes an election, counts the votes, and sends the results to New York. Then the New York office re-counts the votes before sending the actual written ballots to Dharamsala. The entire process takes three or four months. Because Washington tabulates, New York verifies, and Dharamsala authenticates, there is no possibility of election fraud.

The system has a built-in safeguard against ballot tampering. The Tibetan government includes a central election committee in Dharamsala as well as local election committees, one for each exile community. Ballots are counted by the local committees and then sent to the central committee. The ballot is secret, and local committees do not disclose local results. The final announcement comes from Dharamsala.

Tibet has also created a system of voluntary taxation, although this levy can hardly be called a tax because the Tibetan Government in Exile has no territory and thus no way of enforcing payment. The tax has never been mandatory. Tibetans in North America pay about $84 a year; those who live in Dharamsala, where the standard of living is much lower, pay about 100 Indian rupees a year. The successful Tibetan communities in prosperous Switzerland pay more.

Because of China's policy of assimilation, Tibet as an ethnically Tibetan territory is now endangered. For this reason, the Dalai Lama has said he will return to Tibet, acknowledge that Tibet is part of China, and cooperate with any Chinese policy that is ethnically sensitive, includes reinstating Tibetan as the language of education and government, and promises that government will consist mostly of Tibetans within a five-year period. Any acceptable proposal would also have to incorporate a policy of religious toleration and a more sensitive development policy, one that is not destructive of the Tibetan environment. Finally, having thus preserved Tibet from becoming another Han Chinese province, the Dalai Lama would work toward implementing the guarantees of the Chinese Constitution for Tibet's true autonomy.

It is unclear what would happen if autonomy was granted and the Dalai Lama returned to Tibet. He has said that he would dissolve the exile government. He has reassured Tibetans inside Tibet who have held positions in the Chinese government: "None of you who have worked within the system will lose your positions." Should the Chinese leave, an interim government would immediately form inside Tibet. The Dalai Lama would no doubt urge those residing in Tibet that it would be sensible for the new government to include representatives from the TGIE, but he has said that this is a matter for the Tibetan people to decide.

Give the workmanlike way in which the government of Hong Kong—whose democracy is much more developed than Tibet's—was absorbed into the Chinese state, it would seem that implementing a "loose reins" policy in Tibet would be neither as complicated nor as difficult. The old Tibetan feudal system is gone forever.

The question from China's perspective is this: Would changes in Tibet create repercussions in other minority regions? This is a distinct possibility. Judging from the 2009 riots in Urumqi, Xinjiang might also benefit from the "loose reins" model.

The End of the Soft Line

The era of reform saw Tibetans gaining promotions to higher positions in government and education. Tibetan cadres and party members were hopeful that a form of regional autonomy might be in Tibet's future. In 1984, the National People's Congress passed a law granting regional autonomy in Tibet. The law guaranteed local management of internal affairs, but the law was general and limited. Local regional officials still needed permission from the center, but overall the new framework was an improvement. As long as Tibetans did not oppose China's claim to Tibet, Beijing was willing to concede to many of the Tibetans' demands. By 1985, the Party had substantially relaxed its control over Tibet. Tibetans had gained more ground than at any time since the invasion. Not everyone was happy: Chinese and Tibetan leftists disapproved of the reforms.

In 1986, the Party allowed the celebration of the Monlam Festival, the major Tibetan religious festival, the first in two decades. Tibetans came from all over the country to attend. The CCP's official view of religion had not changed: religion was an impediment to economic development and Chinese unity. Tibetans might regard Buddhism as central to their identity, but China saw it as a troublesome national characteristic.

China was willing to allow a limited revival of Tibetan religion and culture. Tibetans, on the other hand, were unwilling to accept government limits on religious freedom. The Party loosened its control over the monasteries, and the population of the monasteries swelled. This was not welcome news to the leadership, who saw monasteries as a potential threat to Chinese political control of the country.

It should be noted that some Tibetan progressives saw the rebirth of monastic institutions as a step backward. Religion in their view was an obstacle to modernization and drained off precious human and financial resources to a non-state enterprise that did not contribute to economic development. Religion was an alternate center of power.

In 1987, a series of riots broke out in Lhasa. Political protests began peacefully but erupted into violence and ended in bloodshed and the imprisonment of protestors.[14] The monks were the first protestors, but after some were arrested, ordinary Tibetans joined the protests. The riots were suppressed by armed Chinese security forces. The demonstrators had been demanding that China quit Tibet. Deng knew that economic reforms had to proceed, but the time of catering to Tibet as a special region within China was at an end. Tibet was to be a multi-ethnic province, not a Tibetan homeland with its own ethnic character.

The riots continued until the 1989 declaration of martial law. Six months later, the Tiananmen protests began, and the army was called out to squash the civil unrest. As Beijing saw it, stability and order were the supreme good; disorder would not be tolerated. Martial law was not lifted until 1990. The Dalai Lama had broken off contact with China following its declaration of martial law.

This was the end of the soft line, hardliners in the Politburo and also in the regional Tibetan government gained in influence, and they decried the liberal policies of the 1980s as a grievous error. They pressed the conclusion upon their more moderate comrades that the result of liberalization was the demand for separatism. From 1989 until the present, the hard line in Tibet has prevailed. The PRC has sought rapid economic development, an end to ethnic accommodation, and rapid integration of Tibet's economy into that of China.

The most scathing critique of the Hu Yaobang policies comes from historian Tsering Shakya.[15] He describes what he terms the "back to square one" phenomenon. In rationalizing the PRC's contemporary state-building—that is, the incorporation of former tribute states into China proper—the Chinese have bent over backwards to make objective reality conform to communist minority ideology. Did the PRC make a real attempt at granting Tibetan autonomy, or was the effort mere window dressing? Shakya states that true autonomy was never implemented; the "autonomy" of regional bodies, such as the National People's Congress and the Political Consultative Conference, existed only on paper.

❧

Tibetans made strides forward in the 1980s. Tibetan was reinstated as the official language of the TAR. The number of Tibetan cadres and senior Party officials in leadership positions in Tibet increased. But old habits die hard. The CCP *appointed* only those Tibetans whom they could identify as faithful apparatchiks (communist bureaucrats with party loyalty, with the pejorative connotation of being cogs in the vast machine of the state apparatus). As a result, the effect of "Tibetanization"—putting a Tibetan face on the Chinese government inside Tibet—has been to appoint cadres on the basis of party loyalty, those who would serve China's interest.

There was no real local authority serving local needs and interests: there was loyalty to Beijing and direction from Beijing. The Tibetans promoted inside Tibet had risen up through the ranks even though some of whom were illiterate in Tibetan. This made political sense for the Chinese, but it did not address Tibetan grievances.

In the end, however, many liberal reforms initiated by Hu were discarded. Shakya observed that, "Chinese cadres . . . refused to surrender their power in the region, or to accept that the last thirty years of their work in Tibet had been, as Hu termed it, 'a mistake.' When Hu and Wu Jinghua later fell from power, these officials celebrated openly and seized the chance to undo all the liberal policies . . . [that Hu and Wu] had established."[16]

Chinese analysis may ascribe problems in Tibet to bad class identity, backwardness, or outside influences, but this analysis has not dealt with the fundamental question of ethnicity. People have lost faith in Communism as a unifying political philosophy. The PRC stakes its claim to legitimacy on a rising standard of living and its "unification" of China. The Tibet Question must be solved in a manner that does not detract from this success. This is the core of the conflict between Beijing and Dharamsala.

The Chinese leadership faces a second problem: the current premier, Hu Jintao, made his reputation (and began his rise to power) during his tour of duty as Party Secretary in Tibet. Hu Jintao dealt with the protests of the 1980s. He and many of his appointees will suffer criticism if a decision is reached for a change of course in Tibet. This would be accompanied by a loss of face and face does play a role. China has finally triumphed over the Century of Humiliation and wishes to be seen as a strong vital player on the world stage.

There are two solutions to this problem: redefine the Tibet Question in terms of Tibet's current state of development and China's responsiveness to historical conditions or wait for the fifth generation of Chinese leadership. Unlike Hu Jintao and his associates, a new generation of leaders may make changes because they do not carry the baggage of the past.

A third complicating factor is that the Chinese leadership does not want to be seen as bowing to international pressure. This is a point of pride in an era that is witnessing China's rise as a regional and global power. The system of "loose reins" suggested by this author has its origins in Chinese history and is a Chinese solution to a Chinese problem. It combines traditional forms of Chinese governance but works through local conditions and is therefore related to conditions on the ground in Tibet:

> The combination of religious faith, ethnic identity and social and economic disadvantage, real or perceived, provide fertile soil for Tibetan nationalism. Despite economic improvements over the last decade, the majority of Tibetans view their position as marginalized and disadvantaged in today's China.... While on the surface the Party has managed to contain the latent nationalistic aspirations of the Tibetan people, these factors, together with the presence of a powerful leadership in exile, do indeed provide a major threat to the CCP. The solution to the Tibetan problem, however, is neither complex nor difficult; nor does it require any major concession by the Chinese government. The notion of Tibet as an integral part of China is a recent invention by the Communist Party in its process of nation building. Tibet has never been central to the Chinese imagination. There was never any Chinese Woody Guthrie to warble, 'This land is our land, from the crest of the Himalayas to the shores of the South

China Sea': the Party conjured up this sentiment after 1950. The spell can vanish as quickly as it was made to appear. Tibet is not Palestine or Kashmir, with extreme passions on both sides backed by centuries of religious bigotry.[17]

A scholar of China, John K. Fairbank, wrote an astute analysis of the Chinese rulers after the Tiananmen Massacre. He remarked that the men who held power in Beijing belonged to the imperial tradition of autocracy. They were a modern version of that tradition, although their rhetoric was dressed in communist ideology. The students and the intellectuals, who would normally be recruited for government service, represented the tradition of modern-minded patriots dating back a century to the beginning of China's modernizing efforts. "In the twentieth century, the institutional successor to family dynasties proved to be Party dictatorship."[18]

The ruler was above the law. Even as he advanced the ideals of Confucianism—benevolence, righteousness, ritual, manners—he ruled by wielding the power of life and death. Loyalty to the emperor took precedence over welfare of the people, for it was only through loyalty to the emperor that an official or candidate for office survived. China's autocratic tradition will eventually be modernized, and the modernization will eventually spread to Tibet. The future for China holds political reform, but the question is, will that change require bloodshed or not?

❧

Will Tibetans ever identify themselves as Chinese? Judging from the history of minorities in the former Soviet Union, especially their reversion to their own traditions once the USSR dissolved, one would say that the odds are against it. The experience of the twentieth century speaks for itself. History has ruled on the issue of ethnicity: Ethnicity is more enduring a part of human identity than economic class. The Chinese are fighting a losing battle.

Tibetans living in eastern Tibetan autonomous provinces and prefectures—parts of Gansu, Sichuan, Yunnan, and Qinghai provinces (formerly the ethnic Tibetan territories of Kham and Amdo)—have been living under Chinese control far longer than those in central Tibet. Though citizens of the PRC, they do not see themselves as Chinese. Neither do those Tibetans who receive schooling in China proper. Young Tibetans receiving Chinese educations are exposed to negative Han Chinese attitudes about (and stereotypes of) Tibet and Tibetans, attitudes nurtured by forty years of state propaganda. One could be polite and call the attitude Han chauvinism, or one could be blunt and call it racism. Either way, the persistence of these attitudes among the Han Chinese populace has tended to reinforce Tibetan ethnic pride and curiosity about the Tibetan heritage.

If China's main interest in Tibet is strategic, would the older model of a "loose reins" autonomy for Tibet threaten China's security or position in the world? If one analyzes China's modern defense structure, the answer to this question must be no. Given China's long-term alliance with Pakistan, the balance of power in the region has shifted from Russia and its alliance with India to China and its alliance with Pakistan. China is the most important regional player in South Asia and will only become more important with the projected withdrawal of the U.S. presence in Afghanistan beginning in 2011.

China's military and weapons superiority—its nuclear capability—are a deterrent to any regional opponent such as India or even Russia. The Chinese military posture is dominant enough to ensure its security.

The modern version of the "loose reins" model is well known in the laboratory of contemporary history. It is the *network* model, the one employed by that student of business administration Osama Bin Laden. This loose, responsive structure, a well-conceived autonomy subject to oversight and accountability, might well serve to transform China's top-down centralized structure.

From the present Chinese leadership perspective, Tibet is the poor stepchild on the multi-ethnic frontier. If one analyzes Tibet from a regional perspective, however, it has the potential to become a vibrant center of trade—perhaps a healing center, certainly a spot for eco-tourism—while retaining its traditional role as a center for spiritual seekers. A bit of new thinking could turn Tibet into a regional exporter instead of region that exports internally, into China. The benefits of restructuring would accrue to both China and Tibet.

The Chinese state is modeled on the Soviet *nomenklatura*—an elite establishment defined by its loyalty to the party. This elite survived the Mao era, even though Mao recognized the problem of an entrenched and privileged bureaucracy. He was so opposed to the emergency of a privileged class within the communist power structure that he launched the Cultural Revolution, in part, to counteract it. The model of a Soviet-style state is a century old. Its structure has been and continues to be a problem for China, and by extension for Tibet. At some point, the state's very size and unwieldiness, let alone its inefficiency, will require streamlining.[19]

The Himalayas has changed in the last sixty years. There are video nights in Kathmandu, and the internet has penetrated Lhasa. Tibet is remote, but not as remote as it had been in former centuries; one need only jet in from Chengdu. Young people in Lhasa listen to rap and wear blue jeans. The high ground does not the guarantee military advantage that it did in former times. China is no longer threatened by colonial encroachment from Britain or Russia. There is economic advantage to be gained if China will allow Tibet to resume its traditional role as a South Asian trading center.

The region has new problems, the narcotics trade, weapons trafficking, and militant extremism. China's leaders have already recognized the need to project smart power in the South Asian region and have already sought closer ties with the Kabul government. China is already an observer member of the South Asian Association for Regional Cooperation.

For some time, Chinese security strategy has been to join regional bodies and work through them. In Central Asia, this is the counter-terror group known as the Shanghai Cooperation Organization.[20] China is a member of similar regional organizations in Southeast Asia and North Asia. Simply by extending that cooperative policy— applying it to Tibet and viewing Tibet not as landlocked but rather as an inland coast—China could serve its own interests more effectively than at any time in the past two centuries.

PART 8

The Twenty-First Century

A New Road Map for Tibet

Back to the Future

As the history of the twentieth century proved, ethnicity is a more fundamental and enduring human characteristic than class. In the former Yugoslavia and the former Soviet Empire, ethnicity came raging to the fore as soon as the strong man and the strong state were gone. In the old Asian republics of the USSR, the ethnics were happy to be rid of the great Russian chauvinists. One might say it was nothing personal. These states gained their independence, but Tibet remained in a chokehold.

The Chinese may blame ethnic unrest in Tibet on outside forces, but after sixty years Tibetans still want to be Tibetans, and for most of them that includes being Buddhist. The answer cannot be, as some in the Chinese leadership maintain, that the Tibetans are simply backward ingrates.

The old clichés no longer apply. Tibetans inside Tibet are a diverse group: Among them are those who are secular, religiously motivated, politically motivated, and economically motivated. There are those who have grown up as nomads and those who have been educated in China. Chinese education has not stripped away their

Tibetan identity; in many cases, their exposure to Han chauvinism has only reinforced their sense of Tibetan pride.

Some of these Tibetans see Buddhism as compatible with modernity. The religion has attracted hundreds of thousands of adherents globally. (According to the statistics of the Chinese Buddhist Association, there are also increasing numbers of Buddhists in China proper, even among Han Chinese.) These Tibetans see Buddhism as being more compatible with modernity than the anachronistic communist ideology that no longer inspires loyalty, even among Han Chinese. Nationalism is the glue that holds China together, and Chinese nationalism is a problem for Tibet because Chinese nationalism has erroneously identified Chinese pride as dependent upon Chinese unity. For the past twenty years, that has meant a hard line in Tibet. The hard line has failed. This means that Chinese nationalism, and Chinese national interest, has to be redefined.

Generational point of view is an important factor in politics all over the world. The younger generation in Tibet is a new breed and has a new outlook. As the late art historian Dr. William Ding-yi Wu commented after a trip to Tibet in the wake of the 1987 Uprising: "Young Tibetans don't want to follow the lamas. They want to wear blue jeans and listen to rock and roll." Shangri-la meets globalization. The revolution in technology has made a huge difference.

Within the past few years, experts on Afghanistan—military and intelligence officers, diplomatic experts, and journalists with long experience—have stated, in interviews and in their writing, that killing the enemy will not work in the absence of economic development. This is a basic principle of counterinsurgency warfare. The same reasoning applies to the cycle of dissent and repression in Tibet.

For China, the Tibet Question has been a political and human rights problem as well as a public relations mess from the day of the invasion to the present. No state can control information for long in the boomerang environment of the global media. China is concerned about its international image. China may throw its weight around, but it will not command respect in the international community through suppression of unrest in minority regions. The globe has simply become too small.

History has brought China to a new moment. With the success of its coming-out party, the Beijing Olympics, China passed from the century-old era of colonial humiliation into its new identity, a modern state wishing to command global respect. As the saying goes, for the Chinese, the 2008 Olympics was the moon shot.

Globalization Comes to South Asia

China has made its relationship with Pakistan the cornerstone of its diplomacy in South Asia. With religious extremism contributing to the instability in both Pakistan and Kashmir, with the rise of a hugely profitable narcotics trade in Afghanistan and a burgeoning weapons trade, with Iran seeking to be the region's hegemon, the time is right for a regional solution based on regional development. China stands to be the beneficiary.

The time is right for China to project its interest in the region in a new manner, applying the economic reforms that have worked so well on China's maritime coast to Tibet. In short: Give jobs, not guns, to the younger generation, who are increasingly a factor in many of these states. Treat Tibet as a coastal province. This is in keeping with millennia of Chinese foreign policy, where China focused on Inner Asia more than on its eastern coastline.

The time is right for change in Tibet. Tensions have clearly been exacerbated by the Tibetans' feelings of economic marginalization in their own country, their loss of ethnic identity, and the religious repression they have endured at the hands of the Chinese military and security police. At the time of the Chinese invasion, no Western government recognized the independence of Tibet. Although the United Nations did pass several resolutions denouncing the invasion, only Ireland, Thailand, Malaysia, and El Salvador supported Tibet's appeal to be heard before UN. Tibet missed its chance for decolonialization.

The Dalai Lama won the Nobel Peace Prize in 1989, but no Western government recognized the legitimacy of the Tibetan Exile Government in Dharamsala, India. To put it another way, Chinese geopolitical concerns have trumped Tibetan human rights concerns. Within the Chinese leadership, China's geostrategic calculations and ideology are the two principal considerations.

An Asian Solution to an Asian Problem

China has successfully raised the issue of sovereignty in international law since the 1950s. Coming out of the Century of Humiliation, the Chinese have argued that no nation has the right to intervene in Chinese internal affairs. Is this approach valid in the current age of interpenetrating influence, or is it simply an anachronism?

Former South Korean Foreign Minister Dr. Han Sung-Joo describes Chinese foreign policy as follows: "The Chinese have a concept of sovereignty in an age of interflow of influence. The zeitgeist of the present age is de-centralization, and China cannot do away with its worldview overnight." Dr. Han believes that it is in China's interest to deal with problems in a multilateral way, just as it is in the country's own interest to open up and liberalize. However, the current generation of Chinese leaders views these developments as concessions rather than as advantages. Even officials who see things from a multilateral perspective are hard pressed to explain their views to colleagues in the current atmosphere of nationalism.

With communism in general disregard among the masses, nationalism has become the glue holding the Chinese state together. Any solution to the Tibet Question must reverse the official line. The leadership will need to reinterpret China's interest in Tibet to the Chinese masses. This will require a public education campaign.

In his public pronouncements, Dr. Han has stressed several principles to which Asian nations (including China) should adhere in order to maintain peace and stability in northeast Asia. These principles apply equally to South Asia.

First among them is that each country should take a pragmatic approach to the issues, not an idealistic (meaning an ideological) one. Speaking at a joint conference of the Baker Institute and the Asia Society, Han stressed that an ideological approach was counterproductive because it rendered every issue explosive and needlessly exacerbated tempers. "Issues can be handled in a more realistic way rather than by rhetoric, saber rattling, or making issues part of domestic politics."

Dr. Han recognizes that countries act in their own self-interest—it would be naive to suppose they act simply on the basis of good will. Han has stressed that in too many instances, domestic factors prevail and domestic audiences are the arbiters, at times when international solutions should not be held hostage to internal politics. Without regional bodies or mechanisms for conflict resolution, domestic audiences become the arbiters of policy in such situations; thus, international solutions are held hostage to internal politics.

Dr. Han advocates a regional approach. In the case of South Asia, a ready-made solution is at hand. The South Asian Association for Regional Cooperation (SAARC) has been in existence for nearly 25 years. It has put forth the plans for a South Asian Economic Union. The original eight members are Afghanistan, Bangladesh, Bhutan, India, Nepal, Maldives, Pakistan, and Sri Lanka. In this approach, Tibet (and also Sikkim) would apply for admission. China already participates in North Asian, Southeast Asian, and Central Asian regional bodies and is the leading force in the Southeast Asian Free Trade Zone, which will soon become the world's largest. China already has observer status in the SAARC.

Most important, the mechanisms exist within the Chinese legal system to reconstruct Tibet in accordance with a historical model that was successful for more than a century: that of Chinggis Khan. With an application of Chinese legal principles drawn from Chinese documents,[1] the Tibet Question could be resolved by a win-win restructuring and reorganization.

The Tibetan protest movement has roots in the monasteries. This is because the threat to Buddhism as an essential part of Tibetan life has forced the locus of protest to the only space that Tibetans have for national expression. In Latin American revolutionary movements, the revolutionaries tacked left to make an end run around the Catholic Church. In the extremist Islamist movements in the Muslim world, the revolutionaries tack right, into the mosques, because the regions' oppressive political climates leave no public spaces for dissent. The same is true in Tibet. Protesting Tibetans carry portraits of the Dalai Lama—not because the Dalai Lama is fomenting splittism, but because he is a symbol of the Tibetan identity that the Chinese have sought to destroy.

The "loose reins" model would be one way to resolve the political restructuring. Chinggis Khan promoted freedom of religion throughout his domains, including Tibet. The religion never proved to be a problem during a century of Mongol rule. The locals got their temples and their freedom of worship and managed their own affairs through the local government; and Chinggis Khan got his taxes, roads, corvée, and military service. When required, force was used to keep the peace. In this period, Tibet was never garrisoned as were the other khanates. Buddhism is nonviolent and pacifist, but Tibetans have shown that even Buddhists can be pushed to violence, as demonstrated by a number of uprisings over the decades. A Tibetan intifada is in no one's interest.

The Great Game of the colonial era and the Cold War between the superpowers have both come to an end. The region's continued turbulence indicates that a new pattern has not yet formed. The situation is fluid. Is it possible to create a stable balance of power in the region and invigorate a combination of new and old patterns of trade? The answer must be yes.

Under a "loose reins" approach, Tibet could become a regional leader. With a smart diversification of its economy, Tibet could export throughout the region rather than being relegated to the less profitable role of merely exporting internally back to China. In colonial times, Tibet's exports were few and related to limited products of agriculture and animal husbandry. With today's global market for Himalayan products, Tibet could multiply its revenue streams. With new forms of sustainable micro-enterprise and a light Chinese hand, Tibet might even have a future as a banking center. The Dalai Lama has a vision of Tibet as a healing center, building on the increased Western interest in such traditional systems of healing as Ayurvedic medicine (popularized in the West by Deepak Chopra). These are new ideas, a promising model and one that has not been tried.

The Mechanics of Change

Because the workings of the uppermost levels of the CCP are conducted in secret, China watchers parse events and media reports
much as the Confucians of old parsed the yarrow stalks to read
the ancient Chinese oracle, the *I Qing*. The conventional wisdom
of China watchers about the fourth generation of China's leadership is that they will not take bold steps in political reform. They
will hold to stability, to the supremacy of party leadership, in the
interests of economic progress. Perhaps the current global financial
crisis might modify the thinking of the current (fourth) generation at Zhongnanhai. (The fifth comes to power in 2012.) Many
of the most reliable China watchers agree that political reform
must come to China—either with the fourth of fifth generation
of leadership.

The think tanks within China that report to the leadership have
been investigating constitutional and governmental reform, including the issues of federalism and different sorts of democracy. Many
within the leadership recognize the obvious: The Leninist-inspired
state apparatus is too vast, too centralized, and too anachronistic to
survive in its present form. Ironically, the huge success of China in
the new environment of globalization has brought pressure on the
old structure, a grossly inefficient behemoth comprising 45 million
employees. That is a staggering figure for a state, even one with a
population as large as China's.

The idea of the leadership has been to abandon the old casti-
gation of class background in order to bring the new middle class
and the newly rich into the Party. How long can the Party survive,
in the face of a growing entrepreneurial class, without reform of
the political structure? Considered purely as a concept and without
value judgment, the most successful model of ideological organization for a non-state player, with the desirable attributes of flexibility
and influence in the age of global media, has proved to be the network structure of Al Qaeda.[2]

The zeitgeist of the age of globalization has been an acceler-
ating trend toward decentralization. A striking example of genius
in innovation is the network model, the polar opposite of a rigid

governmental bureaucracy. The network has flexibility and adaptability, and it makes innovative use of modern communications and transportation. Even though branches (or franchises as they are called on cable television news outlets) operate on slim budgets, the network has been the bane of counterterror experts and law enforcement the world over. It is responsive. It has the ability to swarm manpower to a locus for an event and afterward return to its original shape. It is efficient and responsive and it makes the best use of human, financial, technological, and intellectual resources.

The pre-Olympic crackdown of March 2008 illustrated that the protests have an ethnic component. Perhaps there is also a component of the protests that objects to specific policies, but until the ethnic question is resolved, no amount of force will improve the situation. For sixty years the Chinese have foundered on the shoals of the ethnic question, a result of their own long history and more recent ideology.

International history is a library of political models. The reference for unwinding communism in a post-communist Asian state is already on the shelves. The case study is the government of Mohammed Najibullah installed by Moscow in 1987 after Soviet armed forces departed Afghanistan. "The Najibullah government was able to survive because Najibullah recognized the futility of the early Soviet strategy in Afghanistan. Afghans, he knew, would not fight and die for the Soviet Union." Najibullah realized that a successful strategy lay in winning over local and clan interests. He dropped "the more radical social engineering programs previously championed by the Afghan communist leadership.... [The government] moved away from Marxist reforms from above, embraced Islam as the state religion... [and pursued a program of] quiet modernization rather than reforms from above.... [They] placated local interests, keeping the state's army and state security."[3]

These policies harkened back to traditional Afghan statecraft. Najibullah did not survive for two reasons: the flow of Saudi and American money into the resistance and support for the mujahideen from the ISI, the Pakistan government's intelligence agency in the Pakistani capital of Islamabad. When the USSR imploded in 1991, Soviet aid to Najibullah's government ended and he fell from power.

The fact remains that he was successful for a time in co-opting the Afghan resistance. The analogy to the Tibetan case is obvious: Co-opt the resistance by harkening back to traditional Tibetan statecraft, adapting to present circumstances, and accommodating modern realities.

Longtime Pakistan watcher, journalist, and novelist Tariq Ali has advocated a regional solution for South Asia from the Muslim perspective. Strengthening the regional body would strengthen Pakistan's government. This can only be a positive outcome, as the central government is threatened by takeover from extremists and this causes concern throughout the world community about Pakistan's nuclear arsenal. A regional system of cooperation could provide jobs and this alternative to a career in jihad funded by narcotics money is a better alternative. If China's chief ally in the region is amenable to the regional approach, this is a benefit to China, in practical terms and in terms of prestige.

The hard line employed by the Chinese leadership in the period after the Tibetan Uprising of 1987 exacerbated tensions. The leadership blamed liberalization for fomenting separatism, but the periods of uprisings merely let the valve open to release the steam pent up by failed policies. Since then, China has made some progress. For the first time in the PRC's history, the leaders of all the autonomous regions have ethnic backgrounds. Even so, the top party positions in Tibet are filled by Han Chinese. The leadership wants to illustrate the "Harmonious Society" with affirmative action in government bodies, but it also wants to retain firm control of the Party.

The Tibetan Uprising of 2008 and the subsequent crackdown indicate that reform has not gone far enough in Tibet. Dexter Filkins spent a year reporting on the ground in Afghanistan. In a 2009 television interview, he observed what the American generals have stated about Afghanistan. "You cannot kill your way out of an insurgency. You have to make friends. You have to develop economically and politically."[4]

China is not a perfect state, as the protests over Tibet have shown. Nationalism is the glue that holds the country together, now that faith in communism has waned. China's citizens know that they are propagandized and make allowances for it. China has problems related to the rapid and uneven economic development in China brought about by market reforms. The growth of business has outstripped the growth of business ethics.

It is difficult to imagine, but across China within the past few years, there have been approximately 80,000 protests a year. The issues that create the protests are crony capitalism, the privilege of the princelings (sons and daughters of the Party), the end of the old social safety net, rural-urban inequalities, unrest associated with minority rights, and poor environmental management at the periphery in the service of economic development in the center. The protests add up to what the leadership fears most: social chaos. This is exactly the opposite of what the Party wants, which is social stability and order. The Party is in favor of a harmonious society.

Making Win-Win Work

Reforms that pertain to Tibet concern freedom of religion, a federal system for minorities, and protection of the environment. Much of the world is well aware of the terrible environmental problems in China proper. What is less well known are the consequences of decades of bad policy on the environment in Tibet. In fact, its water has come to the fore as an issue in the global environmental movement. Five of Asia's major rivers have their source in the mountains of Tibet, which could thus be called the water tower for three billion people. There has been much commentary on the subject of using Tibet's natural resources to fuel economic development at the coast. Far less notice has been given to the downstream flooding caused by excessive logging in the Yangzi Basin headwaters.

Because the Chinese have the monopoly of force, they could choose to simply wait in Tibet. Yet even if they wait for the Dalai Lama to die, this would not solve the ethnic question. Any hand-picked successor would not be able to rally the people. In China's calculations so far, the old ideology has distorted modern perception of the ethnic problem.

Although there is distrust between the Chinese and the Dalai Lama, his death might mean the loss of a great opportunity on the Chinese side. For Tibetans, the Dalai Lama is the symbol of their culture. If he returns and accepts Chinese sovereignty, his return would guarantee peace in Tibet and bring the loyalty of the Tibetan masses—loyalty that the Chinese have sought since the time of Chairman Mao. The old lamaist system is gone. In its stead would be a new governmental form, one that could be tolerated just as the government of Hong Kong is now tolerated within the Chinese system.

An analysis of Chinggis Khan's government shows that Tibet was not conquered by force of arms but rather it submitted to Chinggis Khan as a vassal state. Tibet was never garrisoned. Its lamas became teachers to the Khans, the beginning of the *chö-yon* (priest–patron) relationship that lasted through three Chinese dynasties. Although Tibet became a tribute state, the Mongols never ruled it directly. Local forms of rule prevailed.

The "loose reins" system was drawn from Chinese experience and the Chinese system. Its inventor was Confucian in his public life and practiced Buddhism in his private life. His goal was to ameliorate the harsher aspects of Mongol rule. He correctly assessed the character of Chinggis Khan and did not appeal to his compassion but to his self-interest and his desire for revenue. In all conquered areas, the Mongols maintained order by installing a military governor (*darugachi*) and a garrison of troops. Tibet was a special case and had neither governor nor garrison. Free trade was the hallmark of the Mongol Empire, and religious toleration was guaranteed by The Conqueror himself and ensured by his heirs and successors. The main duty of the Mongol military governor was taking a census for the purposes of assessing taxes (remitted to the central government) and assigning unpaid labor and military service. This approach— preserving local culture and continuing the local government for local populations—was successful for a century.

The communist government instituted in Tibet after the 1959 Uprising was a "tight reins" system. The CCP attempted to impose a system of thought and ideology down to the most basic level, that of individual conscience. Social engineering in Tibet had as its goal the creation of a new Tibetan, the new model of the socialist man, as he was called. The goal of creating the revolutionary hero devoted to the welfare of the masses was memorialized in countless plays and posters. The posters featured red-cheeked youths in Mao caps and jackets, staring off into the dawn of a new socialist era. This Marxist utopian project resulted in the most intrusive system in all of Chinese history. Totalitarian attempts at thought control, as practiced in the study sessions and the criticism sessions of the Cultural Revolution era, conflicted with a bedrock truth: The Tibetan identity is bound up with Buddhism, religion, art, culture, costume, food. It's a mix— one doesn't have to be a lama to be a Buddhist.

In traditional times, nothing like this communist system of thought control existed. The social engineering has been a failure. Direct rule has been a failure, despite massive investment by the Chinese and the best of intentions, namely, the improvement of a backward region.

Centralized rule has also created problems in Tibet. In the closely held decisions made by top leadership, one encounters the center versus periphery contradiction. Seen from the capital of China, Tibet is a security risk, a poor stepchild on the dangerous multi-ethnic frontier. From the viewpoint of this frontier, however, Tibet is a potentially vibrant center of regional trade.

These are not new ideas; they have been discussed for a century by everyone from the Thirteenth Dalai Lama to the early Chinese communist leaders. The early theorists of communism in the 1920s believed in a Chinese Federal Republic and believed a federal structure would create harmony with the ethnic nationalities. This belief was deeply influenced by the original Leninist model, which advocated a federal solution for the minorities within the Soviet Union.

Given the early problems in development and his encounter with minorities during the Long March, Mao abandoned these ideas and pursued a solution that was more geopolitical than domestic. The colonial era featured Western colonial expansion into South Asia, and the later Cold War polarization forced a simplistic alignment in the region: Russia backed India and China backed Pakistan, while China had disputes over its long borders with both Russia and India. Tibet, formerly a remote Himalayan country, became a pawn in the game, in colonial as well as Cold War times. Both eras have come to an end. This is a unique historical moment and China and Tibet can both benefit by taking advantage of it.

A relaxation of Chinese central planning in Tibet would parallel the successful reforms enacted in China's Special Economic Zones. These zones (SEZs) have liberal economic policies as well as governmental regulations, for the specific purpose of developing trade and improving the climate for foreign business. They are especially developed along the east coast of China. Since the early 1990s, the government designated a number of border cities as well as provincial capitals and capitals of autonomous regions as SEZs. These are areas where trade is integrated with science and technology, an approach that would make Tibet a regional leader. Tibet might be designated as a Special Ethnic, Trade, and Ecological Zone (SETEZ). This gradual approach to the emergence of a market economy would require loosening the reins of the command economy. Flexibility and adaptivity have proven to be positive assets in the economic sphere. There is no reason why they should not prove to be virtues in the realm of minority relations, too.

Aside from issues of cultural expression and religious freedom, as economic development improves the standard of living and the status of ethnic Tibetans inside Tibet, the problem of unrest will diminish. Black-market economic activities such as smuggling, along with banditry, a time-honored occupation in the cross-border Himalayan region—could be curtailed through modern technology combined with border policing, a task for which the Chinese are well-equipped. With profits on the line for both sides, Tibetan cooperation would be a matter of self-interest. The Tibetans would have something to gain from the new arrangement.

The model for Chinese political reform that is most often cited these days in the upper echelons of the Party's think tanks is that of the European Union, not that of the Canadian commonwealth or the United States. The EU structure is a regional model—shifting to the EU paradigm could create a win-win situation for China and Tibet. If China needs a geopolitical presence in South Asia in keeping with changing situations on the ground, then it could do no better than to reconstitute and expand the region's traditional trade patterns.

South Asia has entered a new historical period. With three nuclear powers in the region, China faces security risks that cannot be met solely by its conventional army. Pakistan's government has been seriously threatened by extremists. India has been vulnerable to many terrorist attacks, culminating in the Mumbai massacre of 2008. The solution to the Tibet Question is in China's security interests as well as in Tibetan ethnic interests. In fact, China has improved its relationships with India and Russia and has made progress on resolving border disputes with both.

In the wake of the terrorist attack in Mumbai, there is a real need to counteract the criminal element that has flourished within the region's expanding and highly profitable narcotics trade. Only by encouraging a robust legal trade can the black-market economy be starved out of existence. China is successfully exporting goods into Central Asia—Tibet could contribute to an already present trend. ABC's Chief Foreign News Correspondent Martha Raddatz has traveled frequently to Afghanistan and has made many appearances on the *Charlie Rose* show discussing the war. As she commented during a December 2009 appearance, "You can't look at the region through a straw."

China is already looking at the big picture. It should expand its view to include a different concept of Tibet's role.

❦

China must take an extremely important factor into consideration. The generational force is operating inside Tibet, China, and indeed the entire region. This may well be a force for secularism. The younger generation is also responsive to the revolution that technology has brought worldwide. The Himalayas of the twenty-first century are not the Himalayas of sixty years ago. One way or another, it's bye-bye to Shangri-la. Tibet has been searching a modern identity for more than century. It can no longer be merely a failed communist experiment, a museum of the Buddhist past, or the baby seal of the human rights movement.

Another phenomenon among the young in China is the new malaise brought about by materialism. Many of the religious tourists to Tibet are Chinese seeking spiritual insight, a break from the new materialism of capitalist China. China has also witnessed the rise of Tibetan pop stars, including one young woman whose song's refrain is *"Om mane padme hum"*—the Tibetan Buddhist mantra. Times have changed, and contradictions abound. Nothing is as it was.

China has always viewed itself as the center of influence in Asia. It modern times it has emerged as a regional power. In conjunction with the Association of Southeast Asian Nations (ASEAN), China is progressing toward creating the largest free-trade zone in the world: China has been a major player in the six-party talks among North Asian states and North Korea.

The creation of a common market—an economic union in South Asia—would usher in a new historical era (and one that replicates with China's traditional model as the Middle Kingdom). If properly implemented, a South Asian economic union would satisfy China's security needs as well as Tibet's concerns about human rights. Thus, the stalemate of a zero-sum game could be replaced with the mutual benefits of a win-win resolution.

The South Asian Common Market would include those Himalayan states that have traditionally been the trading partners of Tibet, formerly Buddhist kingdoms that look to Tibet as a cultural and religious center. These smaller states are the ones that Britain sought to influence in colonial days: Sikkim, Nepal, and Bhutan. This regional common market would also include India, Pakistan, Bangladesh, Sri Lanka, and Afghanistan.

This idea of Tibet as a regional and local leader in the realm of culture and economics represents a restoration of a traditional regional pattern, the first restoration of balance since the end of the Great Game and the Cold War. This is a rare historic moment for the region to reconstitute itself. Russia's push to the South is at an end; Great Britain is gone from the scene. And despite its long-time alliance with Pakistan, China's relationship with India has improved tremendously over the last decade.

The new presence in the region is the United States in Afghanistan. Experts on the scene conclude that economic and political development should be the region's utmost priority, particularly to combat the Afghan narcotics trade and to counteract the extremism that flows, in part, from Pakistan's poor educational system.

As with most historical "tipping points," timing is key. There is but a small window of opportunity, and the situation is tricky.

The instability of Pakistan, the war in Afghanistan, the religious extremism among ethnic groups on the AfPak border and in the Central Asian states—all these factors suggest that a stabilizing force in the region would mitigate the rising problems of displacement, unemployment, and drug-related crime. In an age when weapons are a prized commodity, the resurgence of the ancient career of smuggling is another worrisome and destabilizing phenomenon. It bears repeating that there are three nuclear states in South Asia: China, Pakistan, and India. According to the U.S. Central Intelligence Agency, the greatest likelihood of a nuclear war would be one between India and Pakistan. The mediation of a regional body would allow China to play the role of a balancing force, as it has so often and so successfully with North Korea.

The region is truly at a crossroads. China sits at the intersection of national (domestic) interests, strategic international interests, and human rights abuses. Will China have the courage to come up with a smart power solution? Note that a regional body—such as the South Asian Common Market proposed here—would allow disputes among the three nuclear powers to be settled in the normal course of business, thereby eliminating the need for hypernationalist rhetoric or saber rattling. Tibet, with its tradition of nonviolence, is the perfect regional leader. It is reasonable to suppose that granting Tibetans local control over their own affairs (under the control of the central Chinese government) would resolve the international community's objections to the human rights abuses in Tibet. This would be a public relations victory for China, but there are other benefits as well. Once the human rights questions are resolved by the new autonomy, the World Bank, the Asian Development Bank, and the International Monetary Fund, as well as private capital, would have the way cleared for participation in the Tibetan economy.

A Question of Leadership

Will China wait for its fifth generation of leadership, as the Soviet Union waited for Gorbachev, to make the necessary reforms? One hopes not.

Important China watchers describe the fourth generation of leaders as

> determined modernizers, intent on integrating China's economy with the rest of the world and on maintaining good relations with the United States. They are competent managers with wide experience in China's complex party-state bureaucracy and pragmatic technocrats who are capable of keeping order and promoting development in the world's most populous country. Some of them are willing to subject the ruling Chinese Communist Party to political competition and to trust the state-controlled Chinese media, including the press, radio and television with more freedom to criticize the performance of lower level officials.[5]

These are hard men who believe in authoritarian control to push China through its passage to modernization. They may share Western economic values, but it would be foolish to assume that they share Western moral values—including sympathy for Tibet. This is a dilemma.

Another China scholar Cheng Li believes that the CCP "will face three major challenges in the years to come. The first comes from the need to change its poor international image; the second challenge will result from the changes in Chinese society itself; and the third challenge will come from the new Chinese leadership."[6] Will a new vision of the future triumph over patterns of the past? Will pragmatism finally triumph over ideology in the realm of minority relations, as it has in the economic realm? Only time will tell.

Chinese negotiating behavior requires, at the beginning of a negotiation, an adherence to certain principles. This is how they test the seriousness of their negotiating partners.[7] Once these principles are agreed to, the Chinese become relaxed about the terms of the agreement and the implementation of details. They often prolong a negotiation to test their counterparts' positions and/or employ a series of tactics to gain agreement to their own position. Henry Kissinger has commented on the Chinese method in the various volumes of his memoirs. China's discussions with the United States concerning Taiwan and the normalization of diplomatic relations took decades, and there were many ups and downs.

From the Tibetan perspective, a stumbling block to negotiations has concerned Kham and Amdo, regions that have been incorporated into Chinese administrative units for many decades. Because these areas are ethnically Tibetan, and because in an earlier historical era they belonged to Tibet, the Tibetan Government in Exile claims them as part of Tibet. This dispute goes back to the Simla Convention of 1914. In a speech made on the anniversary of his departure from Tibet, the Dalai Lama stated that Premier Zhou Enlai had said it would be a good idea to incorporate all of the Tibetan areas into one autonomous region. Certainly this would make sense to the diaspora Tibetans, many of whom hail from Kham and Amdo.[8]

Although it would be natural and desirable to unite all those of Tibetan ethnicity, this demand should not become a sticking point, an obstacle to negotiations. The issue could be tabled for future negotiations. Lobsang Sangay, the Harvard-trained Tibetan-American lawyer, in a speech made at an Association for Asian Studies conference in April of 2007, pointed out that the rights of ethnic Tibetans in the majority Tibetan areas of the Chinese provinces of Qinghai, Yunnan, Gansu, and Sichuan are protected under the Chinese constitution and under provincial and county governmental structures relating to minorities. Tibetans in these regions should be allowed to participate in any economic, political, and educational reforms instituted in Central Tibet.

The Chinese might then be able to compromise on several other points—for example, instituting Tibetan as a language in education and government. Around the world there are many recent instances of bilingual education policies. Sangay advocated this as the road to improving economic opportunity for Tibetans and alleviating the systemic inequities that result from promoting Han Chinese over Tibetans in government. If Chinese is a language that would help Tibetans get ahead in a wider sphere, then Tibetans should have the opportunity to learn it. Should Tibetans have to study and take exams in college subjects in Chinese, a second language? Surely this can be perceived as a handicap. Surely it must grate on the nerves to see an "outsider" getting ahead in one's own country, in a language not native to the country.

Another important point of compromise would be for China to reverse its policy of promoting the immigration to Tibet of Han Chinese and Hui "guest workers." The Tibetan Plateau cannot sustain the large influx of outside populations. Immigrants also have problems with altitude sickness because they lack the Tibetans' biological adaptation to the environment. These and other reforms policies were recommended as early as the 1970s—following the Cultural Revolution—by Party Secretary Hu Yaobang.

In implementing to the "loose reins" model of a workable autonomy for Tibet, China's leadership would have legal authority under Article 31 of the Chinese Constitution. This article sets forth the creation and definition of Special Administrative Regions and avoids the pitfalls of Article 4 of the 1982 Constitution and China's Law on Regional National Autonomy (LRNA), both of which are based on the Marxist analysis of minorities.[9]

The hard liners in the Chinese Politburo are fond of saying that the Uprising of 1987 resulted from the liberalization policies of Hu Yaobang. They heap blame upon him for fostering ideas of Tibetan independence. One could as easily argue that the hard-line policy instituted after the uprising has brought about a similar result. After all, the protests in the period leading up to the 2008 Olympics were the worst since 1959. Perhaps the problem is not the liberalization itself, but rather that liberalization allowed the expression of Tibetan resentments fostered by Chinese policies.

In a recent book, Robert Thurman, professor of Buddhist Studies at Columbia, remarks that the Dalai Lama's suggestions for Tibetan development follow the Swiss model—especially with regards to promoting Tibet as a healing center.[10] Tibetan medicine has a long and illustrious tradition of healing and it was a strong influence on traditional Chinese medicine. Such an industry could almost certainly work for Tibet. This idea is part of a trend that reflects the world community's interest in traditional medicine as an alternative to Western medicine. Not far away, in India's hi-tech center of Bangalore, a former film star has created a new resort and spa that offers Ayurvedic medicine to seekers with an interest in traditional and alternative medicine.

The Dalai Lama has a love of nature and has often discussed his concern for Tibet's unique biosphere. With an emphasis on restoration of the environment of the Tibetan Plateau and with a focus on environmental protection, Tibet could become a zone of sustainable eco-tourism. This approach has proved successful in such places as Costa Rica, where the rainforest is a huge tourist attraction.

As a lecturer in Tibetan Buddhism, Thurman is aware of the draw and attraction that this spiritual tradition has for people all over the globe. He has detailed an idea for the development of a world-class tourist infrastructure in Tibet. This would require an upgrade from the fourth-rate tourist infrastructure developed under socialism. The present industry in Tibet mostly benefits Han Chinese. What is needed instead is a Tibetan-hosted tourist industry for the seekers of the world in need of healing—whether of the physical, spiritual, environmental, or psychological variety. Thurman has put forth an original proposal for the diversification of the Tibetan economy into new micro-industries, such as Himalayan water and salt, and the packaging of traditional medicines. Gourmet salt from Pakistan's high mountains is already marketed successfully in gourmet shops and natural foods stores in the West, and such diversification could end Tibet's dependence on the markets for animal products and crafts. All of Thurman's suggested industries would employ economies of scale and sustainable development, in keeping with the environmentally friendly vision of Tibet.

How can such visions be financed? Even with the world economic crisis, there are many financial agencies whose interest in Tibet could be spurred once human rights concerns were eliminated. Given the attention now being paid to the Asian water problem and the issues of deforestation and glacier melt, it would seem that the World Bank, the International Monetary Fund, the Asian Development Bank, and private foreign investment could all have a vital interest in providing the capital necessary to create a Tibetan zone of prosperity.

With respect to Buddhist art, a simple solution has been overlooked. The Chinese urged the United Nations Educational, Scientific and Cultural Organization (UNESCO) to set up a heritage committee. In 1999, China became a member of that World

Heritage Committee (WHC) and began working with it to restore and protect Buddhist sites, such as Dunhuang in Xinjiang. There is a huge traffic in illegal and illicit antiquities, and as many as 300,000 archaeological sites in China are candidates for excavation. Tibetan Buddhist sites could and should come under existing WHC protection, with the cooperation of the Heritage Preservation Department of the PRC's Ministry of Culture.

❦

No agreement will satisfy all the desires of all sides. This is the nature of compromise. There are many who will find fault with one or another of the suggestions put forth here. Any viable road map will naturally require certain conditions, aims, goals, and structure before meaningful negotiations can take place.

China's security needs must be safeguarded, that is a given; but postponing negotiations is no answer because of the new and serious threats to the region from narcotics and extremism. Experts among the Chinese leadership are well aware that they must reform the behemoth of the Leninist state. One reason is that China and the Chinese state apparatus must respond to rapid technological change—a revolution in itself. Reform in Tibet will be just as pragmatic as Deng's economic reforms and will fulfill some of the goals set out by Mao Zedong, among them the goal of permanent revolution.

In China, opinion among the leadership is divided. Moderates in China disagree with the assumptions underlying the hard-line approach, for the very simple and pragmatic reason that the hard line has not produced the stability China desires. The sentiment among moderates in the leadership is that Chinese long-term interests would be better served by returning to an ethnically sensitive model for Tibet. The concept of Tibet as an inland province—one that is re-integrated into the regional economy and that can develop an export strategy to all regional markets—would raise the Tibet Question to a level of strategic *economic* thinking.

ACKNOWLEDGMENTS

This work summarizes eight hundred years of history. While the modernization of ancient cultures is the subject of countless works of scholarship in many languages this volume concentrates on people and events, and the complex interaction of countries in the region in the context of global history.

China has been China for a very long time, and its unity has been the obsession of emperors for many centuries. The imperial bureaucrats who conducted China's foreign policy focused on its Inner Asian frontiers, the minority regions, far more than on its maritime coast in the east. The reasons are simple: Until recent times, China was not an oceangoing nation, and Inner Asia was where the threats emerged. Tibet is part of a pattern that goes back for centuries. This is the context that forms the view of this book. The general reader will come to understand the dynamics of China's interaction with its neighbors. This context makes sense of the present and creates a backdrop for diplomacy in the future

I based twenty years of research on the Mongol Empire on the scholarship of Morris Rossabi, the biographer of Khubilai Khan. The importance of the Mongol Empire, the research trail blazed by Rossabi, formed the core of my thinking and is the origin of this book.

Aside from the Mongol Empire, from my student days, I have been fascinated by China's struggle with modernity, its pre-eminence in imperial times, its disastrous fall, and its struggle to be reborn in the modern world.

Many of the world's problem spots can be traced back to the British Empire and, at the fall of empire, to a Brit with a map and a marker pen. Groups of supremely confident colonial officials used a pen to divvy up the world on maps created by men like Colonel Francis Younghusband, whose expedition included many cartographers. This is true in South Asia, at the Northwest Frontier region on the Pakistan-Afghan border, of the McMahon line that formed the border between India and China, in the Southern Himalayas because the British made it their business to insert themselves in the relationship between China and Tibet. When one examines the history, one realizes that an appreciation of the role of the British is important in understanding modern Tibet. Russian imperialism in North and Central Asia took place over a period of two centuries, as Russia expanded its borders eastward to the Pacific—first under the czars and subsequently under their successor governments. The expansion of Russia into Asia, into China's traditional sphere of influence, created a fear and loathing of foreign imperialism among the Chinese leadership throughout the twentieth century, from the imperial system through the Nationalists to the Communists. The systems of government may have changed but the Sino-Russian struggle for dominance on the Asian continent did not.

This book is built upon the work of giants in the field, and I am indebted to all of them—particularly Hans Bielenstein, former Chairman of the Department of East Asian Languages and Literature at Columbia University, William Theodore DeBary for Chinese history and Burton Watson for Chinese and Buddhist intellectual history. In the field of Indian history, I am indebted to Ainslie Embree of Columbia. I owe a great debt to Robert Thurman for insight into Buddhist thought and into Tibetan history and culture.

The bibliography is extensive but partial. The notes point in the right direction, but there is no way to attribute ideas gained over decades of reading to any one source. Errors and omissions are my own. Academic specialists use a narrow focus and my apologies to them for giving their subjects a general treatment. It simply is not possible to go into detail—richly deserved—in a work of this length.

In order to make narrative sense of complex international history, I have employed the techniques of the novelist, the compression of time, the weaving of story lines and the portraiture of individuals.

I wish to thank my editor, Luba Ostashevsky, for the insight and experience she has brought to bear upon the subject. Luba's assistant Laura Lancaster provided invaluable help in navigating the complexities of acquiring images.

I am indebted to my very first editor, Hugh Van Dusen, for reminding me to keep the narrative flowing. Alan Furst told me that my working title was a clunker and suggested a better one. I am lucky to have the unfailing support of my literary agent, Alex Hoyt. My mother Cathie Grossman does not understand my obsession but loves me. My very close friend Scott Smith understands my obsession. I am grateful to Annie Adams Laumont for giving me a base in New York, with a view of the Hudson River, from which to conduct my research.

❧

A note on the English spelling of foreign words. I follow the current standard Pinyin romanization of Chinese names and place names; thus, for example, I use Chinggis Khan instead of Genghis Khan (Chinggis is the romanization that approximates Mongolian pronunciation, whereas Genghis is the Persianized spelling). For historical names, such as place names, I have used the standard rendering. For names that are familiar from history, I have used the standard spelling. For names familiar from modern history, I have followed Jonathan Spence in eliminating the hyphens from Chinese first names. All of this is an attempt at simplification for the reader.

ONLINE RESOURCES

Portraits

Chinggis Khan: http://afe.easia.columbia.edu/mongols/figures/figures.htm

Kangxi and Qianlong Emperors: http://www.learn.columbia.edu/nanxuntu/html/emperors/

Key Figures: http://afe.easia.columbia.edu/mongols/pop/figures/images_fig.htm

Khubilai Khan: http://afe.easia.columbia.edu/mongols/pop/khubilai/images_kk.htm

Ming Emperors: Hongwu: http://en.wikipedia.org/wiki/File:Hongwu1.jpg; Yongle: http://en.wikipedia.org/wiki/File:Yongle-Emperor1.jpg

Qianlong Emperor, *On Tibetan Buddhism* (1792), Calligraphy handscroll in Chinese, Manchu, and Mongolian (Palace Museum, Beijing): http://www.threeemperors.org.uk/index.php?pid=51

Maps

The empire at the time of Chinggis Khan's death: http://www.nationalgeographic.com/genghis/khanmap.html

Yuan Dynasty as well maps showing the relative sizes of Chinese dynasties: http://www.artsmia.org/art-of-asia/history/yuan-dynasty-map.cfm

Ming Dynasty: http://www.artsmia.org/art-of-asia/history/dynasty-ming.cfm

Qing Dynasty: http://www.artsmia.org/art-of-asia/history/dynasty-ching.cfm

Maps and Images of Tibet

The Tibet Album (British Photography 1920–1950): http://tibet.prm.ox.ac.uk/index.php

Links to various maps and images of Tibet: http://www.ciolek.com/WWWVLPages/TibPages/tib-maps.html

Ethnic Tibet (map embedded in Shakya's reply, "Blood in the Snows," to Wang Lixiong): http://newleftreview.org/?view=2388

U.S. Cartoon of Chairman Mao as Religious Figure

Sixth image, in right-hand column: http://www.loc.gov/rr/print/swann/valt-man/presentation.html

Compare with image of Qianlong Emperor as a bodhisattva: http://www.learn.columbia.edu/nanxuntu/html/emperors/manjusri.htm

Tibet Justice Center

http://www.tibetjustice.org

Complete collection of documents pertaining to Tibet, including Simla Agreement and Seventeen Point Agreement: http://www.tibetjustice.org/materials/#key

TIBETAN TIMELINE

The Imperial Period

7th to 9th century A.D.: Tibet is unified under King Songtsen Gampo. The dynasty lasts for two centuries. During Tibet's imperial period, its borders expand to include Xinjiang province to the north, parts of modern Ladakh and Kashmir to the west, and Amdo and Kham—parts of today's Chinese provinces of Gansu, Qinghai, Sichuan, and Yunnan. Diplomatic relations begin between China and Tibet. Tang China pays tribute to Tibet. When China ceases to pay, Tibetan forces seize Changan (modern Xi'an), the cosmopolitan and international capital of the Tang Dynasty.

822–823: Tibet and China sign treaties and fix the borders between them; a stone pillar in Lhasa memorializes these events. During the imperial period, China and Tibet are two distinct and separate states.

9th century: Buddhism comes to Tibet. Finding itself at odds with the native Bon religion (a shamanist faith), Buddhism struggles to establish itself. Religious conflict causes the Tibetan dynasty to collapse.

10th century: The Tang Dynasty comes to an end in China. Formal political relations between China and Tibet cease until the thirteenth century.

The Medieval Period

1207: Tibet submits to the Mongol Empire under Chinggis Khan without war; Tibet pays tribute to Chinggis Khan. The Mongol Army does not invade Tibet, nor does it place a garrison or military governor there, as it does throughout the rest of its empire.

1240: Ogodei Khan succeeds his father, Chinggis, as Supreme Khan of the Mongol Empire. Tibet fails to send its tribute to the Mongol capital. Ogodei orders the Mongol Army, cavalry forces commanded by his son Godan, into Tibet. Godan's forces advance much of the way to Lhasa and loot monasteries; they also collect intelligence on the political scene in Tibet.

1244: From southwest China (modern Gansu), Godan Khan summons the Sakya Pandit, head of the Sakya sect of Tibetan Buddhism, to the Mongol camp. Godan's camp was both the seat of government and a military camp, as was usually the case with the Mongol Khans.

1247: Sakya Pandit submits Tibet to Mongol rule and in return is recognized as the local ruler of Tibet, a subordinate of the Mongols. This is the beginning of the tradition of investing lamas of the ruling sect as regents or rulers of Tibet.

The Sakya Pandit reportedly cures Godan of leprosy and then converts the imperial Mongol prince to the Buddhist faith. The Pandit promises that Tibet will pay tribute—the beginning of the priest - patron relationship. Tibet's clerics are to provide religious instruction, while the Mongol Khans take the role of defenders of the faith. The Pandit and his nephew, Phagpa, take up residence in a Buddhist monastery in the Chinese capital, and Phagpa comes to the notice of Khubilai Khan. The two Tibetan clerics are, in effect, hostages. Their presence in the capital assured the Mongols of Tibet's loyalty.

1260: Khubilai Khan becomes Supreme Khan of the Mongol Empire and founds the Yuan Dynasty in China. Khubilai experiments with Chinese Buddhism but finds Tibetan Buddhism more to his liking. Khubilai creates the post of Imperial Tutor for the Phagpa Lama, the Sakya lineage of Tibetan Buddhism receives imperial Mongol recognition as the ruling lineage of Tibet and the Phagpa Lama eventually retires from court and becomes the regent of Tibet. Under Khubilai Khan, the government of China creates a Bureau of Tibetan and Buddhist Affairs.

Historians and other Tibetan nationalists interpret this history to mean that both China and Tibet were conquered by the Mongols and came under Mongol rule. Thus, both China and Tibet emerged from Mongol rule. By contrast, the view of the PRC is that Mongol history proves the validity of China's claim to Tibet because Tibet became a protectorate of China during the Yuan Dynasty.

14th century: The great reforming monk Tsongkapa founds the Gelugpa order (sect), later to become the leading order of Tibetan Buddhism and the one that was to produce the Dalai Lamas. The Gelugpa are known as the Yellow Hat sect, in contrast to the Red Hat sects (the Sakya, Kagyu, and Nyingma schools of Tibetan Buddhism).

15th and 16th century: Rival warlords and their monastic supporters engage in civil war in Tibet. The Mongols come to the aid of the Dalai Lama, and his Gelugpa order becomes the ruling sect in Tibet—they replace the Sakya, the sect in ascendance during the time of Khubilai Khan. This marks the beginning of the period when the Dalai Lamas serve as spiritual and temporal rulers of Tibet. The Mongols convert to Buddhism and pledge their allegiance to the Yellow Hat order; from this time forward, the Mongols are closely associated with the Dalai Lama. This close alliance between the lamas and the khans becomes important during the Ming and Qing Dynasties in China. (During the seventeenth and eighteenth centuries, Tibet plays a key role in Qing politics and warfare by serving as mediators for the Qing with the Buddhist Mongols.)

1644: The Qing Dynasty comes to power in China. It is a dynasty installed by the conquering Manchus, who employ Han Chinese, the traditional Confucian literati class, as the governing bureaucracy.

1656: The Fifth Dalai Lama visits Beijing at the invitation of the Qing Emperor. The Tibetan ruler has the Qoshot Mongols as his military backers and a huge following among the Mongol tribes. There is no submission to the Qing, and the Tibetan ruler remains powerful among those who represent a threat to the Qing Emperor.

1682: Dzungar Mongols (associated with the Dalai Lama) attempt to unify all Mongols under their rule and eventually defeat the eastern Mongols, the Khalkas.

1696: The Qing Dynasty is victorious over Dzungar Mongols at the battle of the Kalalun River in Mongolia. The Dzungars no longer represent a threat to the Chinese Dragon Throne.

1717: Qing becomes embroiled in Tibetan politics as Dzungar Mongols conquer Tibet and sack Lhasa. The Seventh Dalai Lama is installed. The Qing Emperor sends an army into Tibet; although this army is defeated by the Dzungars, the Kangxi Emperor still views Tibet as a buffer state for western China. The Qing army ousts the Dzungars in 1720, ending twenty years of political turmoil, and garrison Lhasa with several thousand troops.

The importance of protecting Qing interests against both British and Russian imperial interests (in South Asia and North Asia, respectively) motivates Qing interference in Tibetan affairs and their stationing of an *amban* (bureaucratic official) in Lhasa to protect the Qing sphere of influence on its southwestern flank. For the rest of the eighteenth century, the Qing seeks to protect its national interests by exerting control over Tibet; by the end of the century, the Qing has sent armed forces into Tibet on three more occasions.

1724: Qing Dynasty appoints an *amban* to reside in Lhasa and annexes parts of Kham and Amdo provinces.

1728: Panchen Lama is given control of south and southwestern Tibet (Tsang). The Lhasa government controls less territory as a result of annexations and divisions, a Qing strategy to weaken Tibet by reducing its territory.

1750: Rebellion against amban put down by Chinese garrison in Lhasa.

1788 and 1792: Nepalese Ghurkas invade Tibet. Qing sends troops to protect Tibet.

1793: By Qing imperial decree, henceforth the Chinese *amban* will supervise the selection of senior lamas and the Dalai Lama.

Era of the Great Game: Western Colonial Powers in Asia

1850s: The British colonial empire in South Asia vies with the czarist Russian colonial empire in North Asia in the Great Game for influence on the continent. Tibet closes its borders and bans foreigners.

1865: Britain sends Indians in disguise to map Tibet.

1904: Colonel Francis Younghusband is ordered by Lord Curzon (British viceroy in India) to initiate trade relations with Tibet. Killing hundreds of Tibetans, Younghusband forces Tibet to sign a trading agreement; in response, the Dalai Lama flees.

1906: Britain promises not to interfere in Tibet and signs the British-Chinese convention. The Chinese government pays the Tibetan indemnity to Great Britain.

1907: Both Great Britain and czarist Russia formally acknowledge Chinese suzerainty in Tibet.

1912: The Republican Revolution in China brings down the Qing Dynasty. Chinese troops in Tibet surrender. The Thirteenth Dalai Lama returns from India and declares Tibetan independence, ousting the Chinese *amban* and garrison.

1920s to 1940s: Chinese Nationalists attempt to control Tibet but fail to do so. The Nationalists lose the civil war in the late 1940s.

The Communist Period

1949: Mao Zedong announces the founding of the People's Republic of China as well as his plans for the "peaceful liberation" of Tibet. Chinese unity is now a major goal after the disunity that characterized the warlord period, the Chinese civil war between the Nationalists and the Communists, and the Japanese invasion of 1937–1945.

1950: The People's Liberation Army enters eastern Tibet. The Tibetan provincial forces—no match for the PLA's seasoned troops—surrender.

1951: The Seventeen Point Agreement is signed in Beijing. It guarantees Tibetan autonomy, freedom of religion, and provides for the preservation of the traditional Tibetan government, but it also gives China the right to conduct foreign policy and the responsibility of providing for Tibetan security.

Early 1950s: The Honeymoon Period. At this time, the young Fourteenth Dalai Lama thought Buddhism and Marxism could co-exist: He believed that communism could improve the lot of the Tibetan people in material terms by bringing modernization to Tibet.

This was the period when Mao went slow in bringing socialism to Tibet and courted the elites.

1954–1955: The Dalai Lama spends six months in Beijing, meets with Mao, and takes part in the National People's Congress.

1959: An uprising breaks out in Lhasa and is put down with force by the Chinese. The Dalai Lama flees to India.

1963: Foreigners are banned from Tibet by the PRC

1965: China establishes the Tibet Autonomous Region (TAR); the traditional government of Tibet ceases to exist.

1966: The Cultural Revolution begins in China, leading to the destruction of Buddhist temples as part of its campaign against the Four Olds. According to the Tenth Panchen Lama's 70,000-character critique, the Chinese destruction of monasteries has been underway since the 1950s, even pre-dating the Cultural Revolution.

1976: Mao Zedong dies; the Gang of Four falls and the Cultural Revolution ends. Deng Xiaoping institutes economic reforms in China, initiating the Chinese era of bureaucratic capitalism in which "to get rich is glorious."

1980: Hu Yaobang visits Tibet, deplores the conditions there, and declares that it reminds him of colonialism. A new period of ethnic sensitivity begins in Tibet, and some of the reforms actually work to the advantage of Tibetans. The demise of the Cultural Revolution brings dissatisfactions to the fore, many concerning freedom of religion and the Dalai Lama as a symbol of Tibetan religion and nationalism.

1987: Another uprising in Lhasa results in the imposition of martial law. Liberal reform comes to an end; the hard line is back in place.

1990s: China attempts to improve Tibet's economy and infrastructure, with mixed results. While Tibet gets some modern improvements in infrastructure, its environment undergoes terrible destruction.

2008: Riots break out in Lhasa in the months leading up to the Beijing Olympics. The protests center on Tibetan resentment of Han and Hui nationals in the capital and their unfair economic advantages over Tibetans in the Tibetan homeland.

NOTES

Part 1 Surging Storms

1. LeMiere (2009), 2.
2. Adapted from the 1933 novel by James Hilton and directed by Frank Capra.
3. http://www.mechakgallery.com/about_us.html.
4. Shakya (2002), 55. Shakya remarks that Tibetan life was full of hardship and was rife with economic inequalities. The social system distinguished between commoners and aristocracy, and the former were excluded from state affairs and suffered heavy taxation by lay and clerical landlords. Their only recourse was to petition the Lhasa government.
5. Terrill (2003), 55–86.
6. Fairbank (1989), 3–4.
7. Rossabi (1983), 1–4.
8. Xiung-nu in Chinese.
9. Tu-chŭeh in Chinese.
10. Rossabi (1970), 136–168.
11. Spence (1990), 7.
12. Hopkirk (1984), 447ff.
13. Hopkirk (1984), 447ff.
14. Hopkirk (1984), 447–464.
15. Terrill (2003), 83–85.
16. Spence (1990), xxi; Spence (1981), xii.
17. Spence (1981), 117–123.
18. Cited in Goldstein (1989), 204–205.
19. Dreyer (1976), 139.
20. Shakya (1999), 53–91.
21. Wang (2006), 8–10.
22. Radchenko (2003), 2.
23. Ardley (2002), 46.
24. LeMiere (2009), 2–3.
25. LeMiere (2009), 3.

Part 2 The Mongol Khans

1. The record of this journey is called *Ch'ang Ch'un: Travels of an Alchemist*. See Bibliography, Li Chih-Ch'ang (1979).

2. Rossabi (1988), 36–43.
3. The Uighurs were among the first people to submit to Chinggis Khan's rule. Employed as administrators and translators, they had a special place in the government of the Mongol Empire. The Supreme Khan found Uighur education more suitable than Chinese education for his sons and heirs. At the *khuriltai* (Great Assembly) of 1204, Chinggis Khan decreed that the Uighur alphabet would be used to write down the Mongol language.
4. Van Praag (1987), 3–9.
5. Van Praag (1987), 6.

Part 3   Ming and Qing Dynasties

1. See https://genographic.nationalgeographic.com/genographic/globe.html#/ms010/ for maps detailing the relative size of the territory controlled by Chinese dynasties.
2. Watt and Leidy (2005), 3–10.
3. Watt and Leidy (2005), 3–10.
4. Thurman (2008), 28.
5. Thurman (2008), 30.
6. For a study of how the late Qing ruler Cixi failed to meet the challenge of modernity, see Fairbank (1987), Spence (1990), and Seagrave (1992).
7. Spence (1990), 67–68.
8. Spence (1990), 56.
9. Spence (1990), 117. There were other systems for managing European missionary contact and relations with the south, but all were founded on the basic idea that China was the center and other countries were peripheral.
10. Terrill (2003), 84.
11. Van Praag (1987), 10–25.
12. Van Praag (1987), 13.
13. Van Praag (1987), 25.
14. Farquhar (1978), 23.
15. Farquhar (1978), 24.
16. Spence (1990), 170–178. See also Spence (1996).
17. Spence (1990), 170.
18. Spence (1990), 228–230.
19. Spence (1990), 232.

Part 4   Tibet and the Great Game

1. For a map of the Russian Empire see http://www.wall-maps.com/Classroom/HISTORY/World/ExpansionOfRussianEmpire187.gif.
2. Van Praag (1987), 27–33.
3. Van Praag (1987), 28.

4. See http://www.tibetjustice.org/materials/#key (website of the Tibet Justice Center) for the complete text of the Simla agreement.
5. Van Praag (1987), 30.
6. Anand (2009), 234.
7. Anand (2009), 235.
8. Anand (2009), 227.
9. Interview with the author, 1996.

Part 5   Early Twentieth-Century China

1. Spence (1990), 276.
2. Goldstein (1989), 54, 58, 65–74, 89, 213–224.
3. Fairbank (1987), 167.
4. Goldstein (1989), 213.
5. Sun Yat-sen, *The Three Principles.* Cited in Sloane (2001), 33.
6. Goldstein (1989), 646–661. A little-known split in the British Foreign Office between the Raj faction and the Hong Kong faction explains the British position on Tibet. The Crown Colony of Hong Kong was acquired as a result of British *sea* power and represented British commercial interests in China on the maritime coast. The Raj diplomats, including those in Sikkim and Nepal, viewed the British Empire—from their perspective in the Himalayan region—in terms of *land*-based empire and geopolitics.
7. Border disputes over the eastern provinces remain to the present day. China's border disputes with India led to war in 1962. Border disputes with the former Soviet Union led China to fear a possible war and led the Soviets, under Brezhnev, to place Soviet divisions on the Chinese border.
8. Shakya (1999), 5–6. The contact brought to the fore the issue of the Chinese-Tibetan relationship. The previous occasion was the Simla Conference of 1914, an attempt to define the border between China and Tibet. At the Simla Conference, a face-to-face diplomatic foray, the British mediated. China refused to sign the resulting resolution. Thus China never, in principle, accepted the border.
9. Goldstein (1989), 225.
10. Shakya (1999), 5–6.
11. Goldstein (1989), 213–251. Chiang's Nationalist Chinese government attempted to overthrow the Tibetan government through a Nationalist-backed, socialist-leaning Tibetan political group called the Tibet Improvement Party. The Nationalist Chinese believed that an autonomous Tibetan state would remain part of the new Chinese republic.
12. Goldstein (1989), 406–407.

Part 6   Mid-Twentieth-Century China

1. Goncharov, Lewis, and Xue (1993), 202ff.
2. Radchenko (2007/2008), 342.

3. Radchenko (2007/2008), 343.
4. Radchenko and Wolff (2007/2008), 108.
5. Radchenko (2007/2008), 341.
6. Radchenko (2007/2008), 342.
7. Goldstein (1989), 54, 58, 65–74, 89, 213–224.
8. Norbu (2009).
9. Shakya (1999), 5–6.
10. Shakya (1999), 9.
11. Cited in Dreyer (1976), 50.
12. Dreyer (1976), 59.
13. Dreyer (1976), 150.
14. John Avedon's wrenching account of the Cultural Revolution, *In Exile from the Land of Snows,* is based on hundreds of interviews conducted with refugees with the help of interpreters in Dharamsala, India.
15. Soviet propaganda of the period alleged that the Cultural Revolution was a Maoist plot to exterminate the minorities (Dreyer 1976, 233).
16. Shakya (2002), 53.
17. Shakya (1999), 209. See http://www.tibetjustice.org/materials/china/china3.html for the complete text of the "Agreement for the Peaceful Liberation of Tibet"; see http://www.tibetjustice.org/materials/#key for the Tibet Justice Center's collection of documents pertaining to Tibet.
18. Shakya (2002), 54.
19. *Time* (October 4, 1999), 1. http://www.time.com/time/magazine/article/0,9171,992133,00.html
20. Shakya (1999), 93.
21. Shakya (1999), 94.
22. Shakya (1999), 116.
23. Shakya (1999), 92ff.
24. Shakya (1999), 209.
25. Shakya (1999), 186–192.
26. "The Demise of the Lamaist State" is the subtitle of Goldstein (1989), the first volume of his history of modern Tibet.
27. Shakya (1999), 314.
28. Shakya (1999), 353.
29. Shakya (1999), 289.
30. Shakya (1999), 349.
31. Shakya (2002), 44–45.
32. *Jampa: The Story of Racism in Tibet,* prepared for the United Nations Conference against Racism (Durban, South Africa) by the International Campaign for Tibet; see http://72.32.136.41/files/documents/JampaRacism.pdf (2001).
33. Author interview, summer 1996.
34. Kissinger (1979), 700.
35. For a full discussion of the Panchen Lama and his 70,000-character petition, see Shakya (1999), 271–274.
36. Google in China, see http://www.nytimes.com/2010/03/27/technology/27iht-google.html?ref=technology. Open Net Initiative, "Google's China

Decision Could Have Far-Reaching Implications," http://opennet.net/blog/2010/01/googles-china-decision-could-have-far-reaching-implications (2010), and "Google Filtering: How it Works," http://opennet.net/blog/2006/01/googlecn-filtering-how-it-works (2006).
37. Author interview with Jerome Cohen, Baker Institute Conference, Houston, TX, 1995.
38. Shakya (2008), 26.

Part 7   Late Twentieth-Century China

1. The recently published memoirs of Zhao Ziyang reveal that Zhao was at least an equal partner in theorizing the economic reforms promulgated by Deng. On the occasion of the Tiananmen Uprising of 1989, Zhao urged a soft line with the students while Deng called out the military. Zhao spent more than a decade under house arrest after Tiananmen.
2. Shakya (1999), 369.
3. Shakya (1999), 381.
4. Shakya (1999), 400–402.
5. Shakya (1999), 401.
6. Shakya (1999), 401.
7. After delivering his critique of the Party's policies in Tibet, one of the most scathing in the history of the People's Republic, the Panchen Lama spent fourteen years in prison or under what amounted to house arrest. He was rehabilitated in 1988, a year before his death. The PRC attempted to choose his successor, taking over what was traditionally a religious function of the Dalai Lama. The Tenth Panchen Lama was often called a puppet of the CCP, as his petition was kept a secret for many years and was not made public until after his death. In the petition, the cleric voiced what was regarded as his subversive opinion on the nationality question: "If the language, clothes and customs of a nationality are taken away then that nationality will vanish and be transformed into another nationality. How can we guarantee that Tibetans will not be turned into another race?"
8. Shakya (1999), 383.
9. Shakya (1999), 380.
10. Shakya (1999), 394–395.
11. Shakya (1999), 371.
12. Shakya (1999), 405–406
13. Solomon (1999). This book is a guide to Chinese practice in negotiations.
14. Shakya (2002), 394–430; Goldstein (1997), 79–99.
15. In Norbu (2008c), the Tibetan author and activist critiques Melvyn C. Goldstein, the historian of Tibet. Norbu is an outspoken proponent of Tibetan independence and writes for the website of the Rangzen Alliance: The World Council of Tibetans for an Independent Tibet (www.rangzen.net).
16. Shakya (2002), 1.

17. Shakya (2002), 1.
18. Fairbank (1989), 2.
19. Meisner (1996), 174–175.
20. China has come under criticism for using the Shanghai Cooperation Organization to characterize separatist protests in Xinjiang as terrorism.

Part 8   The Twenty-First Century

1. Davis (2008).
2. Arquilla and Ronfeldt (2001).
3. Nikolas K. Gvosdev, "The Soviet Victory That Never Was," *Foreign Affairs,* http://www.foreignaffairs.com/print/65674.
4. Interview, "Morning Joe," MSNBC, March 13, 2009.
5. Nathan and Gilley (2003).
6. Cheng Li, "China's Leadership," 34.
7. Solomon (1999).
8. Dalai Lama, "Statement on Fiftieth Anniversary of 1959 Peaceful Tibetan Uprising," March 10, 1999, www.dalailama.com/news.350.htm.
9. Davis (2008), 5.
10. Thurman (2008).

BIBLIOGRAPHY

Al-Din, Rashid. 1988. *The Successors of Genghis Khan* (trans. John Andrew Boyle). Ann Arbor, MI: UMI Out-of-Print Books on Demand. [Originally published 1971 in New York by Columbia University Press.]

Ali, Tariq. 2008. *The Duel: Pakistan on the Flight Path of American Power.* New York: Scribner's. [Expounds the idea of a regional South Asian common market. Author interviewed on *After Words,* C-SPAN, October 5, 2008.]

Allsen, Thomas T. 1983. *Mongol Imperialism: The Policies of the Grand Qan Mongke in China, Russia and the Islamic Lands.* Berkeley: University of California Press.

Anand, Dibyesh. 2007. *Geopolitical Exotica: Tibet in Western Imagination (Borderlines).* Minneapolis: University of Minnesota Press.

———. 2009. "Strategic Hypocrisy: The British Imperial Scripting of Tibet's Political Identity." *Journal of Asian Studies* 68(1): 227-252.

Anonymous Group of Intellectuals. 1994. "An Appeal and a Warning from 7 Chinese." *New York Times,* March 11.

Ardley, Jane. 2002. *The Tibetan Independence Movement: Political, Religious and Ghandian Perspective.* New York: Routledge.

———. "Interview with Samdhong Rimpoche, 1997." Unpublished manuscript.

———. "The Movement for Tibetan Independence: Armed Resistance 1949-1974 and the Formation of the Tibetan Government in Exile." Unpublished manuscript.

Arquilla, John, and David Ronfeldt. 2001. *Networks and Netwars: The Future of Terror, Crime, and Militancy.* Santa Monica, CA: Rand.

Barnett, A. Doak. 1994. *China's Far West.* Boulder, CO: Westview.

Barthold, V. V. 1968. *Turkestan Down to the Mongol Invasion* (trans. T. Minorsky), 3rd ed. London: Luzac.

BBC News. "Timeline Tibet: A Chronology of Key Events." http://news.bbc.co.uk/2/hi/asia-pacific/country_profiles/6299565.stm

Beckwith, Christopher I. 1987. *The Tibetan Empire in Central Asia: A History of the Struggle for Great Power among Tibetans, Turks, Arabs and Chinese during the Early Middle Ages.* Princeton, NJ: Princeton University Press.

Benson, Linda. 1990. *The Ili Rebellion: The Moslem Challenge to Chinese Authority in Xinjiang,* 1944-1949. Armonk, NY: Sharpe.

Bergreen, Laurence. 2007. *Marco Polo: From Venice to Xanadu.* New York: Knopf.

Beschloss, Michael, and Strobe Talbott. 1993. *At the Highest Levels: The Inside Story of the End of the Cold War.* Boston: Little, Brown.

Bishop, Peter. 1989. *The Myth of Shangri-la: Tibet, Travel Writing and the Western Creation of Sacred Landscape.* Berkeley: University of California Press.

Bix, Herbert P. 2002. *Hirohito and the Making of Modern Japan.* New York: HarperCollins.

Budge, E. A. Wallis, trans. 1928. *The Monks of Kublai Khan, Emperor of China.* London: Religious Tract Society.

Buderi, Robert, and Gregory T. Huang. 2006. *Guanxi (The Art of Relationships): Microsoft, China, and Bill Gates's Plan to Win the Road Ahead.* New York: Simon & Schuster.

Buell, Paul D. 1979. "Sino-Khitan Administration in Mongol Bukhara." *Journal of Asian History* 13: 121-151.

Chan, Hoklam, and William T. DeBary, eds. 1982. *Yuan Thought: Chinese Thought and Religion Under the Mongols.* New York: Columbia University Press.

Chen Jian. 2001. *Mao's China and the Cold War.* Chapel Hill: University of North Carolina Press.

Chen Jian and Shuguang Zhang. 1996. *Chinese Communist Foreign Policy and the Cold War in Asia: New Documentary Evidence, 1944-1950.* Chicago: Imprint.

Christensen, Thomas J. 1996. "Chinese Realpolitik: Reading Beijing's World-View." *Foreign Affairs* 75(5): http://www.foreignaffairs.com/articles/52434/thomas-j-christensen/chinese-realpolitik-reading-beijings-world-view.

Coll, Steve. 1994. *On the Grand Trunk Road: A Journey into South Asia.* New York: Random House.

Dardess, John W. 1972/1973. "From Mongol Empire to Yuan Dynasty: Changing Forms of Imperial Rule in Mongolia and Central Asia." *Monumenta Serica* 30: 117-165.

Davis, Michael C. 2008. "Establishing a Workable Autonomy in Tibet." *Human Rights Quarterly* 30: 227-258. http://www.press.jhu.edu/journals/human_rights_quarterly/30.2Tibet.pdf.

DeBary, William Theodore, Wing-tsit Chan, and Burton Watson, compilers. 1960. *Sources of Chinese Tradition,* vols. I and II. New York: Columbia University Press. [Discusses the intellectual background to Neo-Confucianism.]

de Rachewiltz, Igor. 1962. "Yeh-lu Chü-tsai (1189-1243): Buddhist Idealist and Statesman." In Arthur Wright and Denis Twitchett, eds., *Confucian Personalities,* pp. 189-216. Stanford, CA: Stanford University Press.

Diplomatic History (Journal of the Society for Historians of American Foreign Relations). 1997a. "Symposium: Rethinking the Lost Chance in China." *Diplomatic History* 21(1).

————. 1997b. "Symposium: Soviet Archives: Recent Revelations and Cold War Historiography." *Diplomatic History* 21(2).

Dreyer, June Teufel. 1976. *China's Forty Millions: Minority Nationalities and National Integration in the People's Republic of China.* Cambridge, MA: Harvard University Press.

Economy, Elizabeth C., and Adam Segal. 2008. "China's Olympic Nightmare: What the Games Mean for Beijing's Future." *Foreign Affairs,* July/August:

http://www.foreignaffairs.com/articles/64447/Elizabeth-c-economy-and-adam-segal/chinas-olympic-nightmare.

Erickson, Barbara. 1997. *Tibet: Abode of the Gods, Pearl of the Motherland.* Berkeley, CA: Pacific View Press.

Fairbank, John K., ed. 1978. *The Cambridge History of China,* vol. 10. *Late Ch'ing 1800-1911, Part 1.* Cambridge, U.K.: Cambridge University Press.

———, ed. 1983. *The Cambridge History of China,* vol. 12. *Republican China, 1912-1949.* Cambridge, U.K.: Cambridge University Press.

———. 1987. *The Great Chinese Revolution: 1800-1985.* New York: Harper Perennial.

———. 1989. "Why China's Rulers Fear Democracy." *New York Review of Books* 36: 14. [http://www.nybooks.com/articles/3904]

Fairbank, John K., and Albert Feuerwerker, eds. 1986. *The Cambridge History of China,* vol. 13. *Republican China, 1912-1949.* Cambridge, U.K.: Cambridge University Press.

Fairbank, John K., and Liu Kwang-Ching, eds. 1980. *The Cambridge History of China,* vol. 11. *Late Ch'ing, 1800-1911, Part 2.* Cambridge, U.K.: Cambridge University Press.

Fairbank, John K., and Edwin O. Reischauer. 1960. *East Asia: The Great Tradition.* Boston: Houghton Mifflin.

Farquhar, David M. 1978. "Emperors as Bodhisattvas in the Governance of the Ching Empire." *Harvard Journal of Asiatic Studies* 38(1): 5-34.

Franke, Herbert. 1981. "Tibetans in Yuan China." In John Langlois, ed., *China Under Mongol Rule.* Princeton, NJ: Princeton University Press.

Franke, Herbert, and Denis Twitchett, eds. 1994. *The Cambridge History of China,* vol. 6. *Alien Regimes and Border States, 907-1368.* Cambridge, U.K.: Cambridge University Press. [Covers Tang to Ming.]

Gilley, Bruce, and Andrew Nathan. 2003. *China's New Rulers: The Secret Files,* 2nd ed., rev. New York: New York Review Books.

Gilman, Benjamin A., and Charles Rose. 1991. "Tibet's Legal Status and China's Sovereignty Claims." http://thomas.loc.gov/cgi-bin/query/C?r102:./temp/~r102FdhjGS

Gleason, Gregory. 1989. "The Political Elite in the Muslim Republics of Soviet Central Asia: The Dual Criterion of Power." *Journal of the Institute of Muslim Minority Affairs* 10(1): 246-263.

———. 1990. "Marketization and Migration: The Politics of Cotton in Central Asia." *Journal of Soviet Nationalities* 1(2): 73-74.

Goldstein, Melvyn C. 1989. *A History of Modern Tibet,* vol. 1. *1913-1951: The Demise of the Lamaist State.* Berkeley: University of California Press.

———. 1990. *Nomads of Western Tibet: The Survival of a Way of Life.* Berkeley: University of California Press.

———. 1997. *The Snow Lion and the Dragon: China, Tibet and the Dalai Lama.* Berkeley: University of California Press.

———. 1998. "The Dalai Lama's Dilemma." *Foreign Affairs,* January/February: http://www.foreignaffairs.com/articles/53606/melvyn-c-goldstein/the-dalai-lamas-dilemma

Goldstein, 2007. *A History of Modern Tibet, vol. 2. The Calm before the Storm: 1951-1955.* Berkeley: University of California Press.

Goncharov, Sergei, John Lewis, and Litai Xue. 1993. *Uncertain Partners: Stalin, Mao and the Korean War.* Palo Alto, CA: Stanford University Press.

Grousset, Rene. 1970. *Empire of the Steppes: A History of Central Asia.* New Brunswick, NJ: Rutgers University Press.

———. 1972. *Conqueror of the World: The Life of Chinggis Khan* (trans. Martin McKellar and Denis Sinor). New York: Viking.

Gvosdev, Nikolas K. 2009. "The Soviet Victory That Never Was: What the United States Can Learn from the Soviet War in Afghanistan." *Foreign Affairs,* December: [http://www.foreignaffairs.com/articles/65713/nikolas-k-gvosdev/the-soviet-victory-that-never-was]

Haeger, John W., ed. 1975. *Crisis and Prosperity in Sung China.* Tuscon: University of Arizona Press.

Halberstam, David. 1992. *The Best and the Brightest.* New York: Ballantine. [Includes history of the U.S. State Department after the Chinese Revolution.]

Hart, B. H. Liddell. 1927. *Great Captains Unveiled.* London: Blackwood. [Reprinted 1996 in Cambridge, MA, by Da Capo Press; audio version available from Books on Tape.]

Heissig, Walther. 1980. *The Religions of Mongolia* (trans. Geoffrey Samuel). Berkeley: University of California Press.

Hoog, Constance, trans. 1983. *Prince Jing-gim's Textbook of Tibetan Buddhism.* Leiden: Brill.

Hopkirk, Peter. 1982. *Trespassers on the Roof of the World: The Secret Exploration of Tibet.* New York: Godansha Globe.

———. 1984. *Setting the East Ablaze: Lenin's Dream of an Empire in Asia.* New York: Godansha Globe.

———. 1994. *The Great Game.* New York: Godansha Globe.

Howorth, H. H. 1965. *History of the Mongols: 9th to 19th Centuries,* 5 vols. New York: Franklin.

Hyer, Paul. 1966. "The Re-evaluation of Chinggis Khan: Its Role in the Sino-Soviet Dispute." *Asian Survey* 6(12): 696-705.

Inaba Shoju. trans. 1963. "The Lineage of the Sa skys pa: A Chapter of the Red Annals." *Memoirs of the Research Department of the Toyo Bunko* 22: 107-123.

Iyer, Pico. 1998. "Lost Horizons." *New York Review of Books* 45: 1. http://www.nybooks.com/articles/961.

Jernow, Allison Liu. 1993. *"Don't Force Us to Lie": The Struggle of Chinese Journalists in the Reform Era.* New York: Committee to Protect Journalists.

Juvaini, Ala-ad Din Ata-Malik. 1958. *The History of the World Conqueror,* 2 vols. (trans. John Andrew Boyle). Manchester: Manchester University Press.

Kahn, E. J. 1974. *The China Hands: America's Foreign Service Officers and What Befell Them.* New York: Viking.

Kahn, Paul. 1981. *Secret History of the Mongols.* Berkeley: University of California Press.

Kamenetz, Roger. 1994. *The Jew in the Lotus.* San Francisco: Harper.

Kissinger, Henry. 1979. *The White House Years.* Boston: Little, Brown.
———. 1994. *Diplomacy.* New York: Simon & Schuster.
Klieger, Christiaan. 2004. "Envisioning a Tibet Outside Tibet." Paper delivered at the Association for Asian Studies Annual Meeting (Atlanta, GA), April 4.
Kristof, Nicholas D., and Sheryl WuDunn. 1995. *China Wakes: The Struggle for the Soul of a Rising Power.* New York: Vintage.
———. 1996. "Asian Tensions Rise Over Sea's Wealth: China's Claims Are Raising Anxiety for Its Neighbors." *New York Times,* May 19.
Kwanten, Luc Herman M. 1971. "Tibetan Names in the Yuan Imperial Family." *Mongolia Society Bulletin* 10(1): 64-66.
———. 1972. "Tibetan-Mongol Relations during the Yuan Dynasty, 1207-1368." Ph.D. dissertation, University of South Carolina, Columbia.
———. 1979. *Imperial Nomads: A History of Central Asia, 500-1500.* Philadelphia: University of Pennsylvania Press.
Kynge, James. 2006. *China Shakes the World: A Titan's Rise and Troubled Future and the Challenge for America.* New York: Houghton Mifflin.
Lam, Willy Wo-lap. 2006. *Chinese Politics in the Hu Jintao Era: New Leaders, New Challenges.* Armonk, N. Y.: Sharpe.
Langlois, John D., ed. 1981. *China Under Mongol Rule.* Princeton, NJ: Princeton University Press.
Lattimore, Owen. 1940. *Inner Asian Frontiers of China.* New York: American Geographical Society.
———. 1962. *Studies in Frontier History.* London: Oxford University Press.
———. 1963. "Chinggis Khan and the Mongol Conquests." *Scientific American* 209(2): 54-68.
Le Miere, Christian. 2010. "Kabul's New Patron: The Growing Chinese-Afghan Relationship." *Foreign Affairs,* March/April. http://www.foreign affairs.com/articles/66194/christian-la-miere/kabuls-new-patron.
———. (2009). "China's Western Front: Can Beijing bring Order to its Western Provinces? http://foreignaffairs.copm/articles/65223/christian-le-mi%C3%83%C2%A8re/chinas'western-flank.
Lewis, Bernard. 1968. *The Assassins: A Radical Sect in Islam.* New York: Basic Books.
Li Chih-Ch'ang. 1979. *Ch'ang Ch'un: Travels of an Alchemist* (trans. Arthur Waley). New York: AMS Press. [Originally published 1931 in London.]
Link, Perry. 1994. "The Old Man's New China." *New York Review of Books* 41(11): 31-36. [A review of four books about Deng's China, including Merle Goldman's *Sowing the Seeds of Democracy* and Allison Liu Jernow's *Don't Force Us to Lie.*]
Mann, James. 2000. *About Face: A History of America's Curious Relationship with China, from Nixon to Clinton.* New York: Vintage.
Martin, H. Desmond. 1981. *The Rise of Chingis Khan and His Conquest of North China.* New York: Octagon.
McLagan, Meg. 1996. "Computing for Tibet: Virtual Politics in the Post-Cold War Era." In George E. Marcus, ed., *Connected: Engagements with Media.* Chicago: University of Chicago Press.

Meisner, Maurice. 1996. *The Deng Xiaoping Era: An Inquiry into the Fate of Chinese Socialism, 1978 to 1994.* New York: Hill & Wang.

Meyer, Christopher. 2008. "A Return to 1815 Is the Way Forward for Europe." *London Times* Online, www.timesonline.co.uk/tol/comment/columnists/guest_contributors/article4656255.ece (September 2).

Meyer, Karl E. 2003. *The Dust of Empires: The Race for Mastery in the Asian Heartland.* New York: Public Affairs.

Ming, Ruan. 1994. *Deng Xiaoping: Chronicle of an Empire.* Boulder, CO: Westview.

Mirsky, Jonathan. 1990. "Lost Horizons." *New York Review of Books* 37: 20. http://www.nybooks.com/articles/3403.

Mote, Frederick W., and Denis Twitchett, eds. 1988. *The Cambridge History of China,* vol. 7, part 1. *Ming Dynasty.* Cambridge, U.K.: Cambridge University Press.

Nathan, Andrew J., and Perry Link, eds. (Liang Zhang, compiler). 2001. *The Tiananmen Papers: The Chinese Leadership's Decision to Use Force against Their Own People—In Their Own Words.* New York: Public Affairs.

Nathan, Andrew J., and Bruce Gilley. 2003. *China's New Rulers: The Secret Files,* 2nd ed., rev. New York: New York Review Books.

Norbu, Dawa T. 2001. "A Struggle in Travail." http://tibetan.review.to/dtn/dn_essay.htm.

Norbu, Jamyang. 1989. *Illusion and Reality: Essays on the Tibetan and Chinese Political Scene from 1978 to 1989.* Dharamsala: Tibetan Youth Congress.

———. 1994. "The Tibetan Resistance Movement and the Role of the CIA." In Robert Barnett and Shirin Akiner, eds., *Resistance and Reform in Tibet.* London: Hurst.

———. 1997. "Non-violence or Non-action: Some Gandhian Truths about the Tibetan Peace Movement." *Tibetan Review* 32(9): 18-21.

———. 2008a. "Barefoot Experts." www.phayul.com (June 11).

———. 2008b. "It's Not the Economy, Stupid." www.phayul.com (June 23).

———. 2008c. "Black Annals: Goldstein and the Negation of Tibetan History (Parts I and II)." www.phayul.com (July 21 and 28).

———. 2009. "Independent Tibet: Some Facts." Rangzen Alliance, http://www.rangzen.net/index.php?s=Foreign+Military+Invasion&x=9&y=8 (February 25).

Norbu, Thubten Jigme. 1986. *Tibet Is My Country.* London: Wisdom Books.

Olschki, Leonard. 1960. *Marco Polo's Asia.* Berkeley: University of California Press.

Ostermann, Christian F., ed. 2007/2008. "Inside China's Cold War." *Cold War International History Project Bulletin* 16. http://www.wilsoncenter.org/topics/pubs/CWIHPBulletin16.pdf.

Pan, Philip P. 2008. *Out of Mao's Shadow: The Struggle for the Soul of a New China.* New York: Simon & Schuster.

Panchen Lama. 1998. "70,000 Character Petition." In *A Poisoned Arrow: The Secret Report of the 10th Panchen Lama* (trans. Robbie Barnett), pp. 50-51. London: Tibet Information Network. [The petition was submitted to the Chinese leadership at their request.]

Petech, Luciano. 1980. "Sang-ko, A Tibetan Statesman in Yüan China." *Acta Orientalia Hungarica* 34: 193-208.

———. 1983. "Tibetan Relations with Sung China and with the Mongols." In Morris Rossabi, ed., *China among Equals: The Middle Kingdom and Its Neighbors, 10th to 14th Centuries,* pp. 173-203. Berkeley: University of California Press.

Peters, Gretchen. 2009. *Seeds of Terror: How Heroin Is Bankrolling the Taliban and Al Qaeda.* New York: St. Martin's Press.

Potomac Conference. 1992. "Sino-Tibetan Relations: Prospects for the Future." www.columbia.edu/cu/lweb/indiv/area/tibet-potomac/editintr.html. [This conference was unique in that its participants included Tibetan, Chinese, and American academics and experts; subjects include the environment, economic development, historical perspectives, and security issues.]

Powers, John. 2004. *History as Propaganda: Tibetan Exiles versus the People's Republic of China.* New York: Oxford University Press. Radchenko, Sergey. 2003. "The Soviet's Best Friend in Asia: The Mongolian Dimension of the Sino-Soviet Split." *Cold War International History Project Working Paper* 42, Woodrow Wilson Center for International Studies, Washington, DC. http://www.wilsoncenter.org/topics/pubs/ACF4CA.pdf.

———, trans. and ed. 2007/2008. "New Documents on Mongolia and the Cold War." *Cold War International History Project Bulletin* 16: 341-366. http://wilsoncenter.org/index.cfm?fuseaction=topics.home&topic_id=1409.

Radchenko, Sergey, and David Wolff. 2007/2008. "To the Summit via Proxy Summits: New Evidence from Soviet and Chinese Archives on Mao's Long March to Moscow, 1949." *Cold War International History Project Bulletin* 16: 105-182. http://www.wilsoncenter.org/topics/pubs/CWIHPBulletin16.pdf.

Rashid, Ahmed. 2008. *Descent into Chaos: The United States and the Failure of Nation Building in Pakistan, Afghanistan, and Central Asia.* New York: Viking.

Reiss, Tom. 2006. *The Orientalist: Solving the Mystery of a Strange and Dangerous Life.* New York: Random House.

Rossabi, Morris. 1970. "The Tea and Horse Trade with Inner Asia during the Ming." *Journal of Asian History* 4(2): 136-168.

———, ed. 1983. *China among Equals: The Middle Kingdom and Its Neighbors, 10th to 14th Centuries.* Berkeley, University of California Press.

———. 1986. *Khubilai Khan: His Life and Times.* Berkeley: University of California Press.

———, ed. 2004. *Governing China's Multiethnic Frontiers.* Seattle: University of Washington Press.

Schell, Orville. 1994. *Mandate of Heaven: The Legacy of Tiananmen Square and the Next Generation of China's Leaders.* New York: Touchstone.

———. 2000. Virtual Tibet: *Searching for Shangri-la from the Himalayas to Hollywood. New York:* Holt.

Schwartz, Ronald. 1994. *Circle of Protest: Political Ritual in the Tibetan Uprising.* New York: Columbia University Press.

Seagrave, Sterling. 1992. *Dragon Lady: The Life and Legend of the Last Empress of China*. New York: Vintage.

Shakya, Tsering. 1999. *Dragon in the Land of Snows: A History of Modern Tibet Since 1947*. New York: Columbia University Press.

———. 2002. "Blood in the Snows." *New Left Review* 15: 37-60.

———. 2008. "Interview: Tibet Questions." *New Left Review* 51: . [http://newleftreview.org/?page=article&view=2720]

Sinor, Denis, ed. 1990. *Cambridge History of Early Inner Asia*. Cambridge, U.K.: Cambridge University Press.

Sloane, Robert, Losang Rabgey, et al. 2001. *Jampa: The Story of Racism in Tibet*. Washington, DC: International Campaign for Tibet. http://72.32.136.41/files/documents/JampaRacism.pdf.

Solomon, Richard H. 1999. *Chinese Negotiating Behavior: Pursuing Interests through 'Old Friends'*. Washington, D. C.: United States Institute of Peace Press.

Spence, Jonathan D. 1981. *The Gate of Heavenly Peace: The Chinese and Their Revolution, 1895 to 1980*. New York: Viking.

———. 1990. *The Search for Modern China*. New York: Norton.

———. 1996. *God's Chinese Son: The Taiping Heavenly Kingdom of Hong Xiuquan*. New York: Norton.

Sperling, Elliot. 2008. "The Mongols, Mao and the Dalai Lama," *New York Times,* April 13. www.nytimes.com/2008/04/13/opinion/13iht-edsperling.1.11935241.html?_r=1&page.

Starr, S. Frederick, ed. 1994. *The Legacy of History in Russia and the New States of Eurasia*. Armonk, NY: Sharpe.

Stephan, John J. 1994. *The Russian Far East: A History*. Stanford, CA: Stanford University Press.

Stoddard, Heather. 1995. "Urban Crisis on the Tibetan Plateau." In *Tibet Transformed: A Pictorial Essay Documenting China's Colonization of Tibet*. Washington, DC: International Campaign for Tibet.

Su Shaozhi. 1993. "A Decade of Crises at the Institute of Marxism-Leninism-Mao Zedong Thought," *China Quarterly* 134: 335-351.

Terrill, Ross. 2003. *The New Chinese Empire*. New York: Basic Books.

The Myth of Tibetan Autonomy: A Legal Analysis. 1994. Washington, DC: International Campaign for Tibet and International Human Rights Law Group.

Thurman, Robert. 2008. Why the Dalai Lama Matters: His Act of Truth as the Solution for China, Tibet and the World. New York: Atria.

———. 2008. Interview, *New York Times Sunday Magazine,* June 29, p. 16.

———. 1996. "The Realpolitik of Spirituality: An Interview with His Holiness the Fourteenth Dalai Lama." *Shambala Sun* 5(2): [http://www.shambhala-sun.com/index.php?option=com_content&task=view&id=2063]

Tibet Press Watch. 1996. "Panchen Lama Selection Dominates Debate over Tibet." Washington, DC: International Campaign for Tibet.

Tibetan Government in Exile, Office of Information and International Relations, Central Tibetan Secretariat. 1989. *Government Resolutions and International Documents on Tibet*. Dharamsala, India.

Tillman, Hoyt Cleveland, and Stephen H. West. 1995. *China Under Jurchen Rule: Essays on Chin Intellectual and Cultural History.* Albany: State University of New York Press.

Tuchman, Barbara W. 1971. *Stilwell and the American Experience in China, 1911-1945.* New York: Macmillan.

Tyler, Patrick. 1999. *A Great Wall: Six Presidents and China, An Investigative History.* New York: Public Affairs.

Van Praag, Michael C. Van Walt. 1987. *Status of Tibet: History, Rights, and Prospects in International Law.* London: Wisdom Publications.

Vernadsky, George. 1969. *A History of Russia,* 6th rev. ed. New Haven, CT: Yale University Press.

Wohlforth, William C. 1997. "New Evidence on Moscow's Cold War: Ambiguity in Search of Theory." *Diplomatic History* 21(2): 229-242.

Yi, Aisin Gioro Pu. 1983. *From Emperor to Citizen: The Autobiography of Aisin Gioro Pu Yi* (trans. W. J. F. Jenner). Beijing: Foreign Language Press.

Yu, Maochun. 1996. *OSS in China: Prelude to Cold War.* New Haven, CT: Yale University Press.

Yun-hua, Jan. 1982. "Chinese Buddhism in Ta-tu: The New Situation and New Problems." In Hok-lam Chan and William Theodore de Bary, eds., *Yuan Thought: Chinese Thought and Religion Under the Mongols.* New York: Columbia University Press.

Wang, Dong. 2006. "The Quarrelling Brothers: New Chinese Archives and a Reappraisal of The Sino-Soviet Split, 1959-1962." *Cold War International History Project Working Paper* 49, Woodrow Wilson Center for International Studies, Washington, DC.

Wang Lixiong and more than 300 others. 2008. "Twelve Suggestions for Dealing with the Tibetan Situation." *New York Review of Books* 55(8): http://www.nybooks.com/contents/20080515.

Watt, James C. Y., and Denise Patry Leidi. 2005. *Defining Yongle: Imperial Art in Early Fifteenth Century China.* New Haven, CT: Yale University Press and Metropolitan Museum of Art.

Wo-lap Lam, Willy. 2006. *Chinese Politics in the Hu Jintao Era: New Leaders, New Challenges.* Armonk, N. Y.: Sharpe.

Wolff, Diane. 1997. "china.com?" *The National Interest* 49: 73-76. [Discusses China and the early internet, the effect of the information revolution on China's economy, and the Tibetan Government in Exile's voice in the virtual world.]

———. 2005. "Asia's Muslim Past." Orlando *Sentinel,* "Insight" section, November 27. [Discusses minority policy in Russia and China under successive systems and compares these policies with the U.S. assimilation of minorities with rights and responsibilities.]

———. Forthcoming a. *The Conqueror Chinggis Khan.* [Details the conquest of North China, the main object of Mongol arms.]

———. Forthcoming b. *Khubilai Khan and Marco Polo: A Novel of Imperial China.* [Details the conquest of Southern China and the reunification of China proper for the first time in 400 years.]

Wright, Arthur F. 1959. *Buddhism in Chinese History.* Stanford, CA: Stanford University Press.

Wright, Arthur F., and Denis Twitchett. 1962. *Confucian Personalities.* Stanford, CA: Stanford University Press.

Xuecheng Liu. 1994. *The Sino-Indian Border Dispute and Sino-Indian Relations.* Lanham, MD: University Press of America.

Zhang Sulin. 2007/2008. "The Declassification of Chinese Foreign Ministry Archival Documents: A Brief Introduction." *Cold War International History Project Bulletin* 16: 10-84. [http://www.wilsoncenter.org/topics/pubs/CWIHPBulletin16.pdf]

Zhao Ziyang, Bao Pu, Renee Chiang, and Adi Ignatius, trans. and eds. 2009. *Prisoner of the State: The Secret Journal of Premier Zhao Ziyang.* New York: Simon & Schuster.

INDEX